MATH EXCURSIONS K

MATH EXCURSIONS K

Project-based Mathematics for Kindergartners
Revised Edition

Donna Burk
Allyn Snider
Paula Symonds

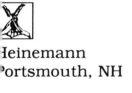

Heinemann
Portsmouth, NH

Heinemann
A division of Reed Elsevier Inc.
361 Hanover Street
Portsmouth, NH 03801-3912
Offices and agents throughout the world

Library of Congress Cataloging-in-Publication Data
Burk, Donna
            Math excursions K: project-based mathematics for kindergartners/
Donna Burk, Allyn Snider, Paula Symonds.
            p. cm.
Includes bibliographical references.
ISBN 0-435-08345-7
            1. Mathematics—Study and teaching (Primary) I. Snider, Allyn. II. Symonds, Paula. III. Title.
QA135.5.B8396 1993   92-16735
372.7-dc20   CIP

The Math Learning Center and its publication *Box It or Bag It Mathematics* are frequently referred to in this publication.

The Math Learning Center is a not-for-profit education corporation dedicated to the improvement of mathematics education. It is founded on the belief that math is an enjoyable—as well as a worthwhile—endeavor and ought to be taught as such. Through workshops, courses, and publications for educators, the Center promotes teaching styles that emphasize the development of conceptual knowledge and problem-solving skills through active-learning experiences.

Box It or Bag It Mathematics is a primary grades program based on the philosophy that children learn best when they are actively involved in hands-on experiences using a variety of materials. Further information about this program and other MLC publications, materials, and workshops is available from The Math Learning Center, P.O. Box 3226, Salem, OR 97302: FAX (503) 370-7961.

For information about workshops for *Math Excursions K*, please write:
Math Excursions
Heinemann
361 Hanover Street
Portsmouth, NH 03801-3912

Design by Impressions, a division of Edwards Brothers, Inc.
Printed in the United States of America
97 96 95   EB   3 4 5 6 7

"Mathematics today involves far more than calculation; clarification of the problem, deduction of consequences, formulation of alternatives, and development of appropriate tools are as much a part of the modern mathematician's craft as are solving equations or providing answers."

National Research Council
Everybody Counts, A Report to the Nation on the Future of Mathematics Education

"There are more kinds of math than just 2 + 2 = 4."

Kristen Sorber
Primary Student
West Linn, Oregon

CONTENTS

Preface

Have you ever wished you could create an environment for at least a few weeks each school year in which your children would be so committed to a classroom mathematics project that they would resent going out to recess? We, too, are teachers who dream of creating totally absorbing math units for our own diverse groups of children, projects that will work even with high-energy, large classes.

Our search for better ways to teach mathematics to young children began many years ago. We each created and tried math games and teaching strategies that felt successful at the time but didn't seem to hold together long enough to go anywhere. We'd drift back to workbook teaching still hoping to find developmentally appropriate instruction we could implement consistently.

Each of us met the late Mary Baratta-Lorton soon after the publication of *Mathematics Their Way®* (1976). Mary so inspired us that we began to implement her ideas in our own classrooms. Once we became Math Their Way® instructors, we all met —Allyn from Portland, Oregon; Paula from San Francisco; and Donna from San Jose, California. Our friendship led us on a constant search for better ways to manage hands-on math instruction and took us on many side trips as we made this teaching philosophy our own. Eventually, we began to share our ideas with other teachers and their encouragement led us to write *Box It or Bag It Mathematics* (Burk et al. 1988).

When Toby Gordon of Heinemann approached us about writing again, we decided to rise to the challenge by stretching the idea of *Box It* "seasonal math." We began to develop projects that integrated math into other curriculum areas. We wanted to involve our students in long-term endeavors that would challenge them to think as well as provide them with a genuine need to work together. After many trials and tribulations, we believe we've put together some projects that make the magic work. We have tried these projects in our own classrooms which reflect very different socioeconomic populations and class sizes, as do the classrooms where friends have so generously field-tested our work.

This kind of teaching definitely requires planning and organization. If you choose to try project-based instruction, we hope our efforts make it easier for you to begin. Try not to give up too soon. It takes more than one unit to be sure the experiences you are providing for children are worth such hard work.

Acknowledgments

We give special thanks to:

Nancy Goldsmith and Jan Marquez
    San Jose, California
Amy Richmond, Anne Kernan, Francis Niebanck, Carol Sweet, Abigail O'Leary,
Lauren Okie, Kate Sculley, Deborah Huysentruyt, and Kathy Callaghan
    San Francisco, California
Peggy Steinbronn
    Altoona, Iowa
Margaret Allen and Carolyn Stringer
    Wilsonville, Oregon

for help field-testing these units;

The children of

Sakamoto School
San Jose, California

George Miner School
San Jose, California

West Portal School
San Francisco, California

Altoona Elementary School
Altoona, Iowa

Wilsonville Primary School
Wilsonville, Oregon

San Francisco Day School
San Francisco, California

for teaching us;

Andy Clark, Cheryl Ogburn, and Jan Gillespie
Portland Public Schools, Portland, Oregon

for asking questions;

Dr. Ken Welch, Dr. Mike Tannenbaum, and Mike Shay
West Linn Schools
West Linn, Oregon

Burns Srigley and Christine Waller
Oak Grove School District
San Jose, California

for support;

Toby Gordon
Heinemann Educational Books, Inc.
Portsmouth, New Hampshire

for suggesting we write something new;

Hilde Howden
Albuquerque, New Mexico

for reading and contributing suggestions;

Dr. Gene Maier and Dr. Michael Arcidiacono
Portland State University
Portland, Oregon

for mathematical advice;

Marilyn Burns and the late Mary Baratta-Lorton

for inspiration;

our families

for their continued patience and loving support.

Artists

Gayle Steinberger and LaVaun Maier

Introduction

What Is *Math Excursions K?*

Math Excursions K is a set of five theme-based units for kindergarten children. Each unit is an exciting departure from the main road of systematic math instruction, an opportunity to drop daily math routines for a week or two and focus on one particular math concept as it relates to a real-world problem.

Each unit revolves around a story in which the main character's dilemma serves as a springboard for teaching mathematical concepts.

"Buttons" (see Lobel, *Frog and Toad Are Friends*, 1985) introduces Toad, who has lost the button from his jacket and must do a great deal of sorting to find it. Children dramatize the story and make cardboard buttons of their own to sort in many ways.

"A House for a Hedgehog" (see Faunce-Brown, *Snuffles' House*, 1983) features Snuffles, a small hedgehog who makes some amusing discoveries about form and function as he attempts to build a new home. After hearing the story, children create a variety of two- and three-dimensional houses for their own tiny hedgehogs.

In "Hansel and Gretel's Path," a white dove creates a magic path that will lead the two children home if they can step on the correct stones in the proper sequence. Students have many opportunities to extend their patterning skills as they learn to navigate a life-sized replica of the dove's path and make their own small paths and pattern cards.

"Are You Sure It's Twenty?" introduces Mrs. Bear, whose inability to count causes quite a stir in the forest, and provides the impetus for plenty of counting practice in the classroom.

In "Teddy Bears Catch a Cold" (see Gretz, and Sage, *Teddy Bears Cure a Cold*, 1984), children use a variety of math skills including sorting, graphing, measuring, counting, adding, and subtracting to care for their sick teddy bears.

Each unit creates a story line for learning; each sets up a situation in which there's a reason to use mathematics. Children must sort through many buttons to find their own in the big button hunt. They must experiment with a variety of shapes to see which works best for a house. Patterns must be tested, eggs counted, and teddy bears measured. Each story carries children's learning forward in a very powerful way. While *Math Excursions K* is not intended to be a complete math program, it is designed to foster the kind of interest and joy in mathematical thinking that youngsters will need throughout their lives.

Why Does *Math Excursions K* Use a Unit Approach?

Because a unit approach is developmentally appropriate

The unit approach mirrors the way young children perceive the world by integrating literacy skills, math, art, science, and social studies in pursuit of themes that provide rich opportunities for concept development. Ideas flow naturally from one lesson to another and lessons extend over a period of days so that connections can be developed.

Because a unit approach creates a meaningful context for learning

While there's little doubt that young children learn more about mathematics by manipulating objects than filling in workbook pages, their learning seems even greater when there's a *reason* to be counting, measuring, or sorting. The *Math Excursions K* units provide purposes for learning. Mrs. Bear thinks she used only six eggs in her cake, but we suspect she used more. How can we find out? The teddy bears are sick and need to be put to bed. How can we make their beds the right size? What's the best shape for a house? How can we use patterning to find our way home? Set in the context of meaningful problems, math becomes a useful and important tool to accomplish many tasks, both in and out of school.

Because the unit approach offers teachers unique opportunities to assess students' mathematical understandings

Many of the tasks posed in *Math Excursions K* provide a rich context for assessment because they require children to apply a variety of mathematical ideas or concepts. In "Hansel and Gretel's Path," for example, children are asked to pick their way home along a path of randomly shaped and colored stepping stones. To do so, they must identify, copy, and extend patterns. Later, they create and test their own patterns. Finally, they learn to predict which patterns will work before they actually move.

Through observation, questioning, and discussion, teachers can learn quite a bit about students' insights and understandings, as well as about their flexibility and persistence in seeking solutions.

How Are the Units Organized?

Although the units vary in difficulty, they share a common format. At the beginning you'll find a preview that lists and briefly summarizes the activities. Next, a planning sheet that may help you schedule the unit in your own classroom. Under "What Do I Need to Know to Begin?" there is a description of the unit, along with some preparation notes. After that, you'll find a description of the math skills that are addressed and a materials list.

We've scheduled one to three activities each day, because these integrated units often involve subjects other than math. You may choose to complete a unit in fewer days or take it more slowly, but be aware that units spread over too long a period tend to lose their momentum.

Each unit begins with a story or lesson designed to establish the central problem.

Instruction then alternates between whole-group lessons and individual or partner work as children pursue ideas and solutions. Work is brought to a close with an activity designed to summarize children's investigations: a button hunt, a house made of all the shapes, a path game to take home for family math, a class-authored book, and dramatic play in the teddy bear hospital.

You'll notice that we use a lot of scripting throughout *Math Excursions K*. This is intended to give you "windows" into our classrooms: to see how discussion might proceed and how children might respond, and to indicate what types of questions might be useful in helping students to become better problem solvers. Every classroom is different, however, and we encourage you to follow the lead of *your* children in discussions and planning.

How Do You Manage Your Classroom During Unit Work?

Although children construct physical and logical mathematical knowledge through spontaneous play, they also learn a great deal from adults as well as other classmates. Our management techniques reflect a firm belief that we need to speak to students, listen to them, and help them interact with one another. Our role is to pose stimulating problems, supply language and materials to support children's discoveries, and facilitate the kind of social interaction they need to test their hypotheses. This is why we alternate whole-group lessons and discussions with independent work, asking children to operate side by side at first, and later face-to-face in partner situations.

In whole-group discussions, children's responses, explanations, and arguments provide us with an ongoing picture of their mathematical understandings. Active student participation in discussions also creates ownership, connection, and community. If you read through the script sections of any unit, you'll become aware that we don't always call on raised hands. Children respond rather freely, sometimes to one another as well as to us. Genuine give-and-take isn't always easy to manage. When everyone wants to talk at once, we occasionally pose a question or make a statement that encourages each student to talk it over with his or her neighbor for a minute or two. Once they've all had a chance to express their views or swap stories, children are more willing to take turns in a group. It also helps to seat youngsters in a large circle where

they can see one another, unless you're reading a story or making a chart. Demonstrations, too, are more effective if you're seated on the floor as a member of the circle.

During independent work sessions, we facilitate children's ability to work together gradually, asking them to cooperate side by side at first, encouraging them to exchange comments and ideas or simply to socialize with one another. In the last three units, we occasionally ask students to work with partners to play games or help one another with tasks that cannot be accomplished alone.

Your role is critical. You must be in constant circulation as children work: listening, observing, responding, redirecting, guiding, questioning, facilitating, encouraging, and assessing their understandings. You'll find that children's investment in the units tends to inspire task-related conversation. It's unusual to find students talking about last night's television show as they're trying to figure out how big their bears' beds need to be or whose collection of twenty weighs the most.

We know this sort of active learning requires more time and energy on your part, but our experiences with children convince us that it's well worth it. In our own classrooms, we might do three or four units a year. Our program of systematic math instruction—*Box It or Bag It Mathematics* (1988)—takes a lot of quality time too.

What About Classroom Setup?

Because *Math Excursions K* features a mix of whole-group and individual or partner work, our management techniques and classroom setups have to facilitate both. The ideal classroom for unit work usually features a fairly large floor area, carpeted if possible, where children can gather to hear a story, see a demonstration, or form an open discussion circle. Furniture is arranged in such a way that children can work side by side, either at desks or tables, or on the floor. It's helpful to have a table or other work space off to one side where children can pursue an investigation by themselves or with a small group as regular classroom instruction proceeds. We also try to have classroom materials such as paper, pencils, glue, paste, tape, crayons, baskets or other small containers, and Unifix cubes, tiles, or other countables centrally located where everyone has easy access.

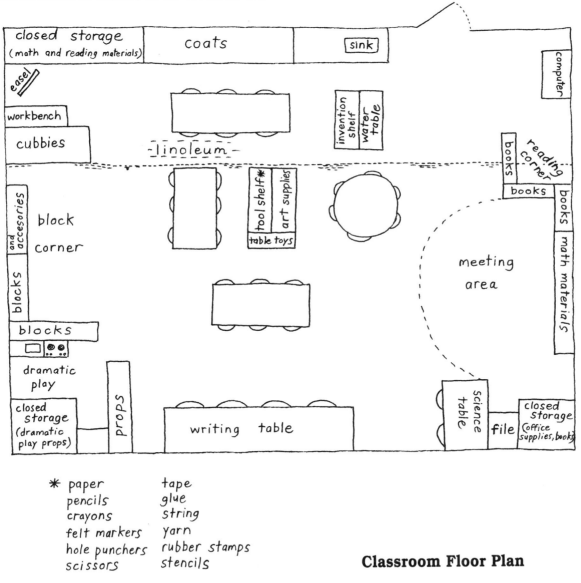

* paper   tape
  pencils   glue
  crayons   string
  felt markers yarn
  hole punchers rubber stamps
  scissors   stencils

Classroom Floor Plan

How Do You Assess Children's Learning?

Because *Math Excursions K* is a series of integrated, theme-based units, rather than a math program intended to deliver systematic instruction, it doesn't lend itself to traditional testing. On the other hand, each unit provides a wonderful opportunity to assess children's emerging math skills, language skills, and ability to generate problem-solving strategies. Assessment methods include observing and questioning students individually and in whole-group interactions and listening to students discuss their ideas and strategies.

The Scope and Sequence of *Math Excursions K*

The scope and sequence chart highlights the skills your students will encounter, practice, and apply. It may also help you focus on children's growing insights and understandings in specific areas. Problem solving is the overall emphasis of the entire book, but each unit has its own focus. "Buttons" features sorting, whereas "A House for a Hedgehog" revolves around geometry. "Hansel and Gretel's Path" focuses on patterning, "Are You Sure It's Twenty?" stresses counting and number sense, and "Teddy Bears Catch a Cold" spotlights measurement and story problems.

Kindergarten Math Skills

	Buttons	A House for a Hedgehog	Hansel and Gretel's Path	Are You Sure It's Twenty?	Teddy Bears Catch a Cold
Problem Solving					
Sort objects by shape, size, color, and other attributes	6+	4–5	3	3	3
Use manipulatives to solve problems	4–5	4–5	6+	3	4–5
Communication					
Share and take turns	6+	6+	6+	4–5	6+
Discuss and demonstrate various approaches and solutions to problems	3	4–5	6+	4–5	3
Use drawing as a tool to clarify thinking and present solutions	3			3	
Estimation					
Recognize the vocabulary of *more/less, the same as*	4–5			4–5	3
Estimate small quantities				3	
Compare weight, length, and size	4–5			3	3
Number Sense and Numeration					
Count by ones to 30	3	3		6+	3
Demonstrate one-to-one correspondence to 20	3	3		6+	3
Recognize and write numerals 0–20				3	
Compare quantities (number sense)	3			4–5	3

3   = Three or fewer lessons in the unit involve this skill
4–5 = Four to five lessons in the unit involve this skill
6+ = Six or more lessons in the unit involve this skill

Kindergarten
Math Skills

	Teddy Bears Catch a Cold?	Are You Sure It's Twenty?	Hansel and Gretel's Path	A House for a Hedgehog	Buttons
Whole Number Operations					
Act out and tell story problems that involve counting, adding, and subtracting	3	3			
Use manipulatives to join or separate groups	3	3			
Measurement					
Use the terms *more*, *less*, and *equal to* compare correctly: length, weight, quantity, capacity, and duration		6+			4-5
Geometry and Spatial Sense					
Construct and identify two-dimensional shapes: squares, circles, diamonds, hexagons, triangles, ovals, and trapezoids	3		3	6+	3
Construct and identify three-dimensional shapes: cubes, cylinders, rectangular solids, prisms, and cones		3	3	6+	
Relate shape and function (Why are cups usually cylindrical? Why are houses usually square or rectangular?)	3	3	3	6+	
Statistics and Probability					
Construct and read a "real" graph (2 or 3 column)	3	3			3
Construct and read a "picture" graph (2 or 3 column)	3	3			

3 = Three or fewer lessons in the unit involve this skill
4-5 = Four to five lessons in the unit involve this skill
6+ = Six or more lessons in the unit involve this skill

Kindergarten
Math Skills

Patterns, Relationships and Functions

	Buttons	A House for a Hedgehog	Hansel and Gretel's Path	Are You Sure It's Twenty?	Teddy Bears Catch a Cold
Copy, extend, and create patterns such as ABAB, AABAAB, ABBABB, ABCABC			6+		
Sort and then pattern objects by color, size, shape, type, texture, and other attributes			3		
Pattern objects by position and quantity			3		

3 = Three or fewer lessons in the unit involve this skill
4–5 = Four to five lessons in the unit involve this skill
6+ = Six or more lessons in the unit involve this skill

Buttons

Buttons: A Preview

What Will Happen in This Unit?

Children will use buttons as a vehicle for practicing sorting and classifying.

Buttons Planning Sheet

	Day 1	Day 2	Day 3	Day 4	Day 5	Day 6	Day 7	Day 8
Sharing, Choosing, Special Classes (Library, Music)				Replace early activities today with Introducing the Button Factory				
Calendar								
Reading and Language Arts		Read "The Lost Button" from *Frog and Toad Are Friends*	Dramatize "The Lost Button"	The Button Factory: Children make their own buttons at the factory in small groups all day				
Unit Work — Science, Social Studies, Art		Make bibs for acting out "The Lost Button"						Have a helper hide the children's buttons right before "The Button Hunt"
Math	Feely Box Sorting				Sort Those Buttons	Is This Your Button?	Which Will Be Left?	The Button Hunt
Closing			Set up the Button Factory					
Notes	Before the unit begins, make the buttons for "The Lost Button" (see Preparation)					Make sure you've prepared button attribute cards for "Which Will Be Left?" (see Preparation)	Prepare a set of button cards to match children's buttons for "The Button Hunt" (see p. 34)	

What Do I Need to Know to Begin?

"Buttons" opens with a feely box sorting activity, in which children describe the attributes of a hidden item as they take turns reaching into the feely box. Once they've discovered that there's a large, ornate button inside, students hear and act out the wonderful story "The Lost Button," from *Frog and Toad are Friends* by Arnold Lobel (1985). Later, children "buy" materials to make their own buttons at the "Button Factory." This shopping activity provides opportunities to handle money, practice counting skills, solve problems, and make purchasing choices on a limited budget. Children then use their wonderful creations in sorting and classifying games. The unit ends with a "Button Hunt": after their buttons are hidden on the playground, children utilize their sorting skills to help each other search for the special button that will match each of their clue cards.

Preparation

Before this unit begins, you'll need to make large buttons for use in acting out the story "The Lost Button" (a chapter from *Frog and Toad are Friends* by Arnold Lobel).

YOU'LL NEED:

- one 12" x 18" piece of white railroad board
- a black felt pen
- two $1/2$" white adhesive dots or cut paper circles
- one $8^1/_2$" x 11" piece of white foam core board or mat board

Cut three circles, each 4" in diameter, from white railroad board for your large buttons. Color black, $1/2$" round "buttonholes" on two of the buttons as pictured below.

Color the third button black and use two adhesive dots or paper circles for buttonholes.

Cut a 4" x 4" square from the white railroad board and color two buttonholes.

Cut one circle, 2" in diameter, from the white railroad board and color two buttonholes.

Finally, cut one circle, 4" in diameter, from the foam core or mat board and color four buttonholes.

Save all of these buttons to use when reading and dramatizing "The Lost Button."

You'll also need to make a set of attribute cards on $8^1/_2$" x 11" oak tag as shown below for "Which Will Be Left?"

What Mathematical Skills Are Addressed?

Buttons—some shiny, some dull; some large, some small; many colored and multi-shaped—fascinate young children. If you give children a handful of buttons they will often sort them spontaneously. This unit utilizes buttons as a vehicle for exploring the skills of sorting and classification. As the children sort in specific ways, they begin to discover many of the skills useful in problem solving. To decide which button to include in a group, they must think logically. By discussing what might happen as a result of sorting the buttons in a particular way, they predict outcomes. By labeling their sorting categories, they build language skills.

Finally, they are encouraged to discuss what they've learned.

The children also have an opportunity to use money, practice counting, and even do some addition and subtraction. Although these intensive experiences may not lead to long-term mastery, "Buttons" is an exciting way to introduce or reinforce some key concepts. Young learners need repeated contact with ideas in varying contexts throughout the early grades. In our own classrooms, we use *Box It or Bag It Mathematics* (Burk et al. 1988) to teach sorting and classification all year long.

What Materials Will I Need?

General Math Materials (Appendix A)

- feely box

Classroom Supplies

- chart paper
- 12" x 18" white railroad board
- white glue
- single hole punch
- 4" x 5" cards cut from card stock or oak tag (one per student)
- four pieces $8^{1}/_{2}$" x 11" white railroad board
- pennies (10 per student)
- eight margarine tubs
- eight clothespins
- black felt-tipped pen
- thirty-five $8^{1}/_{2}$" x 11" sheets of oak tag
- $8^{1}/_{2}$" x 11" white foam core or mat board
- $1/_{2}$" white press-on dots
- crayons
- scissors

Other Things You Will Need

- a large ornate button
- *Frog and Toad Are Friends* (Lobel 1985)
- string
- materials for the Button Factory:
    paper plates in two sizes and two thicknesses
    blue, orange, red, and black construction paper
    black construction paper cut into one hundred and fifty $1^{1}/_{2}$" circles
    two small bottles of glitter with shaker tops
    boxes to hold "Button Factory" materials

Print Materials
(Appendix B)

- Story Bibs black lines (If you prefer a set for children to share, run one copy of each; if you plan to have each child make a bib, run eight to nine copies of each.)

- Starred Paper (Run several copies and cut apart.)
- Circles for buttons: 8" Diameter Circle, 6" Diameter Circle, 1½" Diameter Circles (Run a copy of each sheet and use as patterns to cut orange, red, and blue construction paper circles and black buttonholes.)

How Can I Fit This Unit Into My Schedule?

The activities described in this unit take place over two weeks. It is important that you skim the entire unit before beginning.

We have included a planning sheet that was helpful in our classrooms. We hope this will assist you in charting your course.

Getting Started

The activities in this section set the stage for the rest of the unit.

Feely Box Sorting

Feely box sorting is a great way to stimulate children's interest in a new unit of study. It provides experiences in collecting and using data to form a mental image of a hidden object. Place an ornate button in a feely box and ask children to take turns feeling the hidden object and describing what they feel. Eventually, they will validate that a button is in the box.

SKILLS

- listening
- taking turns
- building language
- thinking logically
- making predictions
- drawing conclusions

YOU'LL NEED:

- a large ornate button placed in a feely box
- chart paper

Gather children in a circle on the rug and show them the feely box. Explain that you have hidden something inside and it is their job to find out what the mystery item is without peeking inside. Put your hand in the feely box to reassure any active imaginations that there is nothing dangerous inside. Then pass the box from child to child. The children will take turns putting a hand in the box and describing what they feel. If they think

they know what is in the box they must try to keep the secret. (A few may need to whisper their guess in your ear to keep from telling.) If someone should happen to announce what is in the box, all is not lost. Try asking, "What makes [Joey] think that? Let's continue passing this box around to see if we agree."

As each child gives a word or phrase to describe what he or she feels, write it on the chart paper. Illustrate the words as you go. Ask children to picture the words in their minds and think about things they know that have those characteristics.

Jeffrey	(sticking his hand in the feely box) *It feels round.*
Teacher	(Writes "round" on the chart paper and illustrates it by drawing a circle.) *Jeffrey says it feels round. Think of things you know of that are round. Don't say what you are thinking out loud.*

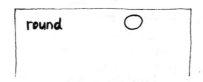

Tabi	*It's kind of cold.*
Teacher	(Writes "cold" and illustrates with an ice cube.) *Okay, so far we know it's round and kind of cold. Think about round, cold things you know about.*
Roshan	*It feels bumpy.*

The teacher writes "bumpy" and illustrates it with a wiggly line.

Michael	*It feels smooth, too.*
Teacher	(Writes "smooth" and illustrates.) *Let's think some more about the thing in the feely box. It feels round, kind of cold, bumpy, and smooth all at the same time!*

Nomi	*It feels kind of hot now. I think it's from all the holding.*
Teacher	(Writes "hot" and illustrates.) *Ah ha! The thing in the feely box gets hot when people hold it in their hand.*
Oona	*I think it's metal.*

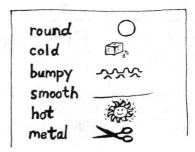

Sometimes children won't be able to come up with a description of what they're feeling. If so, they have the right to pass.

Once everyone has had a turn to feel the item and add some descriptive words to the chart, ask if anyone thinks he or she knows what is inside. List their ideas on the chart paper in question form.

Teacher	*Can anyone tell me what is in the feely box?*
Allen	*Is it a saucer?*

The teacher writes the questions as they are asked on the chart paper.

Sarah	*Is it a pizza?*
Jamal	*Is it french fries?*
Karl	*Is it a coin?*

Is it a....
  saucer
  pizza
  french fries
  coin

18

After the children have asked all the questions they can think of, compare each guess to the list of attributes.

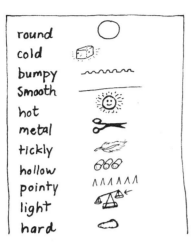

Teacher	*Let's start with the question "Is it a saucer?" Is a saucer round?*
Children	*Yes.*
Teacher	*Is a saucer cold?*
Children	*It could be. Unless it's just out of the dishwasher.*
Teacher	*Is a saucer bumpy?*
Children	*Yes, it could be.*
Teacher	*Is a saucer smooth?*
Children	*Yes.*
Teacher	*Is it a saucer?*
Children	*Maybe. I think it is. Let's peek.*
Oona	*I think the thing in that box is too small to be a saucer.*
Teacher	*I know you're anxious to find out what it is, but let's look at some more of our clues—maybe that will help. Is a saucer metal?*
Children	*Ours aren't. Ours break when you drop them. It's not a saucer.*

Maybe it's a coin. No! Coins aren't bumpy and tickly. I think it feels like my grandma's necklace. It has a round thing that hangs down and it feels about like that thing in the box.

It may be possible to match the attributes with the wrong thing. For instance, it might be very easy to confuse a coin, a medal, or a necklace medallion with a button.

Once all the guesses have been compared to the attributes, remove the button and show it to the children. Compliment them on their detective work, even if they didn't figure it out. Ask if they can think of anything else they might have been able to discover about the button just by touch that would have helped them figure it out. Explain that the unit ahead is about buttons and for the next week they're going to do a lot of things with buttons.

"The Lost Button"

"The Lost Button," a chapter in Arnold Lobel's *Frog and Toad Are Friends*, helps to build classification language and develop the idea of how to go about finding one button among many.

SKILLS

- listening
- story recall
- story sequencing
- comprehension
- building language

YOU'LL NEED:

- *Frog and Toad are Friends* (Lobel 1985)
- buttons cut from poster and foam core board to match the ones named in the story (see "Preparation")

SKILLS

- listening
- story recall
- building language
- performing
- taking turns

Read the chapter "The Lost Button" from *Frog and Toad Are Friends* by Arnold Lobel. Hold up the buttons you've made as they are mentioned in the story.

At the close of the story discuss what happened. Lead students back through the story to answer questions.

1. Where were Frog and Toad going?
2. What happened?
3. What did Toad want to do?
4. What happened then?
5. What did Toad's button look like?
6. How did Toad know the buttons he found weren't the right ones?
7. What did the other buttons look like?

Ask children to look at any buttons they might be wearing. Can anyone describe his or her buttons?

This story is magical and warrants several readings. Many children enjoy supplying the dialogue as it is reread.

Dramatizing "The Lost Button"

Most children love to dramatize stories. Dramatic play allows them to increase their understanding of "The Lost Button" as well as develop specific classification language that will be useful later.

YOU'LL NEED:

- black line patterns for
  Frog
  Toad
  Sparrow
  Raccoon
  (If you want to have more children involved, add a few tree bibs of your own design.)
- 8¹/₂" x 11" sheets of oak tag (four sheets if you want to make bibs yourself ahead of time—you'll need more if you want to make tree bibs; one per child if you want children to make their own.)

YOU'LL NEED: *(continued)*

- 30" of string or yarn for each bib
- glue
- crayons
- scissors
- hole punch
- teacher-made buttons from the previous activity
- feely box containing name cards for each member of the class

To make your own bibs run a copy of each black line and glue it to oak tag. Cut out the bib and color it to match the character in the story. Punch two holes in the top of each bib, thread string or yarn through the holes and tie knots. The bibs will be worn around the children's necks to identify the characters they're playing when it's their turn to act.

The children follow the same procedure as described above in making their own bibs except that each child must first choose a character and glue a copy of the appropriate black line to oak tag. After the glue has dried, children cut out their bibs, color them, punch the holes, and add string or yarn.

Ask children to name the characters in "The Lost But-

ton." As the characters are named, list them on the chalkboard. Show children the bibs you have made or demonstrate how to construct their own costume bibs.

Once the bibs are prepared, explain that you have placed all of their names in the feely box, and you will select the actors by pulling names from the box. Reach into the feely box to pull out one name for each character the children listed and pass out the bibs to the actors before you read the story.

Explain to the audience that they'll provide the sound effects for the play.

Teacher	*Those of you who are watching are an important part of each of our productions. Have you ever been to a play?*
Megan	*When I went to see* Hansel and Gretel, *my mommy said I had to be very quiet and sit still. It was very long.*
Teacher	*We'll make that sitting part a little easier. All of you are going to make the sound effects that go with the story.*
Allen	*How do we do that?*
Teacher	*Well it says in the story that Frog and Toad went for a walk across a meadow. A meadow has tall grass in it. What sound would you make walking through tall grass?*
B.J.	*I've never walked through tall grass. Grass is short.*
Sarah	*We went hiking once and walked through lots of weeds. I got sticky things in my socks. I think the weeds made a kind of "whooshy" sound.*
Teacher	*Rub your palms together. Do you think, Sarah, that is a bit like the sound you remember?*
Sarah	*That sounds a lot like it.*

Teacher   *Whenever Frog and Toad are walking through the meadow, rub your hands together to make the tall grass sound.*

The children practice.

Teacher   *What sound should we make for walking in the woods?*

Children   *We could stand up and walk. But then we couldn't see Frog and Toad so well. We could stamp our feet. Maybe we could hit our hands against our legs like this.*

The child demonstrates, alternating her hands as she slaps her thighs and the sound impresses the class as a good "walking in the woods" sound.

Continue to help the audience develop a repertoire of sounds. When they know what to do, the play begins. Read the story as the chosen actors perform.

Teacher   (reading) *"They looked for the button in the mud."*

Tiffany   *"Is this your button?"*

Joseph   *No! My button is fat, and this button is thin.*

You will probably want to give all the children the opportunity to perform, therefore the play acting may need to stretch over several days.

You will find that your children will begin to notice buttons everywhere. They see them on their clothes. They find them on the yard or at home. They might like to have an area of the room set aside for a button display.

Making Buttons

In this portion of the unit, children visit a class store to purchase supplies to make their own buttons. These buttons will be sorted in a variety of ways as the unit proceeds.

The Button Factory

After the teacher models a shopping trip to the Button Factory, children "purchase" supplies for making their own buttons. Each child will count out ten cents from the bank for his or her purchases. It's helpful to have an older student or parent assist shoppers at the Button Factory.

SKILLS

- making personal choices
- shopping on a limited budget
- counting, adding, and subtracting pennies
- following directions
- working together

YOU'LL NEED:

- paper plates in two sizes (9" and 6 $3/4$" in diameter) and two thicknesses (thin paper and thicker cardboard called "chinet")
  (For a class of thirty, you would need nine large, thin; nine large, thick; nine small, thin; and nine small, thick.)

- 8" Diameter Circles of construction paper in three colors (see Appendix B for cutting pattern)
- 6" Diameter Circles of construction paper in the same three colors (see Appendix B for cutting pattern)
  (For a class of thirty, you would need six of each size and color.)
- at least one hundred and fifty 1$1/2$" black circles for buttonholes (see Appendix B for cutting pattern)
- two small bottles of glitter with shaker tops
- thirty small paper or portion cups for glitter purchases
- ten pennies per child
- eight containers for "factory" supplies (shoebox lids, rectangular plastic baskets, or the like)
- eight clothespins
- 3" x 4" cards for price tags
- eight small margarine tubs
- class list
- price list for helper to check totals
- one piece of Starred Paper per shopper for help in counting out the money (see Print Materials)
- all the children's names in the feely box
- one or two shanked (one-hole) real buttons to show

FOR CHILDREN TO SHARE:

- paste or glue
- half white glue and half water mixture with brush (for sticking on glitter)

To Prepare for the Factory

The day before you plan to do this activity, organize your factory supplies into boxes or other containers. Price each item from one to two cents and write the

---

price on a 3" x 4" label. Attach price tags to containers with clothespins and place margarine tubs inside for money. Set the containers down the length of a counter or table. Have the children make a sign for your factory.

To Model Shopping at the Factory

Show the children the factory you have set up. Tell them they will each make a button with supplies they buy from the button factory. To make it easier for the children to see what is available, move the factory materials to the center of the rug, and ask the children to gather round. Explain that everyone will be given ten cents to spend. Place all the children's names in a feely box and reach in and select a name. Have this child, with the help of the class, count out ten pennies from the class money onto the starred paper. Explain that each person who visits the factory must select one plate and one colored construction paper circle that will fit on that plate. Have everyone look over the available materials.

Teacher *I need to pick one plate for my button. Which plate shall I choose?*

Children *A big plate! Take a big plate!*

Teacher *Okay. Should it be thick or thin?*

Children *Take a thick one.*

Teacher *You want me to take a large, thick plate.*

Children *Yes!*

Teacher *How much will I need to pay for it?*

Children (silence and confusion as the children look carefully for a price tag) *Oh! I see. The card in the clothespin says "2¢." You need to pay two cents for it. That's cheap!*

Teacher *Good for you! Yes, I need to pay two cents. I'll reach into the feely box so someone can take two cents from my starred paper and pay for the plate. Amanda, I chose your name.*

Amanda (taking the two cents from the starred paper) *Where do I put it?*

Teacher *In the margarine tub.* (Amanda pays.) *Good. How much money do I have left?*

Children (All is quiet as the children count.) *Eight cents!*

Teacher   I have to buy the right-sized colored circle to glue to my plate. What shall I buy?

Children   Buy red. No, buy orange. No, blue. Yeah, blue! Do blue.

Teacher   It sounds like nearly everyone would like blue, but what size circle should I get?

Children   Big. You need big because your plate is big.

Teacher   All right I need a big blue circle. How much will it cost?

Children   (All is quiet as the children look.) Two cents. The sign says it will cost two cents.

Teacher   I'll take my big blue circle, and then I'll reach into the feely box to have someone come and count out the correct amount of money to pay for it. (Takes the blue circle and draws a name) Alex, you get to come and pay for the big blue circle. How much money will be left after Alex pays for the circle?

Children   Five cents! No, six cents. I think three cents. I think seven cents.

Alex   (Removes two cents from the starred paper and places it in the margarine tub in the circle box) Six cents are left.

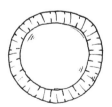

Ask the children if they think you have enough money left to purchase holes and glitter to complete your button.

Talk about the number of holes buttons can have. Ask the children to examine the buttons on their clothing. Have them count the holes of any buttons they find. Show the children the shanked buttons you have. Ask them to help you decide how many holes you should put on your button.

Teacher   How many holes should I buy for my button?

Children   Four, buy four holes.

Teacher   How much does a hole cost?

Children   One cent. A hole costs one cent.

Teacher   How much will four holes cost?

Jeffrey   Four holes—four cents.

Teacher   Does everyone agree with Jeffrey?

Children   Yes. It's four cents.

Teacher   If I spend four cents on holes how much money will I have left?

Children   (All is quiet while some figuring happens.) Two cents . . . No, one cent. No, two cents. It's two cents!

Teacher   Let's see. I'll pull a name out of the feely box for someone to pay for the holes, and we'll see what happens. Chris.

Chris carefully takes one hole and another and another until he has four. He then takes one penny at a time off the starred paper and places each on top of a hole.

Chris   There. Four Holes, four pennies

Teacher   Wow! Did everyone understand what Chris just did?

Nomi   He matched one hole with one penny.

Teacher	*How many pennies are left on the starred paper?*
Children	*Two!*
Teacher	*What can I do with two pennies?*
Tabi	*You can buy some glitter. Glitter costs just one penny.*
Karl	*Boy, glitter is really cheap. I'm going to use lots.*
Teacher	*Wait. There are some words on the price tag with the amount. Does anyone know what they say?*
Sarah	*"Each shake." They say "each shake."*
Nomi	*Oh, you only get one shake of glitter for one penny.*
Teacher	*How much do you think is in a shake?*
Karl	*There's only a little. I use glitter at home.*
Teacher	*Let's see. I'll put one shake of glitter into this cup.*
Children	*Boy! Glitter isn't much in a shake. Maybe you should shake it harder! Yeah, shake it real hard.*
Teacher	*Could I buy a shake for my button? Do I have enough money? I'll try giving it a hard shake.*
Children	*Yes. You can buy two shakes. That will give you more. Buy two!*
Teacher	*(reaches into feely box) Joey, will you come up and pay for the glitter?*
Joey	*(takes the last pennies and drops them in the margarine tub) That's it! No money left.*

That's it! No money left!

Demonstrate how children will brush the surface of the button with a brush dipped in the white glue mixture and then "pinch-sprinkle" the glitter into the wet glue.

Assemble your button so children can see how a finished button could look. Then disassemble the button so children will feel free to make their own choices at the button factory. Their buttons should reflect their own ideas.

The Factory in Operation

The children are now ready to visit the factory. Children briefly interrupt a regular activity as they are called to the factory two or three at a time and resume the activity when they have finished their button. Post a class list by the table to keep track of shoppers. Have starred papers available for counting out the pennies from a general container. If you can, have an aide, older student, or parent helper supervise. After each child has made his or her purchases, they can be checked using the price list. Send children to a construction area after they finish shopping. Save the finished buttons.

Sorting and Classifying Buttons

Children use the buttons they've made to play several sorting and classifying games.

Sort Those Buttons

Children share and then sort their buttons by various attributes including size, color, number of holes, thickness, and presence or absence of glitter.

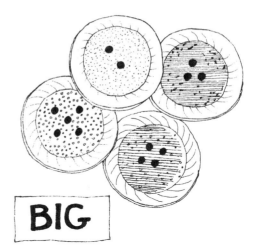

BIG

SMALL

SKILLS

- sharing and taking turns
- solving problems
- sorting by various attributes
- recognizing similarities and differences
- making predictions
- drawing conclusions
- developing language
- counting
- comparing

YOU'LL NEED:

- the children's buttons
- two pieces of chart paper
- index cards for labels

Gather children in a circle. Lay the buttons one at a time in the center of the circle and ask the children to describe each one.

Teacher	*Tell me about the button I've just placed in the center of the circle.*
Alex	*I made it!*
Herman	*It's red.*
Chris	*Yeah, it's thick too.*
Tabi	*It has five holes.*
Megan	*It has glitter on it.*

Teacher	*What about this one? (Placing another button in the circle.)*
Sarah	*That one's blue, and it has no glitter.*
Michael	*It has three holes.*
Nancy	*It's thick like the red one.*
Karl	*That button didn't cost ten cents!*
Teacher	*How can you tell that?*
Karl	*I counted the money up. Two for the plate and two for the circle makes four, and three more for the holes only makes seven. Not ten. Maybe somebody forgot to buy glitter!*

Continue in this fashion until all the buttons have been placed in the circle. Now that the children have had an opportunity to talk about each button, they are ready to begin the task of brainstorming ways the buttons might be sorted.

Teacher   *How can we sort these buttons into groups so that each group will have buttons that are alike in some way?*

Jamal   *We could put all the red ones together.*

Max   *We could put all the blue ones together and the orange ones together.*

Teacher   *You think we should group them by color? I'll write on our chart that we could sort the buttons by red, blue, and orange. That's called sorting by . . .?*

Children   *Color!*

> We could sort the buttons by:
> red, blue, orange (color)

Teacher   *What's another way we could group these buttons?*

Tiffany   *We could put all the big ones here and all the small ones there.*

Teacher   *If we did that, we would be sorting by size. On our chart I'll write we could sort by big and small. That's called . . . ?*

Children   *Size!*

> We could sort the buttons by:
> red, blue, orange (color)
> big, small (size)

Teacher   *Are there any other ways we could group our buttons?*

Nomi   *What about buttons with glitter and buttons that don't have glitter?*

All   *Yeah! I like those glittery ones. That one is mine!*

Tabi   *Is that sorting by glitter?*

Teacher   *That sounds good. I'll write that on the chart. Any other ideas?*

Oona   *What about holes. Some of the buttons have one hole, some two . . .*

Children   *I see one with five holes. There's one with four. There's one with six! Mine has three holes!*

Teacher   *If I wrote that on the chart what would I write?*

Children   *Sorting by holes!*

Jonathan   *Not just holes. How many holes!*

Teacher   *Okay. I'll write how many holes.*

> We could sort the buttons by:
> red, blue, orange (color)
> big, small (size)
> glitter
> how many holes

Teacher   *What else do you see?*

All are quiet. Nearly a full minute passes.

Jonathon   *The plates! The plates are different! Fat, thin. We could put all the fats here and the thins there!*

Teacher What do you call fat and thin? (silence) *It is thickness. One plate is thicker than the other. I'll write fat and thin on the chart, but I'm also going to put the word thickness next to it.*

> We could sort the buttons by:
>   red, blue, orange (color)
>   big, small (size)
>   glitter
>   how many holes
>   fat, thin (thickness)

Continue in this manner. The children may see slight variations in the way the buttons are made. They may see that the glitter is either dumped all in one place or spread out. They may see that the configurations of button holes form different shapes, and so on. Add each new idea to the chart. It is important to have patience. Try not to rush them. Real thinking and careful observation take time.

When the children feel the chart is complete, ask them to choose one way to sort their buttons. For example they might choose to sort by color.

Teacher *All right, if we sort by color, what should we do first?*

Nomi *Put all the red ones in a stack.*

Teacher *Okay. If your button is red, please put it here in a stack.*

Children who made red buttons get them and place them where indicated.

Michael *The orange ones could go here (indicating a spot next to the red group).*

Teacher *If your button is orange, please put it in a stack by Michael.*

Yvonne *All the blue ones should go here.*

Teacher *If your button is blue, please stack it by Yvonne. I'm going to make labels for each of our groups. What should they say?*

Children *One should say red. And one blue. Make that one say orange.*

Blue   Orange   Red

Once the buttons have been sorted and labeled, they can be compared to find out which has the most and which the least. It is important to have your children think about several different ways this can be done.

Teacher *Which group do you think has the most?*

Children *Orange . . . No, red . . . No, blue*

Teacher *What can we do to find out?*

Nomi *We can count them.*

Teacher *What else could we do?*

Jonathon *We could move them right next to each other and the stack that was tallest would have more.*

Tabi *We could lay them out in lines and see which line was longest.*

Teacher *I'll move them right next to each other. Which pile is tallest? Which do you think has the most?*

Children *Red is tallest.*

Teacher *So does red have the most?*

Children *Yes!*

Teacher Let's check by putting them in lines like Tabi suggested. (The buttons are unstacked one at a time from each stack.) *Which stack is going to be the least?*

Children Blue. You only have one blue left and more red and orange.

Teacher (continuing the unstacking process) *What do you see now?*

Children Red isn't the most. There are still orange stacked up and red's all out now. (The children look quite puzzled.)

Though Tabi and several other children understood quite well what had happened, many in the group hadn't a clue what she was talking about. Understanding develops over time as children have many opportunities to compare things with different variables.

Put up the second piece of chart paper. Write "What we learned" at the top. Ask the children to tell you things they have learned by sorting the buttons. Record their observations.

Save the sorting chart. The children might like to try some of the other ways another day.

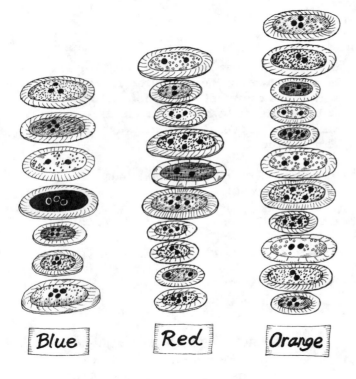

Blue   Red   Orange

Teacher *How did this happen?*

Tabi (very excited now) *I think there are more thick buttons in the red pile. Most of the orange buttons are thin!*

Teacher *How does that make a difference?*

Tabi *Look!* (stacking four thick red plates and four thin orange plates) *The red pile is taller but both piles have the same.*

What We Learned

More were thicker than thinner.
Some had lots of holes.
Almost all had glitter.
Only two didn't have glitter.
The blue were the fewest.
Red and orange were the most.

Is This Your Button?

In this game of elimination, children try to discover the mystery button using clues you give them along the way.

SKILLS

- sharing and taking turns
- problem solving
- sorting by various attributes
- drawing conclusions

YOU'LL NEED:

- the children's buttons

Place the buttons in the center of the rug. Mentally designate one to be the mystery button. Tell the children they can take turns choosing buttons to find the one you picked by asking, "Is this your button?" (If your button is discovered immediately, just choose a new button and begin again.) If the button they guess is not correct, provide a clue by naming one of your button's attributes. Then help the children to see that they can eliminate buttons as they gather clues.

Oona   (pointing to a red button) *Is this your button?*

Teacher   *No, that's not my button. My button is orange, that button is red.*

Children immediately start pointing at orange buttons.

Teacher   *What can you do to the buttons to make it easier to find my button?*

Chris   *We only need orange buttons. We don't need red or blue ones.*

Mark   *Take away the red and blue ones. Just leave the orange buttons.*

Teacher   *Okay. If you made a red or a blue button, take it away. Who would like to choose another?*

Nomi   (pointing to a small button) *Is this your button?*

Teacher   *No, that's not my button. My button is big, that button is small.*

Children are all pointing at big buttons now.

Teacher   *What can you do now to make it easier to find my button?*

Children   *Take away all the small buttons, because your button is big.*

Children who own small buttons on the rug remove them.

Joseph (pointing at a glittered button) *Is this your button?*

Teacher *No, my button has no glitter, and that button has glitter.*

Children (excitedly looking through the remaining buttons) *There's your button!*

Teacher *Which buttons do you need to take away?*

Children *The ones with glitter.*

Teacher *If your button has glitter take it away.*

Children remove their glittered buttons.

Teacher *Tell me about the button that is left.*

Children *It's orange. It's big. It doesn't have any glitter!*

Most children love this game and will want to repeat it many times. Once they have the idea, some enjoy being the "leader," choosing the button and giving their classmates clues.

Which Will Be Left?

Children sort the buttons according to attributes pictured on cards. Before they sort, they try to predict which buttons will remain when they remove the buttons designated by the card.

YOU'LL NEED:

- the children's buttons
- attribute cards (see preparation) made on 8½" x 11" oak tag (as shown below)

Place all of the buttons in the center of the rug. Show the children the cards one at a time. Help the children to identify the attribute on each card and find a button with that attribute. When you have introduced all the cards shuffle them and place them face down on the rug. Have a child draw a card.

Jeffrey *It says "red."*

Teacher *What will be left if we take away all the red buttons?*

Children *The blue ones will be left. So will the orange.*

Teacher *Let's see. If your button is red take it away.* (The children remove their red buttons from the circle.) *What do we have left?*

Children *Blue and orange!*

Teacher *Great. Let's draw another card.*

Tiffany *It says "orange."*

Teacher *What will be left if we take away all the orange buttons?*

Children *There'll be just blue left.*

Teacher	Let's see. If your button is orange take it away. (The children remove the orange buttons.) What do we have left?
Children	Just blue is left.

Teacher	Okay! Let's draw another card.
Joey	It says "big."
Teacher	What will be left this time if we take away all the big buttons?
Children	All the small ones will be left.
Joey	And they're all blue.
Teacher	Let's see. If your button is big take it away. What do we have left?
Children	All small!
Teacher	Great! Let's draw another card.
Mark	Two holes. It says two holes.
Teacher	What will be left if we take away all the buttons with two holes?
Children	All the buttons will be small and blue. Some have three holes, some have four holes, some have five holes, some have six holes.
Teacher	You all are looking and thinking very hard! If your button has two holes, take it away. What do we have left?

Continue in this manner until only a few buttons remain.

Teacher	We only have three buttons left. Can you tell me everything about them?
Children	They are all small. They're all blue. They all have glitter. Two are thick. One is thin. There is one with three holes, one with four holes, and one with five holes.

Teacher	Very good! Could we draw a card that would make all the buttons go away?
Tabi	Blue! if we drew "blue," they would all go away.
Karl	We could draw "glitter" too, and they'd all be gone.
Megan	If we drew "small," they'd all go away too!

Some children in the group may have no idea what these three children have discovered. It may be necessary to test each of their guesses.

Teacher	(looking through the stack for the "blue" card) Here's the blue card. What will be left if we take away all the blue buttons?
Children	Tabi's right! Nothing will be left!
Teacher	Good for you! Let's try that with the "small" card.
Children	Yep! Megan was right. They all go away again.

Finally, ask children if there's any card they might draw that would eliminate all but one button.

Many children will enjoy repeating this game on another day.

The Button Hunt

Have someone hide all the buttons on the playground, weather permitting. (Otherwise, buttons can be hidden in the gym, the library, the cafeteria, or part of your classroom.) Each child must hunt for one special button, using a clue card. As children find their own special buttons, they assist others who are still searching.

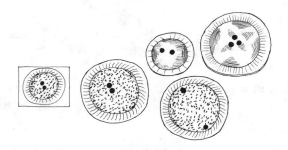

SKILLS

- sharing and taking turns
- problem solving
- sorting by various attributes
- recognizing similarities and differences
- making predictions
- drawing conclusions
- developing language
- visualizing real objects

YOU'LL NEED:

- a set of button cards 4" x 5" (Each card must contain a picture that matches a particular button exactly.)
- the children's buttons

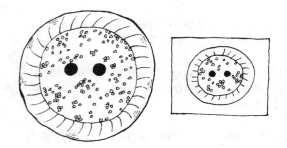

Prior to the lesson you will need to make a set of button cards to match the buttons that the children made. Make sure to place the holes in the same position and configuration as the actual buttons. Use real glitter on the cards for those buttons that have glitter.

Select two cards—one that pictures a large button and one that pictures a small button. Set out four of the children's buttons, one of which matches one of the cards. (Make sure two of the children's buttons you have selected are similar.) Before the hunt begins, have a parent or instructional aide slip out to the yard and hide the rest of the buttons.

Have the children sit in a circle at the rug. Place the large button card in the center so that all the children can see. Ask them to describe what they see.

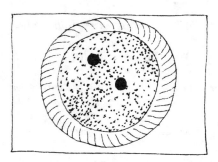

Teacher What can you tell me about this card?

Children It shows a button that is red. The button has two holes. It is thin. It has glitter. It's small.

Teacher How can you tell it's small?

Tabi It just looks small.

Teacher What if I show you this card? (Shows the card that pictures the small button.)

Jeffrey Oh, the button's not small. It's big. That new card has a small button on it.

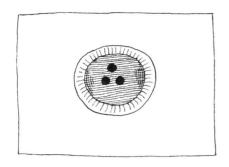

Teacher You're right! What did you need to see before you could know whether the button on the card was large or small?

Jeffrey I needed to see both kinds of buttons so I'd know what a big one and a small one looked like.

Show the second button card and the four buttons you selected.

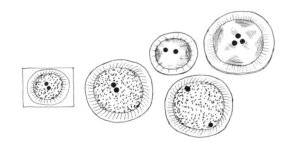

Teacher Can you find the button that matches this card?

Children It matches these two buttons (indicating the two similar buttons).

Teacher Why doesn't it match this button?

Mark That button is blue. The one on the card is red.

Teacher Why doesn't it match this button?

Tiffany That button is small. The one on the card is large.

Teacher Great. Now look carefully at these two buttons. Only one matches the card.

Sarah I see which one. This one matches the card because the holes are real close together.

Teacher Do the rest of you agree with Sarah?

Children Yes! She's right. Look at the holes. They are real close together. You tried to trick us.

Teacher I just wanted you to use your eyes very carefully.

Have your helper quickly hide the last four buttons along with the others.

Pass out a button card to each of the children. Explain that all their buttons have been hidden around the playground, and the card you have given each of them tells which button he or she must find. Each child may pick up only the button that matches his or her card. If a child finds a button that isn't correct, he or she must rehide it and continue searching for the right one.

Have each child look at his or her button card carefully. Have them tell the person sitting next to them everything they can about the button they are to find.

Quickly review a card to make sure everyone understands what to do.

Teacher What color must Megan's button be?

Children Red.

Teacher How many holes will it have?

Children Two.

Teacher Will the button have glitter?

Children Yes.

Teacher Will it be big or small?

Children Big.

Teacher What about thick or thin?

Children Thin.

Teacher So what will the button look like that Megan is looking for?

Children It's red. It has two holes. It's thin and big and has glitter.

Teacher If Megan finds a blue button can she pick it up?

Children No, her button is red.

Teacher If she finds a red button with four holes can she pick it up?

Children No, her button has two holes.

Teacher If she finds a red button with glitter can she pick it up?

Children Yes—No—It depends.

Teacher It depends on . . . ?

Children It needs to be thin, too. Yeah, and big.

Teacher I think you've got it. Are you all ready to hunt?

Children Yes!

Send the children off to hunt. The search continues until everyone has found his or her button. Children who finish quickly may help a friend.

Once all the children have found their buttons, return to the rug to share what happened. Talk with the children about how hard or easy it was to find their button. Which buttons were the hardest to find, the easiest? How many children were helpers? What did they do to help find the buttons? Were there any buttons so alike that it was hard to tell which matched which card? Was the button hunt fun? What did they learn from this unit?

At the close of the lesson, the children may take their buttons and matching cards home to show their families.

A House for a Hedgehog

A House for a Hedgehog: A Preview

What Will Happen in This Unit?

Children will explore relationships between two- and three-dimensional shapes by building model houses.

A House for a Hedgehog Planning Sheet

	Day 1	Day 2	Day 3	Day 4	Day 5	Day 6	Day 7	Day 8	Day 9	Day 10	Day 11
Sharing, Choosing, Special Classes (Library, Music)		Display any hedgehog books and pictures you've been able to find.	Squares Make Cubes: The House Decorating Shop. Have children make their cube houses.	Be sure to make the props for Snuffles' House available to children who want to retell the story.							
Calendar											
Reading and Language Arts	Gathering Information: discuss hedgehogs		Squares Make Cubes: The House Decorating Shop Demonstrate how to shop for supplies and decorate houses. Have children take turns throughout the morning.	Consider reading other books about hedgehogs, houses, and shapes over the next few days.							
Unit Work — Science, Social Studies, Art	Gathering Information: make clay hedgehogs.	Feely Box Shapes		Feely Box Shapes Revisited		Making Circular Houses	Feely Box Shapes Revisited Again	Triangles to Pyramids	Feely Box Shapes Revisited Once Again	Rectangles to Boxes	A Many-Shaped House
Math	Snuffle's House	Picture a Square House		Picture a Circle House	Looking at Round Things		Picture a Triangle House		Picture a Rectangle House		
Closing											
Notes	Cut squares for picturing activity tomorrow. See "Preparation."	Set up materials for House-Decorating Shop and cube houses for tomorrow.	Cut circles for picturing activity tomorrow.	Gather spheres and cylinders and make paper cones for tomorrow.	Prepare materials for children to make round houses tomorrow.	Cut triangles for picturing activity tomorrow.	Run class set of Triangles to Pyramids black line	Cut rectangles for picturing activity tomorrow	Run class set of Rectangles to Boxes black line for tomorrow	Prepare materials for final construction project	If you choose to have your children work with three-dimensional shapes, this final project might take another day or two.

41

What Do I Need to Know to Begin?

Oh, dear! Snuffles the Hedgehog has discovered that his house has burned down and he has nowhere to live. Since he has to start from scratch to rebuild, he'd like to have something a little different than he had before. The children are captivated by Snuffles and enjoy predicting what kind of house he might build next as they listen to his story. They are full of ideas as to why each shape he tries might not work. Their minds race ahead to the final solution, and they are pleased with Snuffles' choice.

Snuffles' House by Daphne Faunce-Brown (reprinted in this unit in its entirety) launches an exploration of shapes that stretches children's understandings and invites new connections.

Throughout the unit, students move from two-dimensional to three-dimensional shapes. They begin by exploring the connection between squares and cubes as they build and then decorate cube houses for the clay hedgehogs they've made. The search for three-dimensional shapes that are round "like a circle" but have space inside for their hedgehogs. After examining spheres, cylinders, and cones, they figure out how to make round houses. Next, they fold large triangles down to form pyramid-shaped houses. Then they cut, fold, and glue rectangular pieces of paper into three-dimensional box dwellings. Such a variety of houses for those little hedgehogs! The final activity allows them to see how all four shapes work together to make houses.

Preparation

Story Props

Make a set of story props to use as you tell and retell *Snuffles' House.*

YOU'LL NEED:

- one 22" x 28" sheet of poster board
- strapping or filament tape
- ruler
- pencil
- a large grocery bag in which to store everything

Cut the poster board into six 3" x 22" strips, one 3" x 21" strip, and one 4" x 8" piece. Coil one 3" x 22" strip into a circle, overlap the ends slightly, **and tape securely with filament tape. Coil a second 3" x 22" strip into a circle, overlap the ends, and tape securely. Compress this circle slightly to make an oval.**

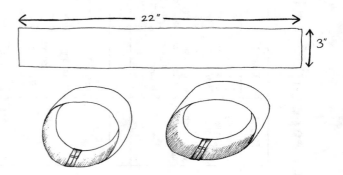

Mark three more 3" x 22" strips at intervals of 5$\frac{1}{2}$". Fold and tape to form two diamonds and a square.

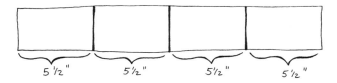

Hint: If you draw each interval line by pressing heavily with a pencil or ball point pen, the poster board will fold more easily.

Finally, fold the 4" x 8" piece of poster board in half widthwise and label it "Rectangular House—Mr. Snuffles Lives Here."

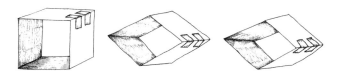

Mark another 3" x 22" strip as shown below. Fold and tape to form a rectangle.

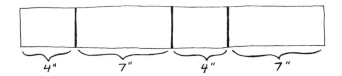

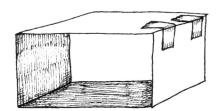

Mark the 3" x 21" strip at 7" intervals. Fold and tape to form a triangle.

You will also need a toy hedgehog. These are commonly sold as soft plastic chew toys for dogs and can be purchased at many pet stores for several dollars. You can also buy them at some toy and baby clothing stores or order them from early childhood supply companies such as Constructive Playthings (1227 East 119th Street, Grandview, Missouri 64030-1117; 1-800-255-6124) or Barclay School Supplies (166 Livingston Street, Brooklyn, NY 11201; 1-718-875-2424). They're usually listed under "Infant Care" and sell for several dollars. The standard size available is about as big as a tennis ball, which fits the proportions of the cardboard "houses" pretty well. If you decide to make one yourself out of fabric or clay, it should be no more than three or four inches in diameter. Put all of your railroad board shapes, the "Mr. Snuffles" sign, and the toy hedgehog into a large grocery bag for storage.

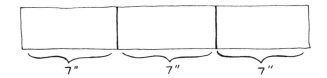

Construction Paper Shapes

These are used with each feely box lesson.

YOU'LL NEED:

- seven sheets of 9" x 12" colored construction paper (We chose to use one color so our children would focus on shape rather than color.)
- the large square, circle, oval, triangle, diamond, octagon, and rectangle templates (see Appendix B)
- the small square, circle, triangle, and rectangle templates (see Appendix B)
- one sheet of heavy 9" x 12" cardboard
- scissors

Use the Large Shape Template black lines to copy each shape onto 9" x 12" colored construction paper. Cut out and label each shape clearly with its name.

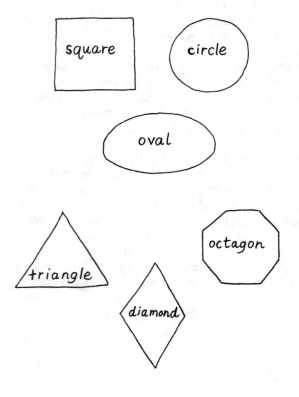

Use the Small Shapes Template black line to cut copies of the square, triangle, circle, and rectangle out of heavy cardboard or mat board to place inside the feely box.

"Picture a House" Cut Shapes

For "Picture a Square House," you will need about fifty construction paper squares in a variety of colors. Cut sizes ranging from 4" x 4" to 12" x 12". You will need similar assortments of circles, triangles, and rectangles for the other three "Picture a House" lessons in the unit.

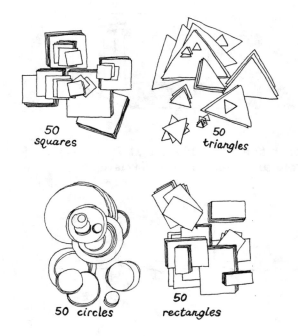

The Cube Houses

To make bases for the cube houses, you will need two half-pint milk cartons for each child. Cut off the top of each milk carton.

Take one graham cracker square and use it to measure and mark each side of the cartons.

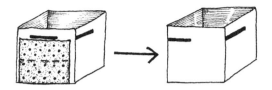

Cut at your markings so that each carton is as tall as a graham cracker.

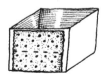

Hold the cartons so the cut tops face each other. Push the cut top of one inside the cut top of the other. You now have a very sturdy cube. Make one for each child in your class.

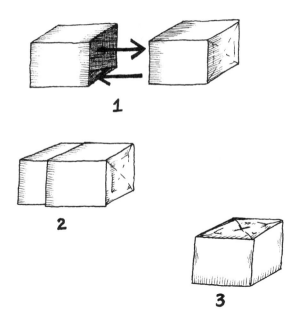

Numeral Cards

YOU'LL NEED:

- seven 3" x 4" rectangles of construction paper

Label each piece with a numeral from 1 to 7.

Spheres, Cylinders, and Cones

Save cardboard tubes and cans for children to explore.

What Mathematical Skills Are Addressed?

The focus of this unit is shape exploration. The children begin a series of discussions about squares, circles, triangles, and rectangles by selecting each shape in turn out of an assortment. They help write a definition of each shape and post it beside a drawing. They explore how the shape works when it is the only one allowed in the construction of a two-dimensional house. Finally, children see how the two-dimensional shape can be used to build its three-dimensional counterpart, which they must do to create snug houses for their little hedgehogs.

As the unit progresses, the children's awareness of shape increases. They talk about shape. They point out the shapes they see everywhere. They discuss how shapes are combined and divided to form other shapes.

In the final activity, children investigate shape combinations as they create two- or three-dimensional houses using all the shapes they have been exploring. Two big triangles can be put together to make a large square. Two rectangles can be stacked one on top of another to form a very large rectangle or sometimes a large square. Two squares can be placed side by side to make a large rectangle. Boxes stack nicely to make two- and three-story houses. Cones and cylinders can be combined to make dandy turrets and pyramids work well for roofs. Students also discover that bending and folding some shapes can generate balconies, awnings, and windows that go up and down.

These intensive experiences serve as an exciting introduction to geometric concepts and make the teaching of shapes lots of fun.

What Materials Will I Need?

General Math Materials (See Appendix A)

- feely box

Classroom Supplies

- 22" x 28" sheet of poster board
- 12" x 18" white construction paper
- crayons
- chart paper
- 12" x 18" construction paper in assorted colors
- scissors
- felt-tip pens
- pencils
- butcher paper
- modeling clay
- white glue
- oak tag

Other Things You Will Need:

- a copy of *Snuffles' House* (Faunce-Brown 1983)
  Note: Snuffles' House is currently out of print. If you are unable to find the book in your school or local library, we have, with the author's permission, reprinted it in this unit.
- *Alice's Adventures in Wonderland*, by Lewis Carroll, was originally published by MacMillan in 1865. Since then, there have been any number of editions, illustrated by various artists. Two of the most recent and most beautiful are
  Alice's Adventures in Wonderland by Lewis Carroll. Illustrated by S. Michelle Wiggins. NY: Ariel Books/ Alfred A. Knopf, 1989.

Alice's Adventures in Wonderland by Lewis Carroll. Illustrated by Michael Hague. NY: Henry Holt, 1985.
- books about hedgehogs or books that show pictures of hedgehogs. Our favorites include
  The Mitten (Brett 1989)
  The Tale of Mrs. Tiggywinkle (Potter 1989)
  Hedgehog for Breakfast (Turner 1989)
  Hedgehog Bakes a Cake (McDonald 1990)
- A *House Is a House for Me* (Hoberman 1978) and other books about houses and house construction
- empty half-pint milk cartons (two per child)
- a sharp knife
- paper plates and cups
- pennies
- margarine tubs or other small containers

Assorted Collage Materials

- paper scraps
- sequins
- ribbon
- pipe cleaners
- feathers
- yarn
- fabric scraps
- toothpicks

House-Decorating Shop Items

- graham crackers
- peanuts
- carob chips
- corn nuts
- peanut butter
- sunflower seeds
- raisins
- miniature marshmallows

Grocery Items (for instruction)

- one 16-ounce can of jellied cranberry sauce
- one very round orange
- two boxes of flat wooden toothpicks
- a toy hedgehog (See Preparation)

Print Materials (See Appendix B)

- one copy of each Large Shape Template (square, oval, circle, triangle, diamond, octagon, and rectangle)
- one copy of the Small Shape Template sheet (contains a square, circle, triangle, and rectangle)
- four copies of Starred Paper
- Counting Mat Price Labels (Run one copy of each sheet. Cut labels apart to use for House-Decorating Shop.)
- Circles to Cones (one per child plus a few extra, run on heavy white paper)
- Triangles to Pyramids (one per child plus a few extra, run on heavy white paper)
- Rectangles to Boxes (one per child plus a few extra, run on construction paper, card stock, or oak tag)

How Can I Fit This into My Schedule?

The activities described in this unit take place over two to three weeks. It is important that you skim over the entire unit before beginning. We have included a planning sheet that was helpful in our classrooms. We hope this will assist you in charting your course.

Who and What Is Snuffles?

The children are introduced to Snuffles the Hedgehog, setting the stage for the rest of the unit.

Gathering Information and Making Hedgehogs

The teacher shares information about hedgehogs with the class and children create simple hedgehogs with clay and toothpicks.

SKILLS

- listening
- collecting information
- building language

YOU'LL NEED:

- your toy hedgehog
- pictures of hedgehogs
- books about hedgehogs
- a copy of *Alice in Wonderland* (optional)
- two one-pound boxes of modeling clay
- two boxes of flat wooden toothpicks
- a "Zoomobile" visit if your local zoo features hedgehogs in its education program

Show your toy hedgehog, Snuffles, to the children. Ask them what kind of animal they think he is and find out if they know anything about hedgehogs. Can they tell anything simply by looking at the toy figure? Show them the books and pictures you have collected. Talk about these wonderful creatures. Tell the children a little about their habits.

For your own information, hedgehogs are found in many parts of Europe but are not native to North or South America. As its name indicates, the hedgehog lives in hedges and thickets and is about the size of a large rat. It sleeps by day and uses its pointed snout to root for insects, snails, and eggs at night. When attacked, it rolls itself into a sharp prickly ball. It spends the winter in partial or complete hibernation.

You might want to read a brief excerpt about the croquet game from *Alice in Wonderland*. Oh! Those poor hedgehogs! If you are able to have a live hedgehog visit, help the children see how Snuffles got his name. (Hedgehogs really snuffle!) Post the pictures of hedgehogs you have collected around the room. Place any books you've been able to gather in the library corner for the children to enjoy at their leisure.

Give each child about an ounce of modeling clay (one quarter of a stick) and some flat wooden toothpicks with which to make a hedgehog. All they have to do is roll the clay into a small ball, shape a snout, and break toothpicks in half to use as prickles. (Flat wooden toothpicks are

easy for children to break and half-lengths poked deep into the clay approximate hedgehog prickles very well.)

Note: It's important that children not be given much more than an ounce of clay for each of their hedgehogs because the houses they'll be making will be quite small. The hedgehogs should be stored at school for use throughout the unit.

Snuffles' House

Children listen to the story of *Snuffles' House* and discover that houses can be made in different shapes, some of which work better than others.

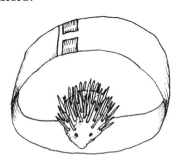

SKILLS
• listening • story sequencing • building language • predicting events • identifying characteristics of geometric shapes

YOU'LL NEED:

- *Snuffles' House: A Story About Shapes*, reprinted here, or a copy of the book if you've been able to locate one
- a paper sack containing the square, circular, oval, triangular, diamond (two), and rectangular forms you made from poster board plus the sign for Snuffles' house (See Preparation)

Read *Snuffles' House* to your class. Use the poster board shapes and toy hedgehog to help students picture what is happening. It is a good idea to practice reading the story before sharing it with the class; handling the poster board shapes and reading at the same time can be challenging. The following is a sample of how the story, modeling, and children's dialogue might fit together.

Snuffles' House
by Daphne Faunce-Brown
(Reprinted by permission of the author.)

Snuffles is a hedgehog, and like all hedgehogs he has long, sharp prickles and black, shiny eyes. Snuffles used to live in a small, square house among some very tall trees.

Remove the square form from the sack. Show it to the children. Tell them that Snuffles' house was square like this shape.

Teacher   Snuffles' house was square . . . like this. It also had an upstairs.

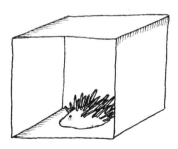

Trevor   You would need stairs to go up.

Teacher   Yes, that's true.

Nancy   He'd need furniture too.

Teacher   You're right! I'm just showing you a model of the shape of the house. Snuffles' house would need all of those things.

One morning when Snuffles came home from a walk, his house was nowhere to be seen. There were clouds of smoke coming from a bonfire on exactly the spot where Snuffles had lived.

The sad little hedgehog walked away. He wandered among the flowerbeds and across the lawn in search of a better place to build a new home.

All Snuffles' friends had square houses, but why not build his house in a new shape?

Ask the children what shape house Snuffles might like to build. After they have given some suggestions, continue with the story.

"An oval house," he thought, "would be beautiful." He set to work straight away. This is what it looked like, and Snuffles felt very proud.

Pull the oval form out of the paper sack and show the children how nicely Snuffles fits inside. Ask them to discuss the pros and cons of living in an oval-shaped house. Can they imagine any problems?

What a fright the poor little fellow had as he walked into his bedroom. The whole house rocked sideways. He could only keep it straight by staying in the middle of the house.

Show the children how the oval teeters.

That night Snuffles slept with his back feet above his head and found it very uncomfortable.

In the morning he thought, "Definitely not an oval house!"

Have the children try to predict which type of house Snuffles might build next.

Teacher   *Do you think that Snuffles will live in his oval house forever?*

Children   *No, it's too rocky! It was like our teeter-totter.*

Teacher   *What type of house might he try next?*

Children   *Square. Rectangle. Something not rocky.*

Teacher   *Let's read on and see.*

"I'll try a round house. Yes, that's it. A big circle like a full moon."

Teacher   *Snuffles is going to build a round house. What do you think about that?*

Thomas   *It's going to roll. I just know it will. Just like the wheel in our hamster cage.*

Snuffles worked hard all day, and in the evening he had finished his round house. It was bedtime and Snuffles was very tired as he climbed the stairs to his new bedroom.

Take the circle of poster board from the paper sack and place Snuffles inside. Ask students to predict what will happen when Snuffles tries to move around in his new house.

As he walked into his bedroom he turned upside down and then began to spin.

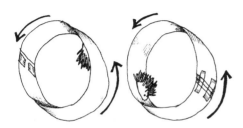

Show Snuffles rolling end over end in his round house.

Children   *I knew he would roll. Why didn't Snuffles know he would roll?*

Teacher   *I guess he hadn't had much experience with round houses.*

Continue reading the story, acting it out as you go.

Snuffles' beautiful round house was rolling, bouncing and bumping. The house stopped with a thump when it hit a tree trunk. Snuffles had to sleep in an upside down house that night.

When he woke up, he felt very sore and miserable. He now knew that his home must have a flat bottom, as his old square house had done.

Ask the children what shape they think Snuffles might try next.

Teacher   *What shape do you think Snuffles might try next?*

Children   *Rectangle. He'll try a rectangle. I think maybe a triangle. It has a flat bottom.*

Teacher   *Let's read some more and see what Snuffles decides.*

A triangular house! It would be exciting, like sleeping in a tent. It would also have an upstairs like his old square house.

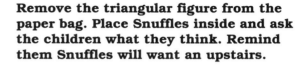

Remove the triangular figure from the paper bag. Place Snuffles inside and ask the children what they think. Remind them Snuffles will want an upstairs.

Teacher   *Here is a model of the triangular house. I'm going to put Snuffles inside. What do you think? Will he be comfortable in this house?*

Annie   *It has a flat bottom. It won't roll or rock.*

Teacher   *What do you think about the upstairs?*

Alan   *It's not going to be very big. He might have trouble fitting his bed in there. It was very hard fitting my new bed in my room. The door was a little too small.*

Teacher   *Let's read on and see what happens.*

Continue acting out the story as you read.

But even this house had a very sad ending. His triangular house had a very very small upstairs. Snuffles could only get to the top of the stairs and squeeze his nose into his bedroom. The point on the triangle did not leave room for a whole hedgehog at the top.

Snuffles went into his sitting room and thought about his new house. He thought about all sorts of shapes and sizes.

Remove the diamond model from the paper sack.

Teacher He thought about a diamond shape.

What do you think? Will this make a good shape for a house? (holding the diamond on one point)

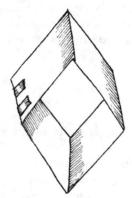

Karl If he makes it that way, it will fall over on its side.

Teacher (letting the diamond fall to one side.) *Oh, oh!*

Yvonne *That looks weird. The walls will be all slanty!*

Continue with the story.

One shape he thought about was an octagon. What a very big and grand word it was!

Teacher *What do you think an octagon is?*

Children *It sounds like octopus. Maybe it has lots of legs. A house with lots of legs! That's funny!*

Tabi *Maybe it has lots of sides.*

Teacher *You are right! An octagon does have lots of sides—eight in all. I'm going to change this diamond into an octagon. Does anyone have an idea about how I might do it?*

This is a very difficult question. Give them a few moments to pursue the problem. Then fold each side of the diamond in half to form the octagon, or use a child's suggestion.

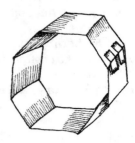

Teacher (placing Snuffles inside the octagon house) *What do you think about this as a shape for the house?*

Children *It looks like it might be hard to build. Some of the walls will slant funny.*

Teacher *Let's see what Snuffles decides to do.*

Continue reading the story.

But he knew that an octagon had eight sides and he felt this would be too difficult to build.

Children *I thought so. Me too.*

At last Snuffles thought of a good and safe shape to build.

Discuss with the children what shape they think Snuffles finally chose. Continue reading.

It was a rectangle.

Children   *I was right! I knew it was a rectangle. Me too!*

It would have a flat bottom, and plenty of room upstairs.

Remove the rectangular structure from the paper sack. Place Snuffles inside. Show how the house doesn't roll or teeter.

Talk about the nice straight sides. Discuss the amount of room Snuffles will have upstairs.

Snuffles' rectangular house was very smart and he painted a sign to stand outside.

Show the little sign you've made.

It said "Rectangular House. Mr. Snuffles lives here." When I last saw Snuffles he was still living there. He had built it as far from the bonfire as possible!

Some students may be very concerned about the vulnerability of the new house. Point out that Snuffles was wise to build his house far away from the bonfire. Ask them to recall what shapes Snuffles used for his houses and what difficulties he had with each of the shapes. Discuss why the first house and the last house were such good choices. Discuss what shapes their own houses are. Do they know of any houses in the shapes Snuffles rejected that would work? Some children might mention Indian tepees, A-frame mountain cabins, or even domes. Explain that they'll be building several different houses for their own clay hedgehogs in the next week or two, and invite students to discuss some good house shapes.

You might leave out the cardboard shapes and the toy hedgehog for the children to retell the story at choosing time.

Squares to Cubes

The children explore the properties of squares and cubes, and they discover that they can use squares to make cubes.

Feely Box Shapes

Children listen to the teacher describe a shape hidden in a feely box. They try to eliminate large construction paper shapes that don't match the descriptions until only the mystery shape remains.

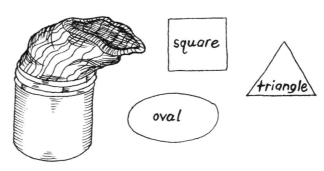

YOU'LL NEED:

- a feely box
- a 2" cardboard square to put in the feely box (See Preparation)
- large construction paper shapes (See Preparation)

Have the children sit in a circle on the rug. Spread the large construction paper shapes out in the center. Help the children identify each of the shapes. Show them your feely box. Explain that you have put a small version of one of the shapes inside, the shape they'll be using to build houses for their hedgehogs. Tell them you are going to put your hand inside and describe what the shape "feels" like. As they listen, they will try to eliminate any of the displayed shapes that don't fit the description.

Teacher I have a shape in my feely box. We'll be using this shape to build houses for our hedgehogs. Can you guess which shape it might be?

Micah An oval?

Kimiko A triangle!

Herman No, a square. Remember his first house was a square?

Teacher Is there anything that would help you know which shape is in the feely box?

Joanna Show it to us!

Traci Pull it out. Then we can see!

Teacher What if I give you a clue about it?

Children Okay.

Teacher Here goes. I'll put my hand in and tell you what I feel. The shape in my feely box has some straight sides. Is there any shape on the rug that doesn't have straight sides?

Tabi The circle doesn't have straight sides—it's round!

Teacher That's true. We can take it away then because it's not like the shape inside this box. Are there any others we could remove?

Michael We can get rid of the oval. It doesn't have straight lines— it has curves.

Teacher Does everyone agree? Okay, Tabi and Michael. Take away the circle and the oval.

Teacher The shape in my feely box has corners.

Children You can't get rid of anything. They all have corners!

Teacher That's true. . . . Here's another clue. The shape in my feely box has more than three corners.

Alan	*You can get rid of the triangle. It just has three corners.*
Teacher	*Okay! Alan, take the triangle away. The shape in my box has four sides.*
Sarah	*(pointing to the octagon) You can get rid of this one.*
Teacher	*What is that shape called?*
Children	*An octopus? No, an octagon.*
Teacher	*Good for you! Sarah, you can remove the octagon. The shape in my box has corners that look like upper case L's.*
Roshan	*You can get rid of this one. (She points to the diamond.)*
Oona	*That's the diamond.*
Teacher	*Do you all agree that the diamond can be taken away?*
Children	*The corners aren't like the big L, they're more like a V.*
Teacher	*Okay, Roshan. You can take the diamond away.*
Teacher	*We have only two shapes left. Which do you think it might be?*
Children	*The rectangle! It's the rectangle because that was how Snuffles made his last house.*
Teacher	*Here's one more clue so you can see if you're correct. The shape in my box has sides that are all exactly the same length.*
Children	*It's the square!*

Take the square out of the feely box and show it to the children. Review the characteristics that make it a square.

Teacher	*Here is the shape that was in my feely box. What is it?*

Children	*It's a square. We were right!*
Teacher	*I'm going to draw a square on this piece of chart paper. Can you tell me what I need to know to be able to draw it correctly? We'll make a list of rules about squares.*
Children	*It has four sides. The corners make "L"s. All the sides are the same length.*

List the characteristics of the square as the children volunteer them. Then use their ideas to draw a square. Post the chart where the children can see it.

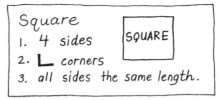

```
Square
1. 4 sides          ┌──────┐
2. L corners        │SQUARE│
3. all sides the same length.  └──────┘
```

Explain that the square is the shape they will be using for the next two days and, just like Snuffles, they will build square houses for their hedgehogs. Give the children a chance to stretch their legs, and then pull them back together on the rug for the next activity.

Picture a Square House

The children create a picture of a square house out of assorted paper squares.

YOU'LL NEED:

- about fifty construction paper squares in a variety of sizes and colors (See Preparation)
- 36" x 36" piece of butcher paper on which to make the house
- glue
- your toy hedgehog

Have the children sit in a circle on the rug. Place the butcher paper in the center. Lay out the squares near the paper. Tell the children they are going to create a picture of a house. Talk about the things needed for a house.

Teacher What are some of the things we need to make a house for Snuffles?

Children We need windows. We need a door. A roof. We need a chimney. We could put a fence around it. It could have some steps up to the door.

Explain that they will each have a turn to add something to the house. They cannot remove anything that someone added before. Each child can add only one or two squares. Call up two children at a time to place their squares.

Teacher What is Michael doing?

Sarah I think he used the biggest square to be the house.

Yvonne adds two small squares.

Teacher What about Yvonne?

Michael She added two windows.

Teacher What's happening now?

Children Alan added a chimney. I'm going to give it a garage. Can I be next? A square car would be funny.

Oona Maybe hedgehogs don't need cars.

Admire the house when it is completed. Count the number of squares used to make it. Leave it on the rug until you have time to glue the squares into place. Once everything is glued down, save the picture for tomorrow's lesson.

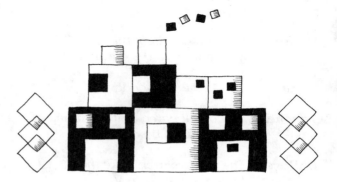

Note: If your students happen to rotate some of the squares as pictured in this illustration, it's interesting to see if they think the rotated shapes are still squares.

Squares Make Cubes: The House-Decorating Shop

The children build cube houses out of graham cracker squares and then visit the House-Decorating Shop to purchase what they need to decorate their houses.

SKILLS

- planning
- coin recognition
- budgeting money
- counting with one-to-one correspondence
- counting, adding, and subtracting money
- fitting two-dimensional shapes together to form three-dimensional shapes
- naming shapes

EACH CHILD WILL NEED:

- two empty half-pint milk cartons with the tops cut off (one pushed inside the other to form a cube—See Preparation)
- six graham cracker squares
- peanut butter (Divide the contents of a very large jar of smooth peanut butter into 8–10 small bowls or margarine tubs.)
- six pennies
- one plastic knife
- one 6" paper plate
- one small paper cup for store purchases
- quart-sized ziplock or paper lunch sack

YOU'LL NEED:

- a small container of peanut butter
- six graham cracker squares
- one milk carton cube
- one plastic knife
- one 6" paper plate
- your toy hedgehog
- the picture children created with squares from the day before
- store items (peanuts, sunflower seeds, carob chips, raisins, corn nuts, miniature marshmallows)
- bowls to hold the store items
- Counting Mat Price Labels for each item (See Appendix B)

- two–four pieces of Starred Paper (See Appendix B)
- six margarine containers for "pay" tubs
- House-Decorating Shop sign

Ask children to sit in a circle on the rug. Lay out their picture of the square house. Set your toy hedgehog on the house and engage students in discussion. Does this flat house pose any problems for Snuffles? As the discussion unfolds, introduce the idea of making a three-dimensional house.

Nancy *Well, it's made out of all squares. Snuffles might get hurt on a corner.*

Kevin *It's a real big house.*

Roshan *And Snuffles is little.*

Sarah *He can't even get in the door!*

Teacher *Why not?*

Sarah   It's only a picture—you can't get inside a picture!

Teacher   Can you think of any way we could build a square house that Snuffles could get into?

Nicole   You could glue some squares together or use tape.

Erlin   If you could get squares to stand up . . .

Teacher   I brought something that might help. (She holds up a milk carton cube.)

Mark   A milk carton?

Jacob   Where's the top?

Oona   It's like a little house. Our clay hedgehogs could fit inside.

Tabi   But there's no door.

Teacher   You're making good observations. What shape is this milk carton?

Children   It's a square!

Teacher   You're right. There's a square on every face. This is called a "cube."

Megan   Like our wooden cubes!

Jory   Like the ice cubes in our refrigerator!

Teacher   We're going to make cube houses for our little hedgehogs with graham cracker squares.

Show them a graham cracker and talk about its shape. Help students see how six square crackers can be used to form a cube house. Be sure to emphasize the relationship between the squares and the cube.

Teacher   Can you think of any way you could use these square crackers to make a cube like the milk carton?

Tabi   Yes, if you could get them to stand up, but that would be hard.

Teacher   How many would you need?

Children   Three. No, four! One for each side!

Teacher   What about the top and the bottom?

Children   Four for the sides. Let's see—one, two, three, four, five, six! But how can we get them to stand up like that box?

Teacher   We'll use the milk carton and peanut butter. The peanut butter will be our glue to attach them to the carton.

Sarah   That's funny!

Trevor   But what about a door? The hedgehog can't get inside without a door.

Teacher   It would be hard to cut a door through a graham cracker, but we'll decorate our cube houses later and you can put a pretend door on yours.

Demonstrate how to take a _small_ dollop of peanut butter, place it in the center of one side of the graham cracker, and gently press the graham cracker square on top of the milk carton.

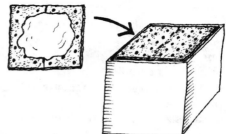

Continue gluing crackers to the carton until you have a graham cracker cube.

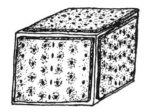

Place crackers, knives, plates (on which to build), milk cartons, and peanut butter for about six children at each table. Send the children out to make their cubes. Have each child write his or her name on the paper plate when finished.

Set up the House-Decorating Shop in a separate area of the room with containers of the store items, "pay tubs," and counting mats by each of the store offerings. You will also need two to four sheets of starred paper, shopping cups, and a large container of pennies. Hang a sign to identify the shop.

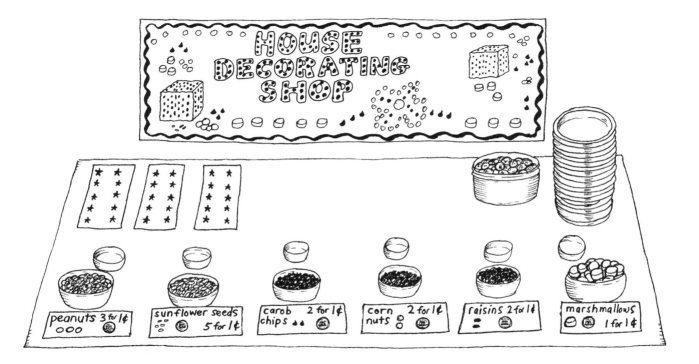

When all of the children have finished making their cubes, have them clean up their tables and gather around the House-Decorating Shop.

Comment that their new houses are currently very plain—no doors, windows, chimneys, and other things such as those the children created in the square house picture. Assure them that they can turn their cube houses into fancy hedgehog homes by making purchases from the House-Decorating Shop. Model how the shopping will work.

Teacher   *Each of you will have six cents to spend. We'll count out six cents on this starred paper.*

Children   *Can we start now? I want some raisins. Do we get to eat all of it?*

Teacher   *We'll use the foods to decorate our houses. If you want to eat it after you take it home, that would be okay.*

Please help me count out six pennies.

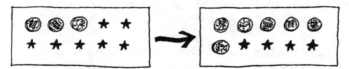

Teacher How many pennies do I have?

Children Six!

Teacher How many pennies are in the top row!

Children Five!

Teacher How many pennies are in the bottom row!

Children One! Five and one—that's six!

Teacher Now that I have six cents, I'm ready to shop.

Talk about the items available for purchase. Discuss the price of each item and demonstrate the use of the counting mats.

Teacher What shall I buy to decorate my cube house?

Children Marshmallows! Carob chips!

Teacher How much do marshmallows cost?

Children One for one cent.

Teacher I'll use this counting mat. What do you see?

marshmallows 1 for 1¢

Children One marshmallow and one penny.

Teacher Let me show you how to use this mat. I'm going to put one marshmallow on top of the picture of the marshmallow. What do you think I'll put over the picture of the penny?

Children Put a penny there!

marshmallows 1 for 1¢

Teacher You've got it! Now I can put the marshmallow in my shopping cup and the penny in the "pay tub." How much money do I have left to spend?

Children Five? Four? No, it's five pennies. See! The top stars are all filled up still.

Teacher How can we be sure?

Children We just know by looking! Let's count—one, two, three, four, five!

Teacher What else can I buy to decorate my house?

Children Carob chips. Buy some carob chips.

Teacher What does this mat tell us?

carob chips 2 for 1¢

60

Children *Two carob chips cost one penny.*

Teacher *Good. What should I do?*

Alan *Put a carob chip on top of each chip picture and one penny on the penny.*

carob chips   2 for 1¢

Teacher *Did I get it right?*

Alan *That's right.*

Teacher *Now what should I do?*

Children *Put the carob chips in your shopping cup. And put the penny in the "pay tub."*

Continue purchasing items until you've spent all your money, but remind children that they don't have to spend all of their money. Demonstrate how to place a tiny bit of peanut butter on the things they have purchased to attach them to the house, but don't finish your house. That way, children will feel free to come up with their own ideas about house decorating.

Set up a table in the room with three or four peanut butter containers and plastic knives. While the rest of the class is involved in another activity, send chil-

dren in partners to the store. It is important to have an adult helper or older student there to help with purchases. After the children complete their purchases, have them tap two more children to shop and then decorate their cube houses.

Have a place for the children to set their completed houses and clay hedgehogs to be admired by all. Children will take their cube houses home at the end of the day in quart-sized Ziplock bags or paper lunch sacks, but their hedgehogs must stay. Be sure to seal your own cube house into a Ziplock bag to save for review in the next few lessons.

Circles to Spheres, Cylinders, and Cones

Children explore some of the similarities and differences between circles, spheres, cylinders, and cones and create round houses for their hedgehogs.

Feely Box Shapes Revisited

The children listen to the teacher describe a circle hidden from view in a feely box. They try to eliminate large construction paper shapes that don't match the descriptions, until only the circle remains.

SKILLS

- listening
- building geometric language
- applying descriptions
- thinking logically
- drawing conclusions

YOU'LL NEED:

- a feely box
- a cardboard circle (2" in diameter) placed in the feely box (See Preparation)
- the paper bag containing your remaining three-dimensional forms and the sign for Snuffles' house (See Preparation)
- your toy hedgehog
- chart paper
- a felt-tip pen
- the story *Snuffles' House*

Have children sit in a circle on the rug and review what they've done so far: made a picture of a house using only squares and used square graham crackers to build cube-shaped houses for their hedgehogs. Explain that they'll be using a new shape to create a picture of a house today. To help them remember some of the possibilities, you're going to read *Snuffles' House* again. Remember to have them predict which shape Snuffles will try each time and explain why each shape won't work. When you're finished with the story, spread out the large construction paper shapes in the center of the circle. Ask the children to identify each of the shapes. Show them the feely box. Explain that you have put a new shape inside and you are going to tell what it "feels" like. As you describe it they will try to eliminate any construction paper shape that doesn't fit the description until the remaining shape matches the one in the box.

Teacher *I have a new shape in my feely box, one that you'll be using to make more houses for your hedgehogs. I'll put my hand in*

and tell you what I feel. The shape in my feely box has less than four corners.

Children *You can take away the octagon. And the square too. No, not the square. It has corners. But she said it has less than four corners. Oh, then the rectangle can go too. The diamond too—it has too many corners.*

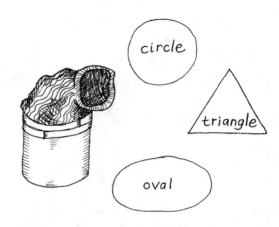

Teacher *If your name begins with T you can take away one of the shapes that doesn't belong.*

Thomas removes the square, Tabi removes the rectangle and Traci removes the octagon. Tarik removes the diamond.

Teacher *The shape in my feely box has a curved line.*

Children *The triangle. We can take away the triangle.*

Teacher *Annie, would you please remove the triangle?*

Teacher *We have only two shapes left. Which do you think it might be?*

Alan *I think it's the circle. The next house after the square that Snuffles built was a circle.*

Teacher *That sounds like a good reason for your guess. What do the rest of you think?*	# Picture a Circle House
	Students create a picture of a house out of assorted construction paper circles.

Teacher *That sounds like a good reason for your guess. What do the rest of you think?*

Children *A circle!*

Teacher *Let's try another clue to be sure. The shape in my box is the same shape as our clock.*

Children *It's the circle. We knew it!*

Teacher *Can we take away a shape?*

Children *Take the oval.*

Teacher *Let's peek into the box and see if you're right.*

Take the circle from the feely box and review the characteristics that make it a circle.

Teacher *I'm going to draw a circle on this piece of chart paper. Can you tell some rules that will help me draw it? We'll list the rules beside it.*

Children *It doesn't have corners. It's round like a clock.*

> Circle
> 1. no corners ✳ (circle)
> 2. round like a clock

Explain that the circle is the shape they'll work with for the next two days. Give them a chance to stretch with a finger play or song game and then pull them back together on the rug for the next activity.

Picture a Circle House

Students create a picture of a house out of assorted construction paper circles.

YOU'LL NEED:

- about fifty construction paper circles in a variety of sizes and colors (See Preparation)
- a 36" x 36" piece of butcher paper
- glue

Have children sit in a circle on the rug. Place the butcher paper in the center. Scatter the circles to one side of the paper. Tell children they're going to make a picture of a house from circles. Review the things a house needs.

Teacher *What are some of the things we need to make a house?*

Children *We need windows. We need a door and a roof. We need a chimney. We could make a stone path with some circles.*

Teacher *Snuffles might like a path leading to his house.*

Brenton	But you said this was going to be a picture. Snuffles can't get into a picture.
Joanna	He could with magic.
Teacher	We'll make a round house later that he can get inside.
Erlin	Like a ball?
Teacher	What made you think of a ball?
Erlin	It's round, like a circle.
Jory	We used to have a ball for our hamster. We'd put him inside and he could roll all around on the floor.
Teacher	What fun!

Explain to the children that they will have a turn, as before, to add something to the circle house picture. They can't remove anything that someone added before them. Each person can add only one or two circles. Call children up two at a time to place their circles. The rest of the group watches and talks about what is happening.

Admire the house when it is completed and initiate a discussion. Was it easy or hard to make a picture of a house using only circles? Why? Have your students ever seen a house that looked round? Pose the problem again that Snuffles won't be able to get inside this flat picture house. Ask children to search the classroom or their homes, if you prefer, to find round things Snuffles could fit inside if there were a way to make a door.

Leave their picture on the rug until you have time to glue the shapes in place. Then post it near your drawing and description of the circle.

Looking at Round Things

Children work in partners to discover the similarities and differences between circles, cylinders, spheres, and cones.

SKILLS

- working cooperatively
- investigating circular forms
- sorting
- comparing circles, spheres, cylinders, and cones

YOU'LL NEED:

- a collection of round three-dimensional objects brought from home or found in the classroom such as
  - balls of all kinds
  - cans
  - cardboard tubes
  - cylindrical blocks
  - a globe
  - jars and other cylindrical containers
  - a balloon
- half a class set of paper cones (You may want to use the Circles to Cones black line in Appendix B.)

Note: Be prepared to contribute enough items of your own so that there will be at least one sphere and one cylinder for every two children in your class.

Ask children to bring the round objects they found to the discussion circle. Allow each to share his or her items and place them in the middle of the rug. Add your own if necessary. Then distribute a spherical object, a cylindrical object, and a paper cone to each pair of children and ask that they move out of the circle a bit and work together to discover as much as they can about each shape—similarities and differences in how the shapes look, how they move, how they balance, how they're made, how they'd work for hedgehog houses. After a few minutes of exploration, draw them together to discuss their findings.

Teacher *What did you discover?*

Jory *They're all round.*

Traci *We got a ball and a can and this paper thing that looks like an ice cream cone.*

Mark *Ours could roll—see!*

Teacher *Do they all roll the same way?*

Children *Yeah! They all roll.*

Teacher *What if I set Traci's can up on one end? Does it roll then?*

Karl *No, it has to be on its side to roll.*

Teacher *Does your tennis ball work the same way?*

Karl *No, it can't! There's no end to put it on. It just rolls all over.*

Teacher *So it seems to be round all the way around?*

Jeffrey *It's just like this Ping-Pong ball. It really can roll far!*

Teacher *So the shapes that are like balls are round all the way around and the cans roll when they're on their sides. What about the cone shapes? Do they roll?*

Kimiko *Sure—look! When I push, it just rolls around in a circle.*

Teacher *What happens when you stand it up?*

Kimiko *Nothing. It doesn't move.*

The discussion in your room could take many directions, but the "big idea" to keep in mind as you listen and respond to children is that each of these round shapes is constructed differently and bears a different relationship to a circle.

As things wind down, ask children if any of the items would make a good house for a hedgehog.

Jeffrey *This can could hold my hedgehog.*

Traci *This jar would work too.*

Sarah *Our tube would be pretty good except the hedgehog might slip out.*

Teacher *What about the cones?*

Hermon	*I'll go get my hedgehog . . . see, he fits right under. All I'd have to do is make a door.*
Megan	*It looks like a little tepee!*
Teacher	*How about the balls? Will they make good houses?*
Karl	*My Ping-Pong ball is too little.*
Nicole	*The red ball would work but how could he get in?*
Joseph	*Cut a door.*
Nicole	*But the ball would pop!*
Jory	*Get a ball that comes apart like my hamster one.*

Making Circular Houses

Now that children have had a chance to explore spheres, cylinders, and cones informally, they'll examine more closely the relationship of each to a circle and discover how to construct cylindrical houses with flat or cone-shaped roofs for their hedgehogs.

SKILLS

- investigating round forms
- comparing circles, spheres, cylinders, and cones
- sorting
- constructing and combining shapes to create circular houses
- working together cooperatively

YOU'LL NEED:

- the circle-house picture your class created
- several paper circles
- a very round orange
- a 16-ounce can of jellied cranberry sauce
- two large paper plates
- small paper plates (one per child)
- a sharp knife, can opener, and spatula
- one 4" x 10" piece of construction paper
- one 5" x 5" piece of construction paper
- one copy of the Circles to Cones black line (Appendix B)
- scissors, stapler, tape, glue
- several cans that have been washed and had tops, bottoms, and labels removed
- your graham cracker cube house

EACH CHILD WILL NEED:

- access to 4" x 10" and 5" x 5" construction paper (enough for everyone to have one of each size plus a few extras)
- access to the Circles to Cones black line (Run a class set.)
- scissors
- crayons

Review the work you've done with circles so far. Use the orange, jellied cranberry sauce and a paper cone to examine the construction of each three-dimensional shape and its relationship to a circle.

Teacher	(laying the circle-house picture down in the middle of the discussion group for all to see) *You've worked together to make a picture of a circle house, but you decided that Snuffles couldn't really live in this house because it's flat. So you hunted at home to find round objects that might hold a hedgehog if you could cut a door.*

	Some of you brought things shaped like this can (holding up can of cranberry sauce). This shape is called a cylinder.
Erlin	*I brought a can, only it was open so a hedgehog could fit inside.*
Trevor	*So did I!*
Nancy	*Me too—from my mom.*
Micah	*Not me. I brought a ball.*
Teacher	*Some of you, like Micah, brought something shaped like this orange. This shape is called a* sphere.
Annie	*What's a sphere?*
Teacher	*A sphere is a shape that's round all the way around like a ball or this orange.*
Oona	*I brought one of those. It can really roll.*
Teacher	*And I gave you paper cones like this to play with.*
Joseph	*Yeah, they rolled funny!*
Teacher	*They rolled around in a circle, didn't they?*
Children	*Yeah!*
Teacher	(holding up the graham-cracker cube house) *Do you remember how we used flat squares to make a cube house the other day?*
Children	*We used peanut butter to stick them on. I put marshmallows on mine. Me too! Not me. I used raisins to make a door.*
Teacher	*How many crackers did you need to make your cube?*
Children	*Three? Four? Six—remember! Four around and a top and a bottom.*

Teacher (holding up several paper circles) *Do you think you could use flat paper circles to make a sphere, a cylinder, or a cone?*

Doubtful silence prevails.

Note: The relationship between each of these round three-dimensional objects and a circle is a challenge for children to understand. If you set any of the three on a table and cut a cross-section parallel to the table, you'll see a circle, just as the cross-section of a cube cut parallel to its base is a square.

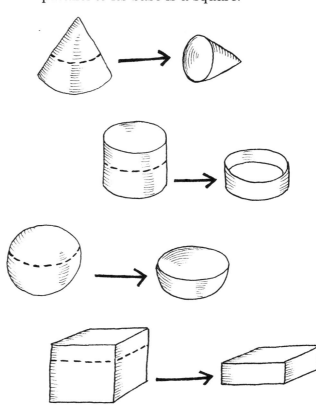

Constructing hollow versions of these shapes as houses for hedgehogs isn't so simple. Although a cube-shaped house is easy enough to make from squares, a cylindrical house is made of two circles and a rectangle.

A cone house can be made by slitting a circle along its radius, pulling it together, and fastening it.

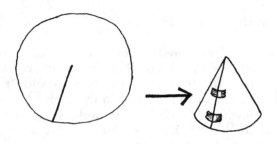

Here's one way to make a hollow sphere. It is very strange indeed.

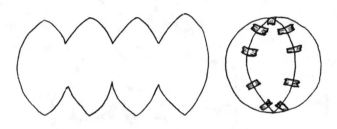

Your kindergartners may be pretty sure there's no way to use flat paper circles to make spheres, cylinders, or cones. On the other hand, some may have ideas possibly based more on wishful thinking than reality.

Alan *I know! If you taped two circles together, maybe it would be like a balloon and you could blow it up round.*

Joanna *Yeah, or stick two together and put stuff in the middle—like a round pillow.*

Kimiko *Maybe I could wrap one around to make a shape like that can.*

If they're eager to try some of their ideas, you could set out a supply of circles along with any other materials they request before you proceed too far with the lesson. You may, however, choose to guide their investigations by examining cross-sections of shapes first. If so, set the orange on a paper plate and propose to

cut it in half, asking children to predict what shapes they'll see if you do.

Teacher *We know that circles and spheres are both round but it's hard to think of how to get a flat circle to turn into a sphere. Let's see what the inside of a sphere looks like. Suppose I set our orange on this paper plate and cut it in half.*

Annie *Can we eat some?*

Michael *Yum!*

Teacher *Sure. Everyone who wishes may have a taste after we're finished cutting. If I cut it in half, what shapes will you see?*

Megan *Seeds!*

Herman (thinking of the orange sections) *Little triangles.*

Roshan *Circles!*

Oona *Half oranges.*

Cut the orange in half. Examine the resulting shapes with your class. If you have a very sharp knife, you can cut a series of cross sections and look at how the circular slices get smaller and smaller.

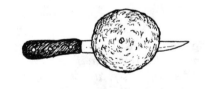

Open the can of jellied cranberry sauce and show the can top.

Brenton   *It's a circle!*

Open the other end of the can, pop the cylinder of sauce out onto the second paper plate and discuss its shape. Have children predict what shapes they'll see when you slice it. Will the circles get smaller, like the orange? Why not? Then lay the sauce on its side and have the children help you cut it into slices. (This is enormously satisfying. If you cook with your class, you might consider making jello cylinders in clean cans and letting children slice their own later.) Examine the resulting shapes.

Why didn't the circles change in size like the orange? Then examine the can. The top and bottom are circles. What shape was used to form the rest of the can? After some speculation on the children's part, slit the label carefully with a knife or razor blade. What shape will it be when you flatten it?

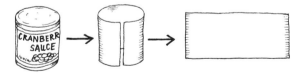

Let children examine several cans that have been opened at both ends and had the labels removed. Can they find the seam where the ends of the metal rectangle were joined?

Look at the cone. What shape do they see at the base? What would happen if you were able to slice the cone? Some children may be able to see that again you'd get a series of shrinking circles.

If the question seems especially intriguing to some of your students, work with them later to form cone shapes out of clay and slice cross-sections.

Show the staple in your paper cone and offer to remove it. What shape will they see when the staple is gone?

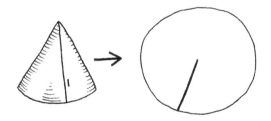

After some discussion, pull the staple out, flatten the cone into a circle, and show students how you cut the circle along its radius, overlapped the two pieces, pulled them together and stapled them to make the cone in the first place.

After a break for recess or other activities, return to the question of making round houses for their hedgehogs. Show your class the construction supplies: rectangles, squares, Circles to Cones sheets, scissors, tape, glue, staples, and crayons. Quickly demonstrate how to make cylinders and cones before you send them out to work.

Some children may choose to make cylindrical houses with cone roofs. Some may be happy with cylinders or cones alone. Others may choose to put a flat floor or roof on their cylinder house by cutting a circle from at 5" x 5" square and gluing it to the top or bottom.

A few may have other round designs of their own they'd like to pursue. Don't discourage them from experimenting even though their finished houses might not resemble cones or cylinders. In any event, remind students to let their hedgehogs watch the construction. Surely the little creatures will want doors and windows and colorful wall decorations for their new houses. Have children store these houses in their cubbies after they've been admired, or set them out for classroom display. Students may need them later in the unit.

Triangles to Pyramids

Children discover that triangles can be used to make pyramids.

Feely Box Shapes Revisited Again

Children listen to several helpers describe a triangle hidden from view in a feely box. They try to eliminate large construction paper shapes that don't match the descriptions, until only a triangle remains.

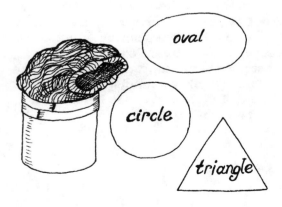

SKILLS

- listening
- building language
- applying descriptions
- thinking logically
- drawing conclusions

YOU'LL NEED:

- a feely box
- a small scalene triangle made of cardboard to put in the feely box (See Preparation)
- the paper bag of three-dimensional forms and the sign of Snuffles' house (See page 72)
- chart paper
- your toy hedgehog
- a felt-tip pen
- the story *Snuffles' House*

70

Have the children sit in a circle on the rug and think about the shapes they've seen and used so far to make houses. Explain that you've hidden a new shape in the feely box, the shape they'll use to create more houses. First you're going to reread *Snuffles' House* with their help. Have students supply key words and phrases as you read and continue to have them predict what shapes Snuffles will try for each house and explain why each shape won't work.

When the story is finished, spread the large construction paper shapes out in the center of the circle. Ask the children to identify each of the shapes. Show them the feely box. Explain that you have put a new shape inside but this time you're going to let them help supply the descriptions.

Generating clues without actually naming the shape is wonderfully challenging to kindergartners; it's almost certain that someone will reach in and simply announce the name of the shape. Nevertheless, it's important to offer your students the opportunity to participate. Explain the game and encourage your helpers to tell something about the shape they're feeling, rather than naming it.

Teacher *I have a new shape in my feely box, but today I'm going to ask a few of you to help describe what it feels like, as the rest of us listen and use the large paper shapes to try to figure out which shape it is. Who thinks they could reach into the box and tell us something about the shape without giving away the secret?*

Many hands shoot up.

Teacher *Joanna, why don't you give it a go.*

Joanna (reaching inside the feely box) *It has points!*

Teacher *Okay. Are there any shapes on the rug we can eliminate? Do you see a shape it couldn't be?*

Yvonne *I think you can get rid of the circle.*

Teacher *Why do you think that?*

Yvonne *Because a circle is smooth around. It doesn't have any points.*

Megan *You can get rid of the oval. It doesn't have points either.*

Teacher *Does everyone agree with Yvonne and Megan? Okay, Yvonne, you remove the circle and Megan, you remove the oval.*

Teacher *Would someone else like to give us a clue? Kevin?*

Kevin reaches into the box.

Kevin *I feel straight lines.*

Children *We can't get rid of anything. They all have straight lines. We need another clue.*

The teacher asks Traci to reach into the box.

Traci *I know it! It's a triangle!*

Teacher *What makes you think it's a triangle?*

Traci *It has three.*

Teacher *Three what?*

Traci *Three points and three lines.*

Teacher *What do you think, class?*

Children *It's a triangle. It just has to be.*

71

Teacher *How do you know?*

Michael *(pointing to the paper triangle on the rug) Look! See, it has three of everything. All the rest have too many.*

Children *Get rid of the rest!*

Teacher *So we can eliminate the . . . ?*

Children *The square, the diamond, the rectangle, and that octagon. It's a triangle in the box.*

Once the children have figured out the secret shape, pull it out of the box. The fact that it's a scalene triangle (no sides or angles equal) rather than the more familiar isosceles triangle (two sides and angles equal) or equilateral triangle (all sides and angles equal) may spark discussion.

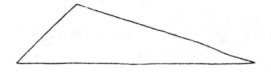

Joseph *Hey, that's not a triangle!*

Teacher *What makes you say that?*

Joseph *Because it doesn't look like the one on the rug.*

Michael *It doesn't look like any triangle. It's too pointy on one side.*

Have all the children leave the rug and search for triangles around the room. Can they find any like this one? Have them bring back any triangles they do find (blocks of various sorts, triangular pieces from building sets, toys or games, paper scraps, a door stop, a prism). Set them in the center of the group and examine them. Do any of them look like the cardboard triangle that came out of the feely box? Do they all look alike? What are some of their similarities and differences? What is common to all triangles?

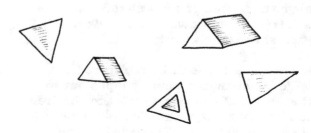

List the characteristics of the triangle as the children volunteer them. Then using these, draw triangles. Post the chart where the children can see it.

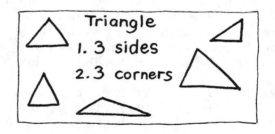

Picture a Triangle House

Students will create a picture of a house out of assorted construction paper triangles.

SKILLS

- thinking logically
- listening
- taking turns
- looking at how shapes fit together

YOU'LL NEED:

- about 50 construction paper triangles in a variety of sizes, types, and colors (See Preparation)
- a 36" x 36" piece of butcher paper
- glue

Have children sit in a circle on the rug. Place the butcher paper in the center. Spread the triangles to one side of the paper. Tell the children they're going to make a house using only triangles. Ask the children to remind you of the things they need to create a house.

Teacher   *Tell me again what things we need to make a house.*

Children   *We need windows and a door and a roof. We need a chimney. We could put a fence around it. We could use triangles for trees in the yard.*

Explain that each child will have a turn to add something to the house. They can't remove anything that someone else has put on before them. Each person can add only one or two triangles. Call children up two at a time to place their triangles while the rest of the group watches and talks about what is happening. Admire the house when it is complete and discuss the particular challenges posed by using only triangles to make a house. How do triangles compare to circles or squares as building materials? Leave the picture on the rug until you get a chance to glue the shapes in place. Post it near your drawing and description of triangles.

This might be a good time to take a walk around the school yard to look at the shapes that are used in neighborhood houses and other buildings. Do students see any triangles? What about squares, circles, or rectangles? Which shapes are used more frequently? Why?

Consider, also, bringing in pictures of various types of houses including tepees, A-frames, domes, yurts, and igloos. You may also choose to feature books about houses and house construction in your reading corner. A few of our favorites are

> *A House Is a House for Me*
> (Hoberman 1978)
> *Building a House* (Barton 1981)
> *Mousekin's Golden House* (Miller 1964)
> *Louise Builds a House* (Pfanner 1989)
> *Christina Katerina and the Box*
> (Gauch 1971)

Triangles to Pyramids

Children make three-dimensional houses for their hedgehogs using triangles.

SKILLS

- making predictions
- using two-dimensional shapes to form three-dimensional shapes
- naming three-dimensional shapes
- following directions
- building spatial awareness

YOU'LL NEED:

- Triangles to Pyramids black lines (See Appendix B)
- several pre-cut paper triangles (Use another copy of the Triangles to Pyramids black line as a pattern to cut four small triangles.)
- scissors
- tape
- one of the children's clay hedgehogs

EACH CHILD WILL NEED:

- access to Triangles to Pyramids sheets (Run a class set plus a few extras.)
- access to pre-cut triangles (Cut about one hundred triangles the size of one of the small triangles shown in the Triangles to Pyramids black line.)
- scissors
- tape
- glue
- felt-tip pens
- crayons
- an assortment of collage materials such as
  paper scraps
  sequins
  ribbon
  pipe cleaners
  feathers
  yarn
  fabric scraps
  toothpicks

Gather the children in a circle on the rug. Have a copy of the Triangles to Pyramids black line, some pre-cut triangles, and a little clay hedgehog ready. Review the houses they've made so far for their hedgehogs and pose the problem of creating a three-dimensional house from triangles. Present the Triangles to Pyramids page as one option and demonstrate how to use it to form a pyramid.

Teacher (holding up the clay hedgehog) *This little guy is very excited. He knows you're going to make a new sort of house for him today.*

Nicole *Out of triangles?*

Teacher *Right. You might choose to work with the paper triangles* (spreading a few out on the rug) *and try to figure out how to fasten them together to make a house for your hedgehog to live in.*

Jeffrey *Can we use other paper too?*

Teacher No, I'd like you to stick with triangles today.

Roshan We could hook them together with tape.

Teacher You sure could. I'd like to show you another possibility.

Teacher sets out a copy of the Triangles to Pyramids Sheet for the group to see.

Herman A big triangle with lines on it?

Teacher I'm going to cut out the larger triangle.

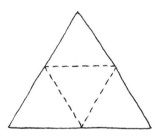

What do you think will happen when I fold along the dotted lines?

Brenton We don't know. Show us.

Thomas It's going to make some kind of house.

Teacher Watch and see what you think.

Bend up the triangles along two of the dotted lines and tape them at the top.

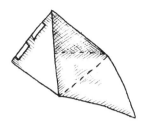

Megan Hey, that looks like a tent.

Oona It's got a door. The hedgehog can walk right in! Can I put him in there?

Teacher Sure.

Kimiko Close his door now.

Fold the third triangle up and fasten it at both sides with a bit of tape.

Trevor Now he's all closed in.

Teacher This is one three-dimensional shape you can make with triangles. It's called a triangular pyramid.

Jory I've heard about pyramids.

Nancy It looks like that pyramid building downtown (referring to the Trans America Pyramid building in San Francisco).

Megan What's 'three-dimensional' mean?

Teacher Well, when I started with the big paper triangle, it lay flat on the floor, remember? (Teacher untapes the pyramid and smoothes it out flat again.) But then I folded up the sides and taped them to make

*a three-dimensional shape—
a triangular pyramid. Three-
dimensional shapes don't
lay flat on the ground.*

If necessary, demonstrate again how
to cut, fold, and tape the Triangles to
Pyramids sheet. Remind your students
that they're welcome to use the pre-cut
triangles instead of the pyramid black
line; some may have other ideas they'd
like to try.

Once students have made their triangular
houses, they can decorate them using the
collage materials placed at each table
while their hedgehogs watch.

When their houses are complete, set them
in a display area for all to admire and
enjoy. Keep them at school until the end
of this unit when children might need
them for their final project.

Rectangles to Rectangular Boxes

Children discover that rectangles can be
used to make boxes.

Feely Box Shapes Revisited Once Again

Children listen to the teacher describe a rectangle hidden from view in a feely box. They
try to eliminate large construction paper
shapes that don't match the descriptions,
until only a rectangle remains.

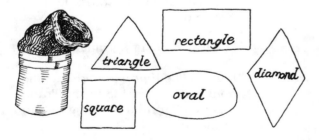

SKILLS

- listening
- building language
- applying descriptions
- thinking logically
- drawing conclusions

YOU'LL NEED:

- a feely box
- a cardboard 2" x 3" rectangle to put
  in the feely box (See Preparation)
- your large construction paper feely
  box lesson shapes (See Preparation)
- your paper bag of poster board house
  forms (See Preparation)
- seven 3" x 4" numeral cards labeled
  1, 2, 3, 4, 5, 6, 7 (See Preparation)
- chart paper
- one felt-tip marker
- the story *Snuffles' House*

Have children sit in a circle on the rug
and think about all the different shapes
they've seen and used so far to make
houses. Explain that you've got one last
shape hidden in the feely box for them
to use in building a new house, but first
they'll work together to tell the story of
Snuffles again. Help students lay out the
poster board shapes in the order they are
presented in the story and label each
shape with a numeral denoting its order.
Encourage them to tell the story using
your toy hedgehog with the posterboard
shapes.

Teacher This time you are going to take turns telling the story of Snuffles' House. I think we should put the house shapes in the order they come in the story. Which shape came first?

Children The square house came first. That was the one that got burned down.

Teacher Let's put the square form here with the numeral one beside it to show it was first.

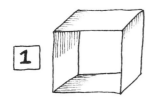

Continue ordering the remaining shapes in the same fashion.

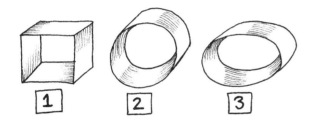

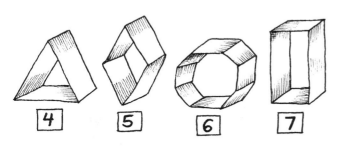

Once all the models have been placed in order, ask for a volunteer to begin recounting the tale.

Teacher Who would like to begin? Michael.

Michael Once upon a time there was a hedgehog named Snuffles. He had long sharp prickles and black shiny eyes. He lived in a little house by some big trees.

Continue calling on children to tell the story and demonstrate what happens each time with the cardboard shapes.

When the story has been told, spread the large construction paper shapes out in the center of the circle. Ask the children to identify each of the shapes. Show them the feely box. Explain that you have a new shape inside. You'll need some children to feel it and help give clues. The rest of the class will try to eliminate any shape that doesn't fit the description, until the shape that matches the one in the box is the only one left on the rug.

Teacher I've put a new shape in our feely box. I'd like a few volunteers to help give clues. Who thinks they could reach into the box and tell us something about how the shape feels without giving away the secret? Thomas?

Thomas puts his hand into the box and thinks for a moment.

Thomas It's got straight lines.

Teacher Straight lines? Can we eliminate any of the shapes on the rug?

Mark You can get rid of the circle.

Teacher Why do you think that?

Mark Because a circle is curved all the way around and sides are straight. So the circle doesn't have sides.

Sarah You can get rid of the oval. It's curved too, not straight.

Teacher Does everyone agree? Okay, Mark, you remove the circle and Sarah, you remove the oval. Who would like to reach into the box and give the next clue? Nancy?

Nancy fishes around for a bit.

Nancy I think it has four corners. They feel pointy.

Annie	*You can get rid of the triangle. It only has three corners.*
Teacher	*All right, Annie. Why don't you come and remove the paper triangle from the rug? Can someone give us another clue?*
Kimiko	*The corners are straight.*
Teacher	*What do you mean?*
Kimiko	*Straight—you know. Not real pointy.*
Teacher	*Do you mean they're shaped like this?*

The teacher draws an upper case *L* on the board.

Kimiko	*That's it!*
Tabi	*You can get rid of the diamond and the octagon. Their corners make Vs.*
Teacher	*Okay, Tabi. You remove the diamond and the octagon. Can someone give us another clue?*
Jory	*I can! Let's see. Some sides are long. The others are short.*
Teacher	*Do you mean the sides are not all the same length?*
Children	*It's the rectangle. We knew it! You can get rid of the square. All its sides are the same. The rectangle's sides are different.*
Teacher	*Sarah, will you remove the paper square from the rug?*

Have a child take the cardboard rectangle out of the feely box and show it to the group.

Teacher	*Roshan, would you like to pull the shape out of the box so we can check our guess?*
Children	*It's a rectangle! We were right!*

Teacher	*I'm going to draw a rectangle on this piece of chart paper. Can you tell me what I need to know to be able to draw it correctly? I'll make a list of the rules for rectangles too.*
Children	*It has four sides. It has four corners. Two of the sides are long. Two are short. The corners all make Ls just like the square.*

List the characteristics of the rectangle as the children volunteer them. Draw a rectangle next to the list. Post the chart where everyone can see it.

Rectangle
1. 4 corners   rectangle
2. 4 sides
3. 2 long sides
4. 2 short sides
4. corners make L s

Picture a Rectangle House

Students create a house from assorted construction paper rectangles.

SKILLS

- thinking logically
- listening
- taking turns
- looking at how shapes fit together

YOU'LL NEED:

- about fifty construction paper rectangles in a variety of colors and sizes (See Preparation)
- a 36" x 36" piece of butcher paper
- glue

Have children sit in a circle on the rug. Place the butcher paper in the center. Spread the rectangles to one side of the paper. Explain that they will be making a house using only rectangles. Encourage them to add the many "extras" a house needs.

Teacher   Tell me again what things we need to make a house?

Children   We need windows and a door and a roof. We need a chimney. We could put a wall around it. We could use rectangles for a garage.

Explain that once again they will each have a turn to add something to the house. They cannot remove anything that someone added before them. Each person can place only one or two rectangles. Call children up two at a time to place their rectangles as the rest of the children discuss the evolving picture. Admire the house when it is completed and discuss the advantages and disadvantages of using rectangles as opposed to triangles, circles, or squares. Leave it on the rug until you have time to glue the shapes in place, then post it near your drawing and description of rectangles.

Rectangles to Boxes

Children cut and fold a rectangle into a box and decorate it to make a house.

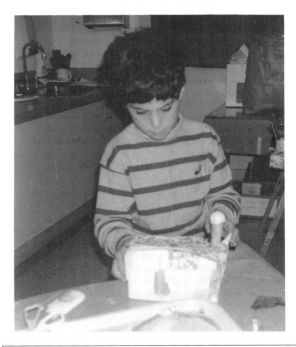

SKILLS

- defining three-dimensional shapes
- planning
- making decisions
- following directions
- building spatial awareness

EACH CHILD WILL NEED:

- Rectangles to Boxes blacklines (Run a class set from the masters in Appendix B on construction paper, card stock, or oak tag—the more durable the material the better.)
- scissors
- stapler
- his or her little clay hedgehog

EACH TABLE WILL NEED:

- an assortment of collage materials
- glue

Have children sit in a large circle. Distribute copies of the Rectangles to Boxes sheets. Talk with children about the shape of the sheet.

Teacher What shape is this sheet?

Children It's a rectangle.

Teacher What shape was the last house that Snuffles built?

Children A rectangle!

Teacher Was it just like this sheet?

Sarah No. It wasn't flat. He could go inside.

Brenton Our rectangle is flat. Snuffles' house was like a box.

Roshan The shape was like a rectangle but it was fat. It had an inside like a box.

Michael His house was really a box.

Teacher Do you agree with Michael? Could we say Snuffles' house was a rectangular box?

Children That's what it was—a rectangle box.

Teacher What could we do to change this flat paper rectangle into a rectangular box?

Herman If you had more than one piece, you could fit them together and tape them.

Megan Like the squares.

Teacher You mean the graham cracker squares we used to make cube houses?

Megan Remember when we got them to stand up?

Teacher I do, but this time I'm going to give you a different problem to solve. Is there any way you could use this one rectangular piece of paper to make a rectangular box?

Tabi I think we should fold it.

Teacher What makes you say that?

Tabi Well, we had to fold that triangle to make that other house.

Mark The pyramid house. We folded the triangles up, remember?

Teacher Do you think that would work this time?

Silence.

Teacher There are probably many ways that would work. I will show a way that I find easy. You'll fold and cut yours along with me.

Pass out scissors to each child and have a stapler available.

Teacher Look at my rectangle. See the four solid lines? I'm going to cut along each solid line but I have to stop when I get to the dotted line. Can everyone show me where I must cut? Point to the line where I must stop cutting. Okay, watch me cut but tell me when I have to stop.

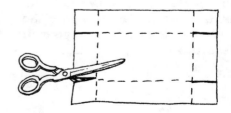

Children *Stop!*

Teacher *Good job. I'll do that for each of the solid lines.*

Cut each of your solid lines with the children's guidance.

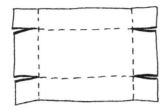

Teacher *Now it's your turn to cut along the solid lines. Remember to stop when you get to the dotted lines.*

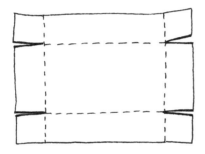

I'm going to fold the top edge down and toward the back along the dotted line.

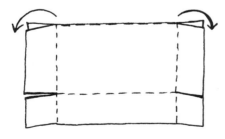

Now fold yours the same way. Please turn it so the bottom is now at the top, like this.

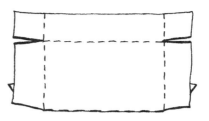

Fold the top down along the dotted line, like this.

Now turn your card vertically, tall like a tree grows.

Fold down all along the dotted lines, like this.

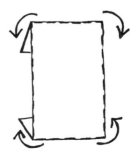

Turn your card so the back is now the front, like this.

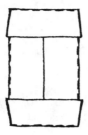

Push the short sides up into place like this, to make the ends of the box.

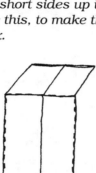

Now push the long sides up like this and wrap the ends around to finish the box.

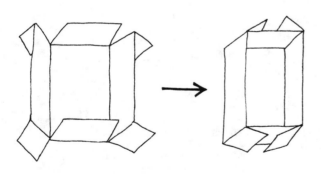

I'll staple my box and then come around and staple yours.

When all the boxes have been stapled, send children out to tables to decorate them using the collage supplies you've provided. Some may choose to leave their boxes open on one side while others will flip theirs over to provide a roof or a floor for the little hedgehog.

Circulate as they work admiring, discussing, and helping where necessary. When the houses are finished, display them for all to see.

Putting It All Together

As a final activity, the children experiment with ways to fit all the shapes they've been exploring together to make very fancy houses for their hedgehogs.

A Many-Shaped House

Children use an assortment of two- or three-dimensional shapes to make houses for their hedgehogs.

SKILLS

- exploring how shapes fit together
- building language
- making choices
- thinking logically
- drawing conclusions

So far, children have had an opportunity to study four shapes in isolation, discovering what happens when you try to make a picture of a house using only squares, triangles, circles, or rectangles and investigating the construction of each of the corresponding three-dimensional shapes. As a final project, we suggest you allow students to create hedgehog houses that combine all four shapes in two or three dimensions, depending on your tolerance and remaining energy. If you choose the two-dimensional route, your children will make pictures of houses with pre-cut construction paper shapes.

If you decide to have your students work in three dimensions, they'll combine the pyramids, cylinders, and rectangular boxes they made earlier with other easily collectible materials such as toilet paper tubes, paper cones, and small boxes of all sorts on cardboard bases.

Either experience will enable children to investigate how shapes work together and provide a pleasurable conclusion to the unit.

FOR TWO-DIMENSIONAL HOUSES, YOU'LL NEED FOR EACH TABLE:

- twenty each of an assortment of construction paper shapes in a variety of colors and sizes (from about 2" squares to 6" x 8" rectangles)
- glue or paste
- crayons
- marking pens

EACH CHILD WILL NEED:

- a piece of 12" x 18" blue construction paper on which to create their house

FOR THREE-DIMENSIONAL HOUSES, YOU'LL NEED FOR EACH TABLE:

- an assortment of easily collected three-dimensional cones, cylinders, and rectangular boxes, such as
    toilet paper tubes
    juice cans
    paper cones
    paper towel tubes
    paper cups
    all kinds of small boxes
      (cereal, gift, drink, etc.)
- white glue
- masking tape

EACH CHILD WILL NEED:

- the cylinder, pyramid, and rectangular box he or she has already made
- a piece of corrugated cardboard roughly 12" square for a construction base
- his or her clay hedgehog

Have the children sit in a circle on the rug. Place an assortment of the shapes and a 12" x 18" piece of blue construction paper or the 12" x 12" cardboard in front of you on the rug. Review the various kinds of houses that have been built so far. Explain that this time, they'll use a variety of shapes to make very fancy hedgehog houses, either on the blue paper or cardboard, depending on whether your class will be using two- or three-dimensional shapes.

Ask the children for their ideas about how to proceed.

Note: Although the sample dialogue below introduces two-dimensional house construction, you might engage students in a similar discussion and demonstration to introduce the three-dimensional project.

Teacher *Who can tell me about the kinds of houses we've built so far?*

Children *We made cube houses. We made rectangular houses. We made pyramid houses.*

Tabi *We made round houses shaped like cans.*

Teacher *You have fine memories. Those were all three-dimensional houses. We also made other kinds of houses. Do you remember what they were?*

Jeffrey *We made big flat houses—those picture kind.*

Children *Out of circles. Squares too. Triangles too. And rectangles.*

Teacher *Now I've mixed up all the shapes and cut them a bit smaller so you can each make your own houses out of flat shapes. Before I send you away to the tables to work, I thought we might experiment with some of the things you could try. Does anyone have an idea of how I might create a house using these shapes?*

Yvonne *You could take some big squares and put them together to make the house part.*

Herman *If you wanted it bigger, you could use two of those rectangles put together.*

Continue eliciting ideas from your class. Let children experiment a bit with how the various shapes can be used together. Encourage them to think about windows, balconies, chimneys, landscaping, and other details that might embellish their creations.

If your class is working in two dimensions, give each child a piece of light blue paper and send them all to the tables to work. If they're working with three-dimensional shapes on cardboard, have them do the construction and trim work all the same day or, if you're feeling very ambitious, have them do the basic construction the first day, paint their creations with tempera the next, and add construction paper windows, doors, balconies, and other embellishments the final day.

In either case, have children dictate or write descriptions of their houses as they finish. Two-dimensional houses might be displayed in the hall or compiled into a classroom book with a cover featuring the four shapes used in house construction. Three-dimensional creations might be displayed on tables or counters in the school library before they go home.

It is a sunny day.

My house has a balcony and a door.

My hedgehog likes his big house.

UNIT 3

Hansel and Gretel's Path

Hansel and Gretel's Path: A Preview

What Will Happen in This Unit?

Children will apply and extend their sorting and patterning skills as they learn to play an intriguing new board game.

After students have heard Hansel and Gretel *and practiced path making, they are introduced to a new version of the story in which Hansel and Gretel are presented with a magic path that will lead them home if they can step on the correct stones.*

Hansel and Gretel's Path Planning Sheet

	Day 1	Day 2	Day 3	Day 4	Day 5	Day 6	Day 7	Day 8	Day 9	Day 10	Day 11
Sharing, Choosing, Special Classes (Library, Music)			Introducing *Hansel and Gretel*: work with a small group to create a story map.		Testing the Pattern Cards	Testing the Pattern Cards, cont. Making the Gingerbread House: meet with a small group to cut doors, windows, etc.	Creating New Patterns	Creating New Patterns, cont.	Testing the Pattern Cards or Creating New Patterns	Meet with children who need to fix up their boards or cards in any way.	
Calendar											
Reading and Language Arts	Introducing *Hansel and Gretel*: read the story.	Introducing *Hansel and Gretel*: read another version of the story	Introducing *Hansel and Gretel*: have children dramatize the story as you tell or read it.	The White Dove's New Path							
Unit Work — Science, Social Studies, Art		Introducing *Hansel and Gretel*: paint trees, characters, houses for a mural.	Introducing *Hansel and Gretel*: have children work in partners to make paths.					Hansel and Gretel's Path—A Whole-Group Game: play again.	Hansel and Gretel's Path—A Whole-Group Game: play a third time.		
Math					Making the Gingerbread House: brainstorm design possibilities.	Making the Gingerbread House: have children work in partners to make trim strips.	Hansel and Gretel's Path—A Whole-Group Game	Making Path Game Boards	Making Pattern Cards	Testing Pattern Cards	Hansel and Gretel's Path—A Partner Game
Closing						Glue the trim strips to the box and put on finishing touches.			Organize children's materials into envelopes.		
Notes	Work on unit preparations: you'll need the path, pattern cards, and box by day 4.										Send children's games home, along with instruction sheets for parents.

91

What Do I Need to Know to Begin?

This unit takes its lead from *Hansel and Gretel*, a powerful tale much loved by young children. Many kindergartners will listen to the story more than once, savoring the details of Hansel's path, the forest, and the gingerbread house, and waiting for the dramatic moment when Gretel shoves the witch into the oven and frees her brother. We've written a new version in which a white dove helps the children home from the witch's house by conjuring up a path that works only when they step on the correct stones in the correct sequence. The dove leaves them with a set of instruction cards, a few rules, and a cheerful good-bye.

Students are able to step into the story at this point because the teacher brings out a life-sized paper replica of the path, a large cardboard box to represent the witch's house, and a set of pattern cards, just like the dove's. The path, pictured below, is made of construction paper "stepping stones" glued onto butcher paper.

There are twenty pattern cards, some of which enable a player to get all the way down the path, and some of which lead into the forest or come to a dead end. The challenge is to try to pick your way among the random stones, following the pattern and the rules. Here's an example:

1. The pattern on this card is green, red, green, red, green, red. Can you use it to make your way home?

Yes! With a combination of forward, sideways, and diagonal moves, you can get to the end of the path. This card "works."

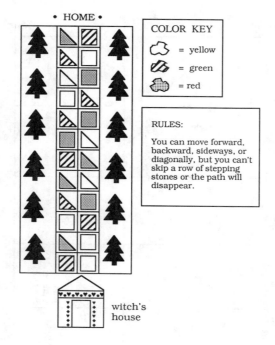

COLOR KEY

◯ = yellow

◿ = green

▨ = red

RULES:

You can move forward, backward, sideways, or diagonally, but you can't skip a row of stepping stones or the path will disappear.

witch's house

• HOME •

2. How about this pattern: square, square, triangle, square, square, triangle?

Whoops—a dead end! There are no squares in the next row and we're not allowed to skip rows. Let's try again.

dead end

• HOME •

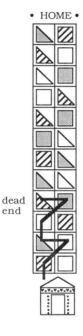

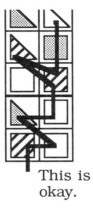

This is okay.

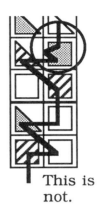

This is not.

3. Let's try another card: triangle, square, triangle, square.

Here's our dead end.

Let's try a backward move, though.

Aha! There is a way to get through. Cards like this take a bit of perseverance, but quickly become very popular with some children. It is okay to step on the same stone again, as long as you don't step on it twice in a row.

• HOME •

dead end

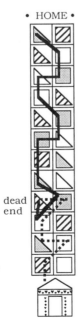

This one doesn't work at all—there are no triangles in the first row so we can't even get started.

• HOME •

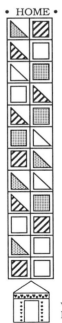

witch's house

4. Here's one more.

Forward to the right, forward to the left,
forward to the right, forward to the left.
This pattern works without a hitch as
long as you start in the left column.

Many children are eager to try the path as soon as it's unrolled. They explore a few of the patterns together and then investigate them more thoroughly during choosing time. After they begin to get a handle on things, the teacher introduces the path game. She divides her students into two teams, seats them on either side of the path and chooses players to represent Hansel, Gretel, and the dove for each team.

The first team draws two cards and tries to predict which is more likely to work. Their first player follows the pattern they choose. If it works and he gets to the end of the path, he's home. If it doesn't, he must return to the back of the line on his side of the witch's house. Then it's the other team's turn. Sometimes, neither card works and the team has to wait for its next turn to try again. The first team to get all three players home wins.

After the game has been introduced, children start working on their own miniature versions of it. They make small path boards

and pattern cards. After they've tested their cards to make sure some work, they play their games with partners and take them home to share with their families.

Preparation

The preparations for Hansel and Gretel's Path are fairly extensive but after you're ready, there's not a lot more to be done during the unit itself. You'll need to make a large butcher paper path, run copies of the pattern cards and mount them on tag board, find a large cardboard carton for the witch's house, make name tags for the whole-group game, and prepare materials for the children's small game boards and cards. See the instructions below and, if you're lucky enough to have them, get parent helpers to do as much of the work as possible.

The Path

YOU'LL NEED:

- a 36" x 96" piece of white or blue butcher paper
- red, yellow, brown, and green construction paper
- a copy of the Tree Outline to use as a pattern (See Appendix B)
- white glue
- scissors
- yardstick
- permanent black wide-tip felt marker

To make the path, use your yardstick and black felt marker to rule off two columns of twelve 8" squares as shown below.

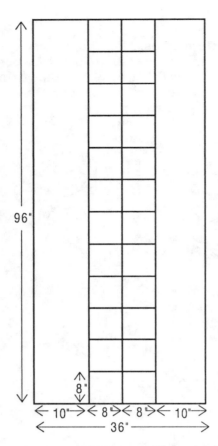

Next, cut seven 6" squares from construction paper in each of the following colors: yellow, green, and red. These are the path "stepping stones." Glue them into place on your grid as shown below, cutting the squares in half to form triangles when necessary.

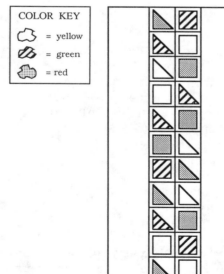

COLOR KEY	
🔺	= yellow
🔺	= green
🔺	= red

Use the Tree Outline black line (see Appendix B) as a pattern to cut ten to twelve trees from green construction paper. (Stack and cut several pieces of green together to make this go faster.) Attach brown paper trunks and glue them along the side strips to represent the deep, dark forest.

Although it seems like a lot of work, the large path goes together quickly and holds up very well as long as children walk on it with their shoes off.

The Pattern Cards

YOU'LL NEED:

- copies of the Teacher's Pattern Cards (See Appendix B: run one copy of each sheet.)
- twenty-one 3" x 12" strips of oak tag
- rubber cement or glue stick
- scissors
- crayons
- clear contact paper if you don't have access to a laminator

Cut your copies of the Teacher's Pattern Cards sheets apart to form twenty-one pattern cards. The shape and direction arrow cards can be glued directly to tag board.

The "blob" cards, on which blobs of color identify color patterns, have to be colored in. Practically any pattern that uses red, green, and yellow will work, but we suggest the following:

1. red, green, red, green
2. green, red, green, red
3. yellow, green, yellow, green
4. yellow, red, yellow, red
5. green, yellow, green, yellow
6. yellow, red, green, yellow, red, green
7. green, red, yellow, green, red, yellow
8. yellow, green, red, yellow, green, red
9. yellow, yellow, green, yellow, yellow, green
10. green, green, yellow, green, green, yellow
11. green, yellow, red, green, yellow, red

Gingerbread House

You will need a box that's large enough for one child to sit inside. The easiest way to get one is to ask parents, particularly if you live in a growing community with lots of people moving in. You could also go to the grocery store and ask for a toilet paper box or other large carton. If you plan to have children decorate it to look like a gingerbread house, you'll need to cut paper strips and candy shapes. (See Appendix B for patterns.)

Name Tags for the Whole-Group Game

YOU'LL NEED:

- six 3" x 9" strips of poster board in two different colors (We used three blue and three orange.)
- six 26" lengths of yarn or string
- permanent black felt marker
- hole punch

Make two sets of name tags by labeling your poster board strips as pictured below.

Punch holes and tie in yarn as shown so children can wear them around their necks. These name tags simply make it easier to identify who's playing for which team.

Children's Game Materials

Run class sets of the Small Path and Children's Pattern Cards (see Appendix B). Cut about two hundred 1" squares in *each* of the following colors: yellow, red, and green. Mix them up and put them in containers for children to use at their tables when they make their path game boards. You're now as ready as you need to be.

What Mathematical Skills Are Addressed?

Like many kindergarten teachers, we ask our students to identify, copy, extend, create, and interpret patterns. (Snap, snap, clap, snap, snap, clap becomes blue, blue, red, blue, blue, red—or any other two colors—if you build it with colored cubes.) When developing this unit, we looked for a way to get children to apply their patterning skills to a problem-solving situation. The idea of a path was intriguing—doubly so when we thought about using *Hansel and Gretel* as a point of departure. At first we thought the path itself ought to be patterned, but then we decided it would be more fun to search out a pattern among randomly placed markers. Our first game board was a humdinger—three columns wide and twelve rows long.

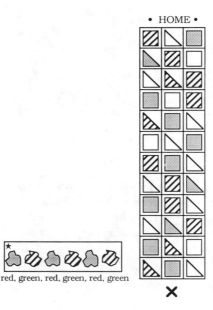

• HOME •

red, green, red, green, red, green

✗

Try threading your way home through this maze! Does the pattern card work?

David, the eight-year-old son of one of us, informed us that it was too hard. "Too much to look at all at once!" he said. We trimmed it down to two columns and handed it back. That was much better. But would it work with kindergartners? It did! By the time we rolled out the "magic" path (after reading *Hansel and Gretel* three times and laying out popsicle stick paths all over the playground), they were absolutely captivated. Did they want to take off their shoes and walk on that path? Absolutely! The pattern cards and rules were confusing the first time around, but it didn't take long for most of them to catch on, especially because they were able to revisit the path during choosing for several days. Many even enjoyed the challenge of making and testing their own color patterns with red, green, and yellow Unifix cubes.

Although a bit cumbersome at first, the whole-group path game smoothed out after several rounds. By the time children had made their own game boards and pattern cards, most understood the game well enough to play in pairs with little or no help. They were thrilled to share it with their families too. Here are some of the comments we received back from parents:

> *As you might have guessed, Zack was very excited to play his Hansel and Gretel game and confidently explained how the game*

worked. He seemed to have the best time using the cards he'd made because I think he knew the outcome without working too hard!

This is a fun game! Lindsay will sit and play for hours.

Grayson was very interested but had trouble with the concept that some [pattern cards] work and some don't. He understands patterning but not why we would want to create a card that would not *work.*

The directions were not clear to me but Jake was able to explain them.

Jory has always loved to play board games. He really enjoys this game, especially since he was able to participate in the making of

"his little game." I think it made him feel important that he had to teach us to play instead of vice versa.

Children had to identify, copy, and extend the pattern from each card as they worked their way down the path. The spatial problem solving required to move forward, backward, diagonally, sideways, and to double back on the path was most impressive. It took perseverance, but eventually they learned to navigate the patterns on nearly every card—even those that at first seemed impossible. Children had to invent and test patterns as they created their own versions of Hansel and Gretel's Path. At all levels of play, students had to predict which pattern would work, so they could select the "best" card for their turn. Overall, it was a fantastic way to reinforce and extend the many pattern concepts taught in kindergarten.

What Materials Will I Need?

General Math Materials (Appendix A)

- Unifix cubes
- feely box

Classroom Supplies

- butcher paper
- tempera paints
- construction paper
- oak tag/tag board
- marking pens
- masking tape
- crayons
- scissors
- yarn
- large manila envelopes (10" x 13")
- poster board
- white glue

Other Things You Will Need

- several different versions of *Hansel and Gretel* (preferably with large colorful illustrations). Some suggestions are:

  Hansel and Gretel retold by Ruth Belov Gross. NY: Scholastic, 1988.

  Hansel and Gretel by The Brothers Grimm. Illustrated by John Wallner. Englewood Cliffs, NJ: Prentice-Hall, 1985.

  Hansel and Gretel by James Marshall. NY: Dial Books, 1990.

  Hansel and Gretel by The Brothers Grimm. Illustrated by Susan Jeffers. NY: Dial Books, 1980.

- pictures of gingerbread houses from magazines, kits, and or cookbooks (Ask parents to contribute to this collection.)

Other Things You Will Need *(continued)*

- small blocks
- dollhouse figures
- a large cardboard box, such as a moving carton or a toilet paper box from the grocery store—something that might hold one child
- small baskets, boxes, or trays for materials distribution
- a pound of lima beans and two small cans of fast drying, high gloss spray paint in blue and orange or other materials to make markers for children's take-home games

Print Materials (Appendix B)

- one copy of each Teacher's Pattern Cards Sheet (See Preparation.)
- several copies of Candy Shape Patterns (if you plan to have children decorate your cardboard box to look like the gingerbread house.)
- The Small Path Game Board (Run a class set plus a few extra.)
- Children's Pattern Cards—three sheets (Run a class set of each sheet plus a few extra.)
- Sorting Sheet (Run a class set.)
- Game Instructions Sheet for Families (Run a class set.)

How Can I Fit This Unit into My Schedule?

The activities described in this unit are designed to run a little over two weeks. It is important that you skim the entire unit before beginning. We have included a planning sheet that was helpful in our classrooms. We hope it will assist you in charting your own course.

Getting Started

The activities in this section set the stage for the rest of the unit.

Introducing *Hansel and Gretel*

You'll want to take some time to familiarize your students with *Hansel and Gretel* and be sure they understand the idea of a path.

SKILLS

- listening
- dramatizing a story
- map making
- working with partners

YOU'LL NEED:

- several different versions of *Hansel and Gretel*
- butcher paper and tempera paints if you plan to have children make a mural
- blocks and dollhouse figures if you plan to have children build a story map
- Unifix cubes, pattern blocks, bottle caps, popsicle sticks, or natural materials children can collect outside such as stones, leaves, pine cones, or twigs, if you plan to have them make some simple paths of their own

Open the unit by reading *Hansel and Gretel* to your class. Kindergartners revel in the power of this fairytale no matter how many times they hear it. They love the idea of the path, the magic of the gingerbread house, the cleverness of the children, and the ignorance of the witch.

They listen eagerly for the moment Gretel shoves the witch into the oven and they don't appear to be as troubled by the stepmother's behavior as are older children. To five-year-olds, Hansel and Gretel is a tale of action, trickery, crime, punishment, and reward. Everyone gets what he or she deserves in the end.

To enhance children's understanding of the story and to be sure they know how paths work, you might choose to do some or all of the activities listed below.

Dramatize the Story

Have children take turns acting out *Hansel and Gretel* as you retell it. Provide simple costumes (hats, headbands, or story bibs) to identify the players and a few props to add magic (pebbles, a chicken bone, and some costume jewelry).

Create a Mural

Have children paint characters and scenery to depict a scene from the story. Hansel, Gretel, the witch, the woodcutter's cottage, the gingerbread house, trees, pebbles for a path—your students will probably add to this list. When their paintings are dry, cut them out and arrange them on your bulletin board.

Make a Story Map

Work with a small group of children to brainstorm and then build a story map of *Hansel and Gretel* with blocks. This is a bit like building a miniature stage set; it involves thinking about where the various parts of the story take place and how the locations might be arranged in relation to one another. One group decided to set up the woodcutter's cottage and the gingerbread house, with a forest and a pond in between. Later they added Hansel's path, a fence around the gingerbread house, and a large bake oven and kennel in the witch's yard.

After the set is built, children can use dollhouse figures to reenact the story on the map (see Johnson and Louis 1987).

Make Paths

After reading *Hansel and Gretel*, discuss Hansel's paths. Why did he leave the pebbles and bread crumbs? How did he arrange them to form a path? What is a path? Why didn't his second path work? How did the children get home in the end? After some discussion, model the path-making activity described below and have your students try it in partners. Work in the gym, multipurpose room, or outside if possible. If you work outside, children can designate pieces of playground equipment, trees, or bushes—instead of chairs—to be home and woods.

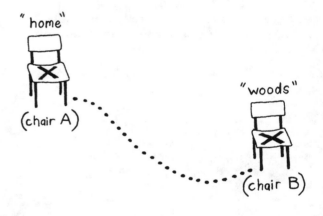

One partner is Hansel, the other, Gretel. As Hansel and Gretel walk from home into the woods (from chair A to chair B), Hansel leaves a trail of Unifix cubes, pattern blocks, popsicle sticks, twigs, pebbles, pine cones, or the like. When they reach the woods (chair B), the partners turn around and follow their path back home picking up the markers as they go so they won't be discovered. Have them repeat the activity, trading roles so that both children get to make a path. The second child may choose a different route.

The White Dove's New Path

After children are familiar with the story, introduce a new version in which a white dove conjures up a path of magic stepping stones to help Hansel and Gretel find their way home. As you describe the path, unroll the paper replica you've prepared along with the pattern cards that must be followed. After a brief discussion of the path and rules, children start testing the cards to see which "work" and which do not.

SKILLS

- identifying colors and two-dimensional shapes
- identifying directions—forward, backward, sideways, diagonal, left, right
- identifying and extending color, shape, and directional patterns
- searching for patterns
- problem solving

YOU'LL NEED:

- a copy of *Hansel and Gretel*
- your *Math Excursions K* guide opened to page 103
- a large butcher paper path (See Preparation)
- a set of Teacher's Pattern Cards (See Preparation)
- a large cardboard box to represent the witch's house (See Preparation)
- a ruler to use as a pointer
- a feely box of children's names (See Appendix A)

Begin by reading *Hansel and Gretel*. If your students have already heard several versions, they'll know that each one is a bit different. Tell them to listen for a very different ending this time. When you get to the part where Gretel has disposed of the witch and freed Hansel, switch to the text below:

Hansel and Gretel ran out of the witch's house, eager to get home. They started through the tall fir trees but soon realized they didn't know which way to go. Gretel suggested they return to the witch's house and try to think of a plan. Hansel agreed, and back they went. As they approached the house, a lovely white dove fluttered down from the roof top.

"Look, a dove!" cried Hansel.

"Can you help us get home?" cried Gretel. "We don't know which way to go."

"I am a creature of the forest," replied the dove. "I can make a path for you, but you'll have to find your own way home."

With that, the dove cooed softly three times and a double path of brightly colored stepping stones appeared.

Unroll the paper path you've prepared and let the children examine it for a minute before you continue.

Teacher   Here's what the dove's path looked like.

What do you notice about it?

Amanda   It's got trees on it.

Teacher   Yes, those are to show the deep, dark forest on either side of the path.

Damon   It has different colors—red, yellow, and green!

Gary   And shapes—triangles and squares.

Teacher   Those colored shapes are the stepping stones.

Jacob   They go in twos—two, two, two, two . . .

Daniel   There are twenty-four. I counted them.

Katie   I see a pattern (pointing along one column)—green, red, yellow, green, red, green, red, green, yellow . . .

Teacher   Do you all agree there's a pattern in this column?

Children   Yes! No! It doesn't go over and over. It starts, but then it stops. This part does—green, red, green, red, green, but then it stops. No— these aren't in a pattern!

Megan   Can we walk on it?

Teacher   Yes, later on, if you take your shoes off, but let me go on with the story right now.

As they stood looking at the path, the dove said, "You might think you can follow the stepping stones straight home, but this is a magic path." She handed the children a set of cards like these (display your pattern cards briefly and continue) and explained that they must follow the patterns.

"Some will lead you home, but others will take you deeper into the forest or come to a dead end. Then you'll have to go back to the witch's house and try again. As you use these cards, be sure to remember: you can step for-

104

ward, backward, sideways, and diagonally, but you cannot skip a row of stones. If you do, the path will disappear. Good luck."

And with that, the dove flew away.

Set the cardboard box at the beginning of the path to represent the witch's house and suggest the children try the cards to see if any work. Most will be eager to walk on the path so pull a name out of your feely box to choose a helper.

Teacher   *Stacy, I've pulled your name out of the box. Why don't you take off your shoes and come stand at the beginning of the path? I'll bet Stacy will need help from all of you boys and girls, since she's the first to try the path.*

Once you have someone ready to go, display one of the cards.

Teacher   *Here's our first card—what do you see?*

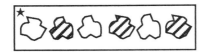

Children   *Yellow, green, yellow, green, yellow, green. It's a pattern!*

Timmy   *What's the star for?*

Beth   *It probably shows where to start!*

Teacher   *That's right. The star is a start signal. So what color should Stacy step on first?*

Children   *Yellow!*

Teacher   *Now what?*

Children   *Green! She needs to step on a green but there's no green next— it's another yellow.*

Damon   *I see a green! See?*
(He jumps up and points to the green stepping stone beside the yellow in the first row.)

Teacher   *Is that fair? Can Stacy step sideways?*

Damon   *Sure! (He takes the ruler the teacher is holding and lays it across the first two stepping stones.) She can go this way!*

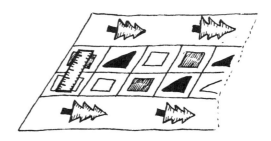

As your first student attempts to walk the path, you'll be able to repeat and demonstrate the rules.

Teacher   *You're right. The dove said Hansel and Gretel could go sideways, forward, backward and diagonally (positioning the ruler to show each direction).*

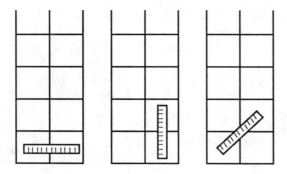

Can Stacy skip over a whole row of stepping stones like this?

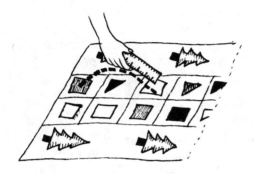

Zack   *No! The path will disappear!*

Teacher   *Where should Stacy step next then, if she can't skip a row?*

Grayson   *There's a yellow in the next row—see?*

Teacher   *Can she step diagonally?*

Children   *Yes!*

Teacher   *Now where?*

Children   *Green! There's another green straight ahead.*

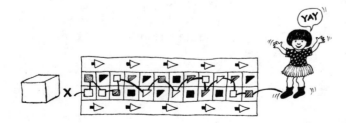

Have everyone watch and try to help the first child navigate the path.

Children   *Yellow, green, yellow, green, yellow, green, yellow, green, yellow, green, yellow, green. Yes, she made it home!*

Try a few more cards, using the feely box to select helpers to walk the patterns each time. Not all the cards will work. Some will lead off the path, while others will come to a dead end.

Teacher   *Let's try another card. How about this one?*

Taunice   *Hey, wait a minute! We don't have any black squares or triangles on our path!*

Teacher   *You're right. This card shows a shape pattern. Can you read it to me?*

Children   *Triangle, square, triangle, square, triangle, square.*

Teacher   *Grayson, I've pulled your name out of the feely box. Take your shoes off and come give this pattern a try.*

Stefani   *Grayson can't go. This card won't work!*

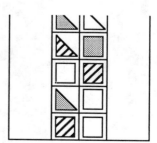

106

Teacher	*Why not?*
Stefani	*See!* (She points to the first row.) *There are no triangles to step on.*
Grayson	*That's okay. I can just step here* (pointing to the triangle in the second row).
Zack	*No, don't do that! The path will disappear!*
Grayson	*What?*
Zack	*The rule! You can't skip!*

Teacher	*Are you telling Grayson he can't skip over the first row of stepping stones?*
Zack	*Yeah!*
Teacher	*You're right. This card doesn't work at all. Let's try another.*

Picking out patterns from a random assortment of shapes and colors can be very challenging. Some children will be fascinated, while others may seem a bit bewildered at first. Rest assured that most of them will figure it out in the next few days.

Learning to Play The Game

In this section, children experiment with the dove's pattern cards, create and test new color patterns, and transform the large cardboard box into a "real" gingerbread house. Finally, they learn to play a whole-group, life-size version of Hansel and Gretel's Path.

Testing the Pattern Cards

Children take several days to become more familiar with the path and pattern cards, working individually or in small groups during choosing time.

SKILLS

- identifying and extending patterns
- learning to move in different directions: forward, backward, sideways, diagonally, left, right
- sorting
- problem solving
- sharing and taking turns

YOU'LL NEED:

- the large butcher paper path
- Teacher's Pattern Cards
- manila envelopes
- the large cardboard box you're using to represent the witch's house
- a sorting sheet (Fold a 12" x 18" piece of white construction paper in half. Label one side "yes" and the other side "no.")

yes ☺	no ☹

Now that you've established the story line and introduced the path, pattern cards, and rules, children will need time to experiment—to find out which cards work and which don't and simply to learn how to navigate the path while searching out a pattern among the stepping stones. We find this exploration stage works best during choosing time with an adult or older child available to help.

Teacher *This week I'm going to set out the paper path and pattern cards during choosing time. This is your chance to try out the patterns and find out which cards work.*

Children *Yeah! I want to try it! Do we still get to take our shoes off? Where's that witch's house? Can I use the blocks? I want to go to the invention table. Can we use the playhouse?*

Teacher *You can use the blocks or invention table or any of the other things during choosing, although I will ask all of you to try the path at some time.*

Jory *How come?*

Teacher *You'll need to know which cards work to play the game we'll learn later. Also, it's fun. I'll be around to help you get started. Who wants to give it a try?*

Several hands go up.

Teacher *Lindsay, Ashley, Nicole, Carl, why don't you stay here with me on the rug? We'll set things up as soon as everyone else is situated.*

Plan to work with the first few students who volunteer. Your presence and their enthusiasm will draw others. After they've removed their shoes, let each choose a card from the pile and try walking the path with it.

Cards that work can be placed on the "yes" side of the sorting sheet, while those that don't can be placed on the "no" side.

Expect intense concentration and joy—children's faces often shine as they walk off the end of the path, because the card they chose worked. Expect also some frustration when things don't work out quite right. If children seem confused, offer help but try not to jump in too soon. Encourage students to help one another. They'll often try the same card several times or choose one from the "yes" side of the sorting paper. Some children will come to this activity on their own and stay with it for a long time. We had about twelve hard-core path enthusiasts in one class of twenty-five. Others will come with a friend and return on their own once they catch on. A few may need to be encouraged to give it a try.

Creating New Patterns

Children's path explorations can be extended by encouraging them to create and test their own color patterns with green, red, and yellow Unifix cubes.

SKILLS

- creating patterns
- learning to move in different directions
- sorting
- sharing and taking turns

YOU'LL NEED:

- the butcher paper path
- as many red, yellow, and green Unifix cubes as you can gather (100 or more of each is ideal)
- the "yes"/"no" sorting paper you prepared for the last lesson

After children have had a day or two to investigate the pattern cards, replace them with baskets of red, yellow, and green Unifix cubes. Challenge students to create and test their own color patterns during choosing time.

Teacher *Boys and girls, I've put away the pattern cards today and set out red, green, and yellow Unifix cubes. I'd like you to make your own patterns with the cubes and test them on the path to see if they work during choosing either today or tomorrow. Can you think of a pattern that might work?*

Nickolas *Yellow, yellow, green? I looked at the path. See? It starts yellow, yellow, green!*

Teacher *Do you think it will work?*

Jake	Hey, I know one! Green, red, green, red!	**Teacher**	Try it out and see if it works on the path.
Teacher	Do you think it will work?	**Brenton**	Oh no! I'm stuck!
Jake	I don't know. I've got to try it out first.		

Most kindergartners, in fact, can't think of a pattern that will work just by looking. They have to build it and walk the path holding the cube pattern in their hands.

Teacher   That's just what I'd like you to do. Make a pattern and then test it. If it works, put it on the "yes" side of our sorting sheet. If not, put it on the "no" side. Then try making another.

Many children will proceed in a trial-and-error fashion, building simple color patterns without regard to the path and then testing them. Those who do consider the path as they work may use the first several colors they see, only to discover that their pattern doesn't extend all the way down the path.

Brenton   I made yellow, yellow, green, yellow, yellow, green, 'cause see . . . the path starts yellow, yellow, green.

Teacher   So even though the path started with yellow, yellow, green, it didn't continue that way?

Brenton   Yeah!

Teacher   Try a different pattern. Maybe you can make something that will take you all the way home.

Even if you've done lots of patterning with your students prior to this unit, some may build trains that aren't patterns at all, especially if they're looking at the path as they work.

Lindsay   Look what I made! Green, red, yellow, green, red, green, red, green, yellow, green.

Teacher   Your cubes match the left side of the path perfectly. Do they make a color pattern that repeats?

Lindsay   Well, there's green, red, green, red, in the middle.

Teacher *That's true. Is there a pattern that repeats all the way through your train?*

Lindsay *Oh yeah. It's not a pattern.*

Teacher *What would happen if you changed your train to green, red, green, red, green, red or green, red, yellow, green, red, yellow?*

Lindsay *I'll try it.*

Be sure to allow several days for this investigation. The fact that it's fairly complex will draw some children back again and again. Others will need encouragement to try it at all, but will find that many of their patterns work, especially as they become more skillful at making diagonal and backward moves and doubling back as they walk the path. The more time they spend searching out patterns now, the easier the path game will be to learn later.

Making the Gingerbread House (Optional)

In this lesson, children work together to transform your cardboard box into a "real" gingerbread house.

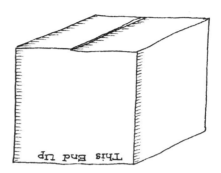

This End Up

SKILLS

- identifying two-dimensional shapes
- problem solving
- creating patterns
- working with partners
- sharing and taking turns

YOU'LL NEED:

- several versions of *Hansel and Gretel* (See References)
- pictures of gingerbread houses from magazines, kits, and cookbooks (Ask parents to contribute to this collection.)
- your large cardboard box
- brown butcher paper to cover the sides of the box if it's printed or beat up
- a 22" x 28" sheet of brown or white poster board for the roof (If your box is quite large, you may need to use two sheets and tape them at the roof gable.)
- masking tape
- white glue
- tempera paints

YOU'LL NEED: *continued*

- thirty–forty strips of white construction paper or butcher paper—3" wide and as long as one side of your box
- Candy Shape Patterns (See Appendix B for patterns and cutting instructions; fifty of each shape will probably be more than enough.)
- glue sticks or student glue bottles
- crayons

Although a plain cardboard box or even a chair will serve perfectly well to represent the witch's house when children play the path game, a decorated box adds a touch of magic, helps preserve the story line, invites children to become more involved, and gives them another chance to use their patterning skills. Later, when the unit is over, it will make a dandy reading space for one child at a time. If you decide to go this route, gather your children and examine any pictures of gingerbread houses you've been able to find. Then set the cardboard box in the middle of your discussion circle and brainstorm ways to use paint, paper, glue, and tape to make it look more like a gingerbread house. They may suggest doors, windows, a roof, and decorations of various sorts.

Sam   *It needs candy. All gingerbread houses need candy, like candy canes and lollipops and stuff.*

Beth   *Are we going to use real candy?*

Teacher   *Not on this gingerbread house. The whole thing is going to be made of cardboard and paper. But we can cut paper to look like candy shapes. What sort of candy shapes did you have in mind?*

Stacy   *Hearts!*

Sam   *Candy canes and lollipops!*

Teacher   *Let me list your ideas here on the board. Anything else?*

Carl   *Round things like cookies for the roof.*

Gary   *M & Ms. My mom used M & Ms when she made our gingerbread house.*

Nicole   *Diamond shapes would be good.*

After children have made some suggestions, begin to guide their thinking about how things are generally placed on a gingerbread house. They may be able to tell you that the candies are usually arranged in patterned rows. If not, tell them.

Teacher   *(sketching as she talks) You have lots of ideas for decorating our box. When people make gingerbread houses, do they usually put the decorations on like this?*

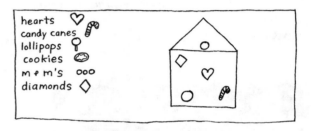

Amanda   *No! They put them in rows!*

Lindsay   *And they have to be in patterns.*

Teacher   *Oh, you mean like this?*

Children   *That's right! Yeah! Rows on the roof and by the doors and windows.*

After many suggestions have been volunteered, meet with a small group of children to do some of the basic structural work: cut a door and windows,

cover the sides of the box with brown butcher paper if necessary, fold the poster board in half and tape it on for a roof, paint the door, and so on.

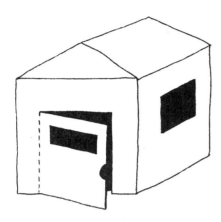

Present the basic house to the class the following day and have them work in partners to make patterned trim strips.

Katie　　*It looks more like a house today.*

Jory　　*But where's the candy? It's not very fancy yet.*

Teacher　　*Everyone can help put on the candy shapes, but since we can't all fit around the box at once, I'm going to have you prepare trim strips by gluing paper candy shapes on these long pieces of white paper. When they're dry, we'll glue them onto the house.*

Gary　　*That's like the frosting on our gingerbread house. My mom put on lines of white frosting and we got to stick candies on.*

Give each pair of children a strip of white paper and a collection of cut paper candy shapes. Have them work together to develop a pattern and glue it down the length of their strip. If they finish early, they can make another. You'll need twenty to thirty in all.

When the strips are dry, glue them to the roof and sides of the gingerbread house. It will have a charming patchwork appearance when it's complete because nearly every pattern strip will be different. You can use white tempera paint for any final touches.

Hansel and Gretel's Path—A Whole-Group Game

Now that they've had several days to investigate the path and prepare a gingerbread house, children learn to play the whole-group version of Hansel and Gretel's Path.

SKILLS

- identifying and extending patterns
- making predictions
- searching for patterns
- discussing and demonstrating various approaches and solutions
- sharing and taking turns

YOU'LL NEED:

- your gingerbread house (or a large cardboard box, a chair, or something to represent the witch's house if you didn't have the children make a gingerbread house)
- the large butcher paper path
- Teacher's Pattern Cards
- six name tags for team players, three in orange and three in blue (See Preparation)
- two chairs at the end of the path, one marked with a square of blue paper to represent "home" for the blue team, the other marked with a square of orange paper for the orange team.

Explain to your students they're going to use the path, pattern cards, and gingerbread house to play a new game called Hansel and Gretel's Path. Divide them into two teams and seat them on either side of the path. Establish team identities by setting color-coded chairs at the end of the path.

Choose three children from each team to be Hansel, Gretel, and the Dove and give them color-coded name tags. Have them remove their shoes and stand on their side of the gingerbread house at the beginning of the path.

Explain that the first team to get all three of its players down the path and "home" will win, but everyone will help and all the players will make it home eventually. (Most kindergartners are less concerned about winning than making sure no one is left behind.)

To begin, have a player from one of the teams draw two pattern cards from the stack in your hand. Display both cards and ask all the team members which one they think is most likely to get their player home.

Teacher *Let's start with the orange team today. Ashley, will you please pull two pattern cards from my stack?*

Ashley *Sure!*

Teacher *Great! Let me hold both of them up so everyone can see. Orange team, which card would you like to use? Which one do you think will work to get your first player all the way down the path?*

Jake	*The arrows! The arrows always work!*
Megan	*They're too hard. Do the shapes!*
Stacy	*Yeah! Square, triangle, square, triangle!*
Brenton	*That shapes one will work. I know it!*
Teacher	*It sounds like several of you think the shapes pattern card is a good choice. Sam, you're the first player on the orange team. Why don't you try the shapes pattern? We'll help you.*
Children	*(reading the pattern as Sam steps on the shapes they name) Square, triangle, square, triangle, square, triangle, square, triangle, square, triangle, square, triangle, square. Yeah! He made it all the way!*
Teacher	*Good job, Sam and Orange Team. Sam, you can sit right here in the orange chair at the end of the path. That's "home" for your team.*

Let the other team draw two cards from your stack and decide which one to have their first player try. Only a few children are likely to volunteer opinions initially and you'll have to work a bit to draw a decision from the group. It's possible that a team will choose the wrong card or that neither pattern will work. If so, their player must return to the gingerbread house to wait for his or her next turn. Play reverts to the other team. Continue back and forth until one team gets all their players home. Declare that team the winner and continue drawing pairs of cards until any remaining players on the other team are home too.

Plan to play the path game two or three more times with your entire group. Children's enthusiasm and participation seems to grow as they become more familiar with the rules and procedures. Be sure to pick different players each time and let students know that they'll each be making a miniature version of the game to play at school and home.

Making the Game Their Own

In this third and final section of the unit, children make their own miniature game boards and pattern cards for Hansel and Gretel's Path. After testing their cards and practicing playing their games at school, they take them home to share with their families.

Making Path Game Boards

First, each child glues construction paper squares and triangles on a small, predrawn grid and then sketches in trees and a gingerbread house to create a game board.

YOU'LL NEED:

- red, green, and yellow construction paper cut into 1" squares (200 of each color will be more than enough) and divided into baskets for each table

EACH CHILD WILL NEED:

- a copy of the Small Path Game Board black line (See Appendix B)
- scissors
- paste or glue stick
- crayons

Gather your students into a large circle. Show them a blank grid and a basket of paper squares. Explain that they'll each make their own path game board by gluing squares and triangles onto a grid. Have someone demonstrate how to cut the squares into triangles.

Timmy   *Where are the triangles?*

Teacher   *Good question! Does anyone have any idea how we could make triangles?*

Jacob   *Sure! You can get triangles by just cutting a square. I'll show you. You can get two!*

Teacher   *Okay. (She hands him a square and a pair of scissors and he demonstrates.)*

Nickolas *I knew that!*

Beth   *Yeah, I've done that before.*

Explain that the paper stepping stone shapes have to be placed randomly to make a path that works well.

Teacher   *The secret to making a really good path is to use both shapes and all the colors as often as you can. Try to mix them up so you don't end up with a bunch of yellows altogether or a whole line of reds; always try to put two different colors next to each other.*

Megan   *What?*

Teacher   *Let me show you what I mean. I'll start with a red square. (She glues a red square to the paper as she's talking.) What should I use next?*

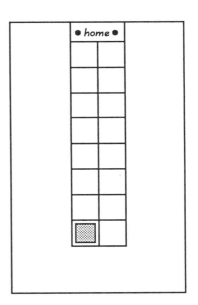

Stefani   *Where's the big path? We could just copy it!*

Teacher   *We could, but it's more fun to invent our own.*

Stacy   *Put on a yellow now.*

Teacher   *A yellow square or a yellow triangle?*

Stacy   *Square.*

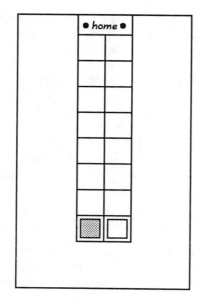

Teacher   *Okay. Now what?*

Daniel   *You need a green next. You haven't used green yet.*

Teacher   *That's true. I haven't used any triangles either. So I'll cut a green triangle and stick it on. Now what?*

Brian   *You've used all three colors. There's nothing left.*

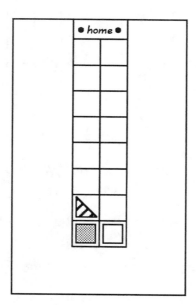

Teacher   *Well, the main thing is not to put the same two colors right next door to each other. What if I used red?*

Jake   *Now there are two reds by each other this way* (pointing diagonally). *See!*

Teacher   *That's okay. You just don't want to have a whole line of yellows or reds like this* (placing some shapes without gluing them).

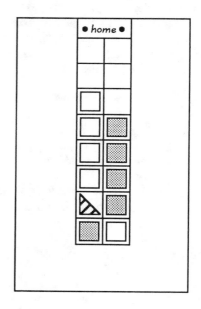

Ashley   *How come?*

Teacher   *If I have too many yellows or reds or greens in a line, I'm afraid not many patterns will work on my path.*

Taunice *You could do red, yellow, red, yellow, red, yellow.*

Teacher *That's true. I wonder if other patterns will work. Oh, oh! I've forgotten to use triangles on my path.*

Work with your students to make a path of randomly placed shapes and colors. Then put the path away and send them out to make their own. This is not an easy task for some children. Even though most will be able to do the actual cutting and gluing, a few will have trouble with the idea of random placement. You'll have to circulate as children work and may even have to help children make needed adjustments.

We did consider having everyone copy the same path, but decided against it because children seemed more invested in their own. They had to think a little harder and we had to move a little faster, but it was worth the effort.

Once their boards are dry, have students draw in trees along the sides and a ginger-bread house at the bottom to show where to start.

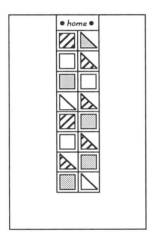

Colors and shapes have been evenly distributed in a random mix. This path will work fine.

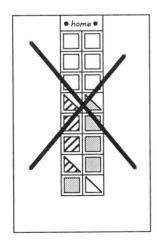

Shapes and colors are too bunched up here. It will be difficult to find patterns on this path.

Making Pattern Cards

When their path game boards are complete, children make pattern cards.

SKILLS:

- creating patterns

EACH CHILD WILL NEED:

- copies of both Children's Pattern Cards black lines (See Appendix B)
- scissors
- a large manila envelope
- crayons (red, green, and yellow *only*)
- access to red, green, and yellow Unifix cubes

Have children meet you in the discussion circle. Explain that the next step in preparing their own path games is to make pattern cards. Show them both of the Children's Pattern Cards sheets. Demonstrate how to cut the first apart.

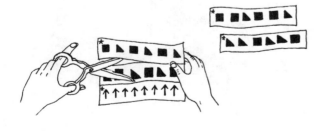

Cut the second sheet apart and show students how to fill in the "blobs" to create their own color patterns.

Teacher *I wanted you to have pattern cards like mine for your own games, but I felt it would be too hard and take too long to draw the shape and arrow cards, so I made copies for you to cut apart. I knew you'd want to make your own color patterns, though, so I just drew blank "blobs" for you to fill in.*

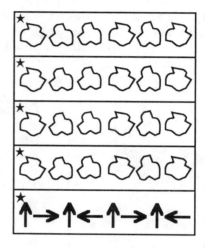

After you've cut these cards apart, you can go ahead and color in a different pattern on each. What three colors will you need to use?

Children *Red, green, and yellow.*

Teacher *Why?*

Nicole *Because those are the three colors we used on our paths.*

Teacher *Can you think of a pattern we could color using red, green, and yellow?*

Amanda *Red, green, red, green, red, green . . .*

120

Teacher (coloring as Amanda talks) *Sure, that's a good pattern. Do you think it will work on your game board?*

Amanda *I don't know.*

Teacher *How could you find out?*

Amanda *Try it out?*

Teacher *Good idea! That's exactly what we'll do tomorrow—test out all our pattern cards.*

Jory *What if they don't work?*

Teacher *Some will and some won't—that's part of the game*

Katie *Yeah, like on the big game, sometimes we pick cards that don't work. Then we have to wait another turn.*

When you think they understand what to do, send children off to cut and color their pattern cards. Be sure they have access to red, green, and yellow Unifix cubes as they work; some children find it helpful to build the patterns before they color their cards. You might also want to give children the option of working with their own game board in sight. Some like to search out color patterns that "work" first and then color in their cards. Others find this terribly confusing and do better simply coloring a variety of red, green, and yellow patterns and testing them later.

Note: **Before you go on, it's a good idea to place each child's game board and cards in a large manila envelope. Scan students' work quickly as you organize it. Is there a pattern on every card? Are the stepping stones on their board randomly placed or have some used all squares or glued lots of one color in a line? If you spot problems, meet with those children before the next lesson and help them make needed changes.**

Testing the Pattern Cards

Some of the cards the children have just made will not work; that's what drives the game. Before they can play, however, students need to find out if any of their cards do work. In this lesson, each child tests his or her cards and makes adjustments if necessary.

SKILLS

- identifying and extending patterns
- searching for patterns
- sorting

EACH CHILD WILL NEED:

- his or her path game board and pattern cards in a large manila envelope
- a Sorting Sheet (See Appendix B)
- a Unifix cube or other small object to use as a game marker

Have children gather in a circle and show them how to test and sort their cards.

Teacher *You've made your game board and cards—you've really been working hard. Your games are almost ready, but you need to test your cards to be sure that some of them work. Taunice agreed to let me borrow his things so I can show you how.*

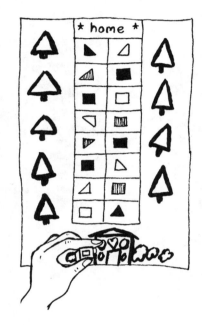

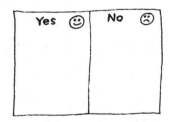

Teacher *His first pattern card is red, green, yellow, red, green, yellow. I'll try to follow that pattern with my game markers. Here goes . . .*

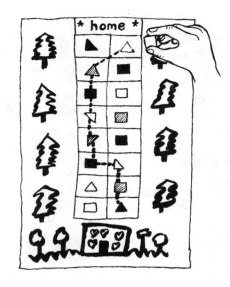

Teacher *That card worked, so it goes on the "yes" side of the sorting sheet.*

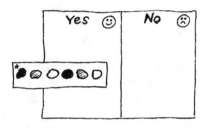

Teacher *The next card is . . .*

Children *Green, red, green, red . . .*

Teacher *Will it work?*

Grayson *No.*

Teacher *How do you know?*

Grayson (pointing to the first row) *There's no green here.*

Teacher *Grayson's right. There's no green shape in the first row. Now what?*

Children *Put that card on the "no" side. Try another one. Yeah, get a different one.*

When you think children understand what to do, send them off with their own materials. As you circulate, you might find a few children who don't "get it" yet, who aren't able to bear a pattern in mind as they try to search it out, or who skip rows in their determination to make every card work. Note what you see, but don't despair; this is not their last chance to make sense of it all. Children who do "get it" might be asked to help those who don't.

There may also be a few children who discover that none of their cards work. If so, plan to meet with them before the next lesson and help them figure out what to do. Their problems are usually due to the fact that the stepping stones on their boards aren't randomly placed. You can help them fix their boards.

Hansel and Gretel's Path—A Partner Game

Children play their games with partners in school and then take them home to share with their families.

SKILLS

- identifying and extending patterns
- making predictions
- searching for patterns
- working with partners
- sharing and taking turns

EACH CHILD WILL NEED:

- his or her path game board and pattern cards in a large manila envelope
- three small game markers in one color and three in another (see *Note* below)
- a copy of the Game Instructions Sheet for Families (See Appendix B)

Note: There are many things you can use for game markers. We bought a pound of lima beans and painted half of them orange and half blue using high gloss, fast-drying enamel spray paint. Each child was able to take three orange beans and three blue beans home with his or her game and we had plenty left over.

Gather your students in a circle. Choose a child to be your partner and demonstrate how to play the game, using his or her materials. The rules and procedures are just the same as the whole-group game. Each partner chooses a color and sets his or her game markers to one side of the gingerbread house. The pattern cards are shuffled and placed face down in a pile beside the game board.

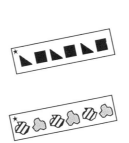

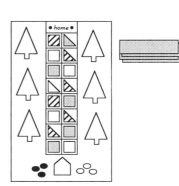

Partner A takes the top two cards off the stack, sets them face up, and decides which one to use. Both cards may work, but the player must choose just one. If only one card works but the player chooses incorrectly, or if neither card works, both cards must be returned to the bottom of the stack. Whether Partner A is able to move a marker home or not, the next turn goes to Partner B. Play continues back and forth until one of the players gets all three of his or her markers home, though most kindergartners like to continue until both partners have "won."

When you think children understand how to play the game, send them out by twos with their materials. If you're willing to take the time, you might partner children and have each pair play one child's game the first day and the other child's the next. This gives you time to model the activity twice and to emphasize that everyone's game plays out a little differently, because their game boards and some of their cards are different. The triangle, square, triangle, square card that worked on one partner's board might not work on the other. Again, it seems that to a certain point, children's enthusiasm for the game increases as they get more familiar with the rules and procedures.

After a day or two of partner play, send children's games home along with Game Instructions Sheets for Families. You might even send a short note explaining the project and encouraging parents to play the game with their kindergartners. We feel this provides good closure; children are proud of their games and excited to share them with their families. If you are feeling extravagant and just a little crazy, however, you can really finish with a flourish by having children make small edible gingerbread houses to take home too. To do this, you'll need:

- student-size milk cartons (One per child; scrounge these from your cafeteria) Cut off the tops, trim them down to the height of a graham cracker square, and run them through the dishwasher.

- graham crackers (four squares per child; that's two crackers broken in half)

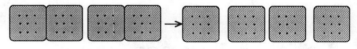

- several batches of "cement" frosting (See recipe below; each batch is enough to frost eight houses.)
- three or four different kinds of tiny candies (We used cinnamon red hots, chocolate chips, and the tiny pastel dots you find in the cake-decorating section at grocery stores.)
- plastic spoons (one per child)
- sturdy paper plates (one per child)
- napkins (one or two per child)
- portion cups or other small containers to hold the candies and frosting
- 3" x 5" white index cards to use for roofs
- crayons

"Cement" Frosting for Gingerbread Houses

(each batch is enough for eight children)

Use an electric mixer to beat three egg whites and $1/2$ teaspoon cream of tartar until frothy.

Gradually add one pound (one box) of powdered sugar. Beat on low until mixed well. Then beat at high speed for 3 to 5 minutes longer. This takes a good mixer and lots of patience. Store the frosting in a tightly sealed container. It will keep up to two weeks in the refrigerator.

Children used the backs of their spoons to smear frosting on the sides of their milk cartons to hold their graham crackers. They used more frosting to anchor candies to the fronts of their graham crackers. We asked that they pattern their candies in some way. Most of them did.

When they were finished, they folded index cards in half, colored designs and patterns, and popped them on top of their houses for roofs.

We gave each child a gingerbread house "kit"—four graham crackers, a cut and washed milk carton, a cup of frosting, three small cups of candy, a spoon, and napkin all on a large paper plate.

This was truly, a grand finale!

UNIT 4

Are You Sure
It's Twenty?

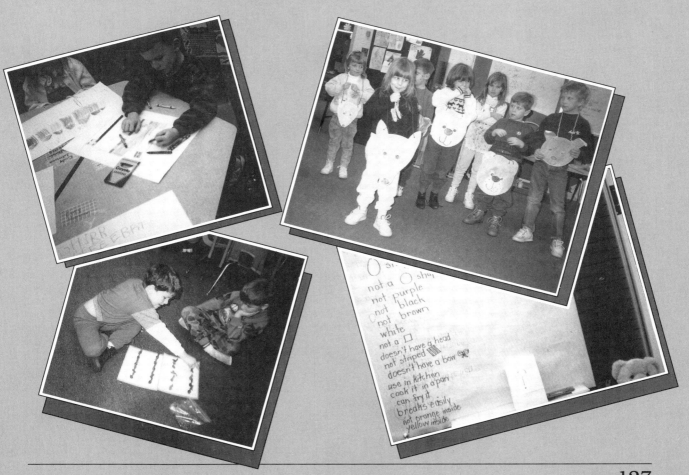

127

Are You Sure It's Twenty?: A Preview

What Will Happen in This Unit?

Children will have many opportunities to develop number sense to twenty as they act out, solve, and extend some of the problems posed in "Eggs for Breakfast," a story we've written for you to tell and enjoy with your class.

Are You Sure It's Twenty? Planning Sheet

	Day 1	Day 2	Day 3	Day 4	Day 5	Day 6	Day 7	Day 8	Day 9	Day 10
Sharing, Choosing, Special Classes (Library, Music)			The Forest Home Art Store—have children "purchase" their supplies and create their forest scenes throughout the morning	The Forest Home Art Store—have children work together to staple or tape their forest scenes into cylinders, or have a parent helper do it.	Make sure children have access to pan balances and other simple scales, along with items to "weigh" during choosing today, and for the next few days.	Gathering Collections of Twenty—have children who brought in their collections show them to the rest of the class.	Gathering Collections of Twenty—let the rest of your students show their collections; help those who didn't bring anything count collections of twenty out of your supplies.	Do All Twenties Weigh the Same? Introduce and explore the question together, letting small groups of children experiment with the scales and collections throughout the morning.		Making Breakfast at School
Calendar										Are You Sure It's Twenty? Our Favorite Things
Reading and Language Arts		Eggs for Breakfast		Gathering Collections of Twenty—have children brainstorm a list of things they could collect at home.						
Unit Work – Science, Social Studies, Art		Making a Mrs. Bear Counting Puppet								
Math	Mystery Box Sorting	The Forest Home Art Store—Introduce the task and show children the store supplies.			Mrs. Bear's Secret Eggs Game	How Many Eggs?	Are You Sure It's Twenty? How Many Children Have Twenty?	Do All Twenties Weigh the Same? Send partners out to compare their collections.	Which Collection is Heaviest?	
Closing										
Notes	Set up supplies for the counting puppets and art store.	Line up a parent or upper-grade volunteer to supervise the art store tomorrow.		Compose, type, and run copies of a letter home requesting parents to help children gather collections of twenty.	Send letter home to parents today.	Make sure you have extra items on hand for children who forget to bring their collections tomorrow.			Gather all the materials you need for tommorrow's class breakfast.	

131

What Do I Need to Know to Begin?

Winter is finally over! Mr. and Mrs. Bear have been asleep for so long that they've developed ravenous appetites. The door is open to let in the fresh spring air and animal friends begin dropping by for breakfast. Sweet Mrs. Bear—she gets so mixed up whenever she's cooking eggs. The poor dear counts each of the cracked shells as one egg and thinks there may be too many eggs. The animals are not sure there will be enough eggs for everyone and urge Mrs. Bear to pay closer attention to her counting.

This amusing story is a perfect springboard for helping kindergarten children develop their counting and problem-solving skills; goodness knows they don't want to end up like Mrs. Bear. An egg in the mystery box leads to a dramatization of "Eggs for Breakfast." As the story unfolds, the teacher asks the children to help Mrs. Bear figure out how many eggs she has in her bowl and how many more she'll need to feed the extra guests. Students go on to create Mrs. Bear puppets and forests to use in several counting games. Next, they bring their own collections of twenty from home to count, weigh, and compare.

The unit comes to an end as children prepare eggs and fruit for their own breakfast at school. Finally a class big book is created to record their favorite parts of the unit.

Estimating, counting, comparing, measuring, weighing, sorting, graphing, reading prices and spending money, listening, telling, drawing, and writing are the tools children use to pursue and solve the many problems posed in this unit.

Preparation

If you are lucky enough to have parent volunteers, you might have them run copies of the printed materials you'll need, make story bibs, and put together a sample Mrs. Bear puppet and "forest." You might also want to write a note to parents requesting craft materials for the puppets and forest homes children will be making. (See "What Materials Will I Need?" page 133.)

What Mathematical Skills Are Addressed?

Although Mrs. Bear has good rote counting skills and seems to understand the concept of one-to-one correspondence, something is missing. She keeps trying and trying to figure out how many eggs she has in her bowl by counting each half eggshell as one egg. She doesn't seem to understand that two shells mean one egg. The children are astonished at her mistakes. The issue here is number sense, a complex math skill that involves a firm understanding of number meanings, a feel for the relationships between numbers, a sense of their relative magnitudes, and an idea of what happens when you operate on them.

"Are You Sure It's Twenty?" gives kindergartners a chance to begin to develop such understandings. Rote counting, one-to-one correspondence, estimation, comparison of quantity, and operation sense all come into play as they figure out how many eggs Mrs. Bear has really broken into the bowl, spend ten cents to make a forest home for a counting puppet, to play several counting games, and examining collections of twenty they've brought from home also contribute to growing mathematical understanding.

These intensive experiences will not lead to long-term mastery, however. Young learners need repeated opportunities to develop number sense throughout the early grades.

In our own classrooms, we use *Box It or Bag It Mathematics* (Burk et al. 1988) to teach and review estimating, counting, comparing, sorting, and measuring all year long. "Are You Sure It's Twenty?" is a joy-filled way to introduce or reinforce these key concepts. Children love project-based learning and bring lots of energy to units such as this.

What Materials Will I Need?

General Math Materials (Appendix A)

- feely box for children's names
- simple scales for weighing
- a few extra countable items for children who may forget to bring their collections from home
- Unifix cubes
- individual chalkboards, chalk, and erasers

Classroom Supplies

- chart paper
- marking pens
- scissors
- pencils
- writing paper
- colored construction paper
- glue
- stapler
- crayons
- large paper clips
- white construction paper
- chalk
- oak tag
- 3" X 5" index cards
- envelopes

Other Things You Will Need

- an apron
- a basket
- a hard-boiled egg sealed in a box or bag
- a large plastic bowl
- ten hollow plastic Easter eggs
- ten large yellow craft pom poms
- Ziplock sandwich bags
- graph labels: "Exactly Twenty" and "Not Twenty"
- supplies to decorate Mrs. Bear puppets (use what you can easily gather— curled pieces of paper ribbon, paper ribbon bows, pieces of lace, tissue paper, fabric, tiny straw or plastic flowers)
- Forest Home Art Store supplies (again, use what you can easily gather; choose a variety of free and inexpensive things, such as the following, which are meant only as suggestions):
  Forest Trees (Appendix B),
  Animal Houses (Appendix B),
  small pieces of gift wrap (birds, wild animals, flowers, etc.),
  small stickers,
  cotton balls,
  small plastic or straw flowers
- popsicle sticks or coffee stirrers
- six containers for art store supplies (shoe box lids, cut-down boxes from the grocery store, rectangular plastic baskets, or the like)
- six margarine tubs

Other Things You Will Need *(continued)*

- six clothespins
- 300 pennies
- supplies for making breakfast at school (eggs, bread, apples, margarine, oranges, bananas, paper plates, napkins, plastic forks and knives)
- a donut or biscuit cutter
- an electric skillet or griddle
- spatula
- several small bowls
- a sharp knife

Print Materials (Appendix B)

- Working Space Paper (Run a class set.)
- 1-20 Counting Grid (Run a class set.)

- Heavier/Lighter Labels (Run half a class set.)
- Mrs. Bear Counting Puppet (Run a class set on brown construction paper.)
- Forest Trees (Run about fifteen sheets on green construction paper.)
- Animal Homes (Run about twenty copies.)
- Story Bibs (Run a copy of each character and use them to make story bibs for "Eggs for Breakfast." See page 138 for instructions.)
- Attribute Signs for "Mystery Box Sorting." (Run one copy of each. If you think you might want to use these for future sorting activities, color, mount, and laminate them.)
- Paper eggs (Run a class set.)
- Fruit for Breakfast Worksheet (Run a class set.)

How Can I Fit This Into My Schedule?

The activities described in this unit take place over two weeks. It is important that you skim the entire unit before beginning. We have included a planning sheet that was helpful in our classrooms. We hope this will assist you in charting your course.

Mrs. Bear's Dilemma

As the unit opens, children discover there's an egg in the mystery box and are introduced to "Eggs for Breakfast," the story around which many of the subsequent activities are centered.

Mystery Box Sorting

We often begin a new unit with "Mystery Box Sorting." Something related to the unit—in this case, an egg—is hidden in a box and students ask questions to determine what it is. Although they have to think very hard to figure it out, the mystery of it all never fails to intrigue young learners.

> **SKILLS**
>
> - listening
> - taking turns
> - sorting information
> - drawing conclusions

YOU'LL NEED:

- a hard-boiled egg
- a paper bag or small box in which to place the egg
- chart paper
- access to a chalkboard
- chalk and eraser
- Attribute Signs, one copy each (see Appendix B)

Show the children the box with the egg hidden inside. Explain that you have something in the box and you want them to find out what it is, but they will not be allowed to peek. Tell them there are many things that would fit in the box and they will need to pretend they are detectives and collect clues about what the mystery item might be. To do this, they need to ask questions that can be answered with a yes or no.

Tell children the best questions to ask are ones about what might be in the box—its color, size, shape, or even how or where it is used. In kindergarten it is very difficult for the children to ask this type of question without practice. Early in the year, children want to know immediately if it's a mitten, a dog, a pencil, a toy, a candy bar, and so on.

Even when the children ask an attribute question such as, "Is it square?" that question is immediately followed with, "Is it a circle?" "Is it a triangle?" and "Is it a rectangle?" no matter how each question has been answered. Many youngsters this age cannot rule out other shapes, even after one seems to be strongly affirmed. It takes many experiences before children will be able to attend to the information they've already gathered.

You may need to stop occasionally and focus their questions. It's helpful to put up simple signs showing color, size, shape, living/nonliving, function, and the like in order to help children refine their questioning. You can draw your own or make copies of the ones we've included in Appendix B and color them in.

Don't despair! This activity is so solid that we do it at least once a month in our classrooms with a variety of hidden items because it involves tremendous problem solving. They do get better at questioning and dealing with information they've gathered.

Make a drawing on the board similar to the one below. Hang a piece of chart paper next to it.

Explain to the children that every time they ask a question, you'll erase one part of the drawing. When the drawing is completely erased, they'll have gathered many clues to help them guess what's in the box.

Teacher   *Does anyone have a question to ask?*

Joey   *Is it a ball?*

Teacher   *(erasing one ear from the drawing) No, it is not a ball. Can anyone ask a question about the color, size, or shape of the object in the box?*

Karrie   *Is it round?*

Teacher   *(erasing another part of the drawing) Yes, you might say it is somewhat round.*

Gerge   *Is it red?*

Teacher   *(erasing) No, it isn't red. What do we know so far?*

Children   *It's not red, it's kind of round. It's not a ball.*

Teacher   *You all have such good memories! I'm going to record what we've learned so far. Any more questions?*

Kimi   *Is it blue?*

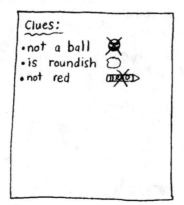

Teacher   *(erasing) No, it isn't blue.*

John   *Can you eat it?*

Teacher   *(erasing) Yes! Okay, let's add these new clues to our list. What shall I write?*

Children   *You can eat it! It's not blue.*

Teacher   *Any more questions?*

Justin   *Is it candy?*

Teacher   *Justin, can you think of an "about question" that would give you a clue about whether it is candy or not?*

Justin   *Is it sweet?*

Teacher   *(erasing) Great! No, it's not sweet.*

Continue the game in this fashion until the picture you drew is completely erased. Review the list of clues and allow the children to make specific guesses.

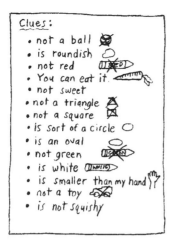

Clues:
- not a ball
- is roundish
- not red
- You can eat it.
- not sweet
- not a triangle
- not a square
- is sort of a circle
- is an oval
- not green
- is white
- is smaller than my hand
- not a toy
- is not squishy

Yusuke   *Is it a slice of bread?*

Teacher   *Let's use our clues to help us decide. Can we eat a slice of bread?*

Children   *Yes.*

Teacher   *Is bread sweet?*

Children   *Sometimes.*

Teacher   *Is bread little?*

Children   *Not usually.*

Teacher   *Is bread white?*

Children   *Yes.*

Teacher   *Is it roundish?*

Children   *No—it can't be bread!*

Continue having the children guess and test their hypotheses. If they are unable to determine what is in the box, tell them you are going to put the box away until tomorrow. They should think about what might be in the box and even talk it over with their families to figure out new questions to ask tomorrow. If they don't get it on the second day, we usually give them hints or show them what's in the box and talk about what kind of questions would have helped them figure it out.

Eggs for Breakfast

Winter is finally over! Mr. and Mrs. Bear have been asleep for so long, they've developed ravenous appetites. The door is open to let in the fresh spring air and animal friends begin dropping by for breakfast. Sweet Mrs. Bear— she gets so mixed up whenever she's cooking eggs. The poor dear counts each of the cracked shells as one egg and thinks there may be too many eggs. The animals worry about whether there will be enough eggs for everyone and urge Mrs. Bear to pay closer attention to her counting. As the story moves along, the teacher asks the children to help Mrs. Bear figure out how many eggs she has in her bowl and how many more she'll need to feed the extra guests.

SKILLS

- listening
- estimating and discussing
- counting
- comparing quantities
- problem solving

YOU'LL NEED:

- a basket for eggs
- a plastic mixing bowl (not clear—you don't want the children to see through it)
- ten plastic eggs, each with a large yellow craft pom-pom inside
- a simple headband with bear ears
- an apron
- story bibs for each character (see Appendix B and instructions below)
- your feely box with each child's name inside

EACH CHILD WILL NEED:

- a chalkboard, chalk, and eraser

137

To make story bibs, run a copy of each blackline and glue it to oak tag. Cut out the bib and color it to match each character in the story. Punch two holes in the top of each bib, thread a 30" length of string or yarn through the holes and knot the ends. The bibs are to be worn around the children's necks to identify the characters they're playing when it's their turn to act.

Before telling the story, find out what your children know about bears. How might bears feel when they first awaken from that long nap? What other animals might be found in the forest? You may want to explain that in your story, Mr. and Mrs. Bear have been unusually friendly and whenever other animals see their door open, they love to drop in. The bears in your story are also unique in that Mrs. Bear likes to cook. Explain that other animals will be dropping by who are considerably better at solving hard counting problems and they'll just shake their heads in amazement at how hard it is for their dear friend to figure things out. Tell them you'll be using the feely box to select animal friends. Don your apron and bear ears because you will be starring as Mrs. Bear in this story. Then set your props nearby and begin.

(Mrs. Bear is just waking up from her long winter's nap. As she is stretching, she discovers that Mr. Bear is already up and has opened the door to let in some nice fresh spring air. Select a name from the feely box to wear the Mr. Bear story bib. Be sure to "ham it up" a bit as you tell your story.)

Mrs. Bear *Are you up? Is it spring already? Oh, you've even opened the door. Look at that sunshine! Winter **must** be over. I'm so hungry my stomach is growling. How about you?* (Have all the children make growling noises to help Mr. Bear unless the feely box has given you a born actor or actress.)

Look at that! Someone has left us a basket of eggs. I think I'll crack some of them for breakfast. Maybe some of our friends will come by and we can find out what's been happening in the forest.

*Let's see. Where's that bowl? Since we're hungry, we're going to need **a lot** of eggs. I hope I don't smash these shells. Cracking eggs is kind of hard.* (Tap the rim of the bowl with your plastic egg and split the shell in half letting the yellow pom pom fall into the bowl. Put the half shells down beside the bowl in clear view, but keep the bowl in a place where the children can't see how many "yokes" have been added.)

One...two...Oh, look, there's Rabbit. Come in, I'm cooking eggs. Please stay for breakfast. (Select another name from the feely box to wear the rabbit story bib.) *Oh, dear, I forgot how many eggs I put in the bowl. Oh, I see.* (Point to the shells as you count.) *One, two, three, four...that's it—four eggs! Rabbit, why are you looking at the bowl like that? Did I make a mistake?*

Children, Rabbit seems to think I've made a mistake. Can you help me figure out how many eggs I've put in the bowl? (Once they've had a chance to talk about it, ask them if they can show you how they're figuring it out by drawing on their chalkboards.)

Look at that, Rabbit. Some of the children think I've only put in two eggs. Wait a minute, we could look in the bowl. Oh, oh! There are only two yokes. What happened to the others? (Give the children a minute to explain your errors.)

You're right. I'll try to be more careful. We definitely need more eggs. I'll crack some more. (Tap the bowl and "crack" three more eggs, letting the "yokes" fall into the bowl, and displaying the shells.) *Oh, look! There's Owl. She'll know about counting these eggs. Come in! Stay for breakfast. Look, I'm fixing eggs. I hope I haven't put in too many. Will you help me count?* (Point to the shells and count each of them.) *One, two, three, four, five, six, seven, eight, nine, ten. That's about right! Ten eggs for four of us.* (Owl shakes her head and looks at Rabbit. Rabbit shakes his head too.)

Oh, oh. You're shaking your heads. Children, did you watch me count? I didn't leave out any numbers. Look! One, two, three, four, five, six, seven, eight, nine, ten. (Wait for children to straighten out your thinking and counting! After a few youngsters point out the fact that you're counting two shells for every one egg, have them draw it on their chalkboards to help you and those who don't see your mistakes to understand.)

I'm not sure. Maybe we should count the yokes. (Tip the bowl and remove the "yokes" so children can count them.) *How did I get so mixed up again? Five eggs, I'm not sure that's enough. We'll need some more. Here comes Fox. Perhaps she'll want to stay for breakfast too.* (Pull the name from the feely box for Fox.) *Fox, you like eggs. I'm fixing breakfast. See, we have some eggs already in the bowl. Won't you stay?*

Rabbit and Owl think maybe I don't have enough so I'm going to put in some more. I'll be very careful counting this time. How many of us are going to eat? I should crack two eggs for each of us. I have five yokes in the bowl. That's enough for one each. How many do I need if we each get two eggs? (Rabbit, Owl, and Fox may be able to help you, but if not, explain to the children that you'll need their help. How many eggs will it take if each character gets two? Ask them to try figuring it out on their chalkboards. It has been our experience that a number of children can figure this out.)

My goodness! I'm going to need ten eggs. How many more will I have to put in? (These "how many more" questions can throw children a curve at first, but give them a bit of time and a few will solve it. Encourage them to explain how they did it. We often hear things like, "I just counted. You had five so I just counted on my fingers, six, seven, eight, nine, ten, and I knew it was five more." Or, "I just knew it." Or, "I know five and five are ten." A few children may note that when you thought you had ten eggs and it was really five, there were ten half shells. But they may not be able to explain exactly how they know this relates to the problem.)

Okay, here goes. One, two, three, four, five. ("Crack" five more eggs into the bowl, carefully setting the half shells beside the others.) *Oh, oh. I think I've cracked too many eggs. Please help me count these shells. One, two, three, four, five, six, seven, eight, nine, ten, eleven, twelve, thirteen, fourteen, fifteen, sixteen, seventeen, eighteen, nineteen, twenty! That's too many eggs. I'll have to take some out of the bowl.*

(By this time, children are aware of the problem of counting the shells to determine the number of eggs and some will try very hard to point out your mistakes. Take a minute to create a chart of how many eggs they think are in your bowl.)

How many eggs did Mrs. Bear really use?			
5	15	13	25
14		100	
9	19	11	7
20		30	6
	10		

Wait a minute, here come Sparrow and Raccoon. Let's see if they can figure it out. How many eggs do you think I've put in my bowl? (Often the "animals" head straight for the bowl to count the yokes but encourage them to show the errors in your calculations with the shells, stopping them part way and looking back at the chart to see if there are any numbers that can be eliminated.)

Teacher *We'd better take a look at our estimates. Are there any numbers on there that may not work?*

Children *It's not five. Five isn't enough. It can't be one hundred. You don't even have that many eggs. Maybe it's not thirty. That's a lot of eggs. I don't think it's six. I think it's twenty! Me too!*

Teacher *Maybe we should put a red dot by the numbers you think might not work now that we know more.*

Return to your helpers and let them finish figuring out how many eggs you've really cracked. Then return once again to look at the chart to examine the numbers that are still there. Why did so many people think it was twenty? Which guesses were too high? Which guesses were too low?

Thank you so much for helping me figure it out! Ten eggs! I think we'll need some fruit with our breakfast since there are so many of us. Will all of you go see if you can find any wild strawberries out there while I make some toast?

Counting Practice

By now, children should be convinced that even bears need to be able to solve counting problems. In this section, they practice and develop their own skills as they create props to play a puppet counting game and act out another counting story.

Making a Mrs. Bear Counting Puppet

To begin, each child constructs and decorates a Mrs. Bear stick puppet. On another day, children visit the classroom store to purchase materials to create a "forest" for Mrs. Bear. They make choices to fit their limited budgets, read prices, and count out money for each material.

<table>
<tr><td>

SKILLS

- decision making
- combining simple shapes and materials effectively

</td></tr>
</table>

EACH CHILD WILL NEED:

- a brown construction paper copy of the Mrs. Bear puppet (Appendix B)
- a popsicle stick, coffee stirrer, or tongue depressor
- scissors
- masking tape and glue to share

YOU'LL NEED:

- an assortment of decorator items for Mrs. Bear such as:
    - curled pieces of paper ribbon,
    - paper ribbon bows,
    - pieces of lace,
    - small pieces of tissue paper for dresses, aprons, or skirts,
    - small cut pieces of fabric for dresses, aprons, or skirts,
    - tiny straw or plastic flowers,
    - several large Styrofoam packing blocks or shoe boxes

Demonstrate how to cut a Mrs. Bear puppet and attach it to a popsicle stick with masking tape. Discuss the various items you've been able to provide and brainstorm how children might use them to create a truly unique Mrs. Bear. Have students display their finished bear puppets by anchoring them in a Styrofoam block or poking them into holes you've prepunched in shoe boxes.

Note: Although children "purchase" supplies to make a forest home for Mrs. Bear in the next lesson, all the materials to decorate Mrs. Bear are free.

The Forest Home Art Store

The Mrs. Bear puppets are complete and dry. Now it's time to make "forest homes"—decorated paper cylinders that will serve as portable puppet theaters later. In this lesson, children purchase supplies (predrawn trees, cotton balls, tiny flowers, stickers, and the like) to create forest scenes on long strips of construction paper. When dry, the strips will be rolled and stapled to form cylinders.

SKILLS

- planning
- discussing various approaches to a problem
- reading prices
- counting money
- taking turns and sharing
- constructing cylinders

YOU'LL NEED:

- a "bank" of about three hundred pennies
- four to six sandwich-size Ziplock bags
- six containers for art store supplies (shoe box lids, rectangular plastic baskets, or the like)
- six clothespins
- 3" X 4" cards for price tags
- six small margarine tubs
- materials for the art store:
  - green construction paper trees (Appendix B),
  - construction paper animal houses (Appendix B),
  - small pieces of gift wrap (butterflies, flowers, animals, etc.),
  - small stickers,
  - cotton balls for clouds,
  - small straw or plastic flowers

Note: The possibilities for your art store are endless. Choose a variety of free and inexpensive things. The items listed above are meant only as suggestions.

EACH CHILD WILL NEED:

- one 9" X 18" piece of blue construction paper
- one 3" X 18" piece of brown construction paper
- glue and a stapler to share
- scissors
- crayons

To Prepare for the Art Store

The day before you plan to do this activity, organize your art store items into boxes or other containers. Price each item from one to two cents, and write the price on a 3" X 4" label. Attach price tags to containers with clothespins. Set the containers down the length of a counter or table and place margarine tubs alongside for money. Have the children make a sign labeled "Forest Home Art Store."

To Model Shopping at the Art Store

When you're ready to demonstrate forest decoration and construction, move the materials to the center of the rug and ask children to gather round. Explain that the supplies in the boxes will be used to make forests for their Mrs. Bear puppets. Each child will have a chance to visit the store with ten cents (which you will provide), but it's important to think about how they want to decorate their forests and what purchases they want to make. Of course, most will want to buy everything. There are many times when one must shop on a limited budget, however, so it's important to think about how they'll spend their money.

Teacher *Each of you will have ten cents to spend at the store. Though you'll be able to choose several items to decorate your forests, it's important to think about how you'll spend your money.*

Children *I can't wait. Me, too! I want lots of those stickers. Yeah, and some of those trees and flowers.*

Kimiko *That's a lot of stuff. Maybe it won't all fit. What does it go on?*

Teacher *Good question. You'll each begin with a long blue piece of construction paper, which will be your sky, and a long narrow piece of brown construction paper, which will be your ground.*

Children *Do we have to pay for those too?*

Teacher *No, those are free. Let me show you how you'll assemble them.*

The teacher carefully glues the brown strip at the very bottom of the blue and demonstrates how the long rectangle will be rolled into a cylinder after it's decorated.

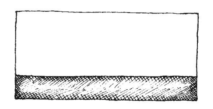

Teacher *I have a "purse" of ten pennies here just like you'll be getting. Let's see what I can buy to decorate my forest. I think I'd like some trees. How much are the trees?*

Children *It has a one. That's one cent...it's like a real store.*

Teacher *Good reading. The trees costs one cent each. I think I'd like to buy two trees. How much money do I need to pay for the trees?*

Children *Two pennies. Yeah, two cents. Put them in that yellow tub.*

Teacher *Good job! You've been shopping before. What else shall I buy? Let's see, I think my woods should have some clouds. I'll try that. I only want to buy one cotton ball. How much money will I need?*

Children One penny, put it in the tub by the cotton balls.

Teacher Good. How much money do I have left?

Children Count it.

Teacher Okay, could you help me? One, two, three, four, five, six, seven cents. That will buy many more things. Hmmm...these look like animal houses. I could color them and cut them out. They'd look nice in my woods. They cost one cent each and I'd like to buy three of them. How much will three cost?

Children Three cents...yeah, three pennies. Put them in the tub.

Teacher How much more money do I have?

Children Count it. Yeah. Let's see.

Teacher I had seven cents and I just spent three cents. Can anyone figure out how much I have left before we count it?

Children Maybe you have six cents...no, eight cents.

Hermon I think it's four cents 'cause I just know about that.

Teacher Let's count and see. One, two, three, four...four cents! Oh, there are so many things left to buy and I don't have much money. I have to choose carefully. I have some trees, some clouds, and animal houses. What else do I want in my woods? I know...if I bought some of these little pieces of gift wrap, I could cut out these animals and have them in my woods. It says they are two for one cent. I think I'd like to buy four. How much money will I need?

Children Four cents! Yeah, four pennies. No...not four cents, not if you get two for a penny.

Teacher How could I figure it out?

Kimiko What if you got two and put a penny in and then got two more and put in another penny?

Teacher Let me see...Take out two pieces and pay a penny, that's one cent. And then, take out two more and pay another penny, that cost two cents altogether...four for two cents, what a good deal! How much money do you think I have left?

Children Count it! You have three cents. No, two cents.

Teacher Let's check...One, two...two cents. Oh, I have to think real hard how I want to spend my last two pennies. I have trees and animal houses. I have pieces of gift wrap so I can have animals in my forest. I have a cotton ball to make some clouds. Boy, I sure like these little balloon stickers! They would make my woods look like I was having a party. They costs two cents each. How many can I buy?

Children You've got two pennies left. You can only buy one sticker.

Teacher I sure wish I could have more but one will still look good and it would make it seem like there was going to be a party with some cake. I'll spend my last two pennies for a sticker.

The Art Store in Operation

When you feel most of the children understand the procedure, they're ready to visit the art store on their own. Set the materials back on the counter or table and plan to have the store open all morning.

Children will briefly interrupt a regular activity to go to the store and will reusume the activity when they have finished their forests. Post a class list by the store area to keep track of who has come. As each shopper comes through he or she will count ten pennies from the bank into a Ziplock "purse," make his or her purchases, take them to a table where blue and brown background paper, glue, scissors, crayons, and staplers are available, and assemble a forest scene. Allow children to visit the store in twos. Have an aide, older student, or parent helper supervise if possible.

Once everyone has shopped, decorated their forests, and labeled them with their names, ask children to store them in an area far enough apart that wet glue won't cause them to stick to each other. When they're dry, have students work together to staple or tape them into cylinders before you continue, or have a parent helper do so.

Mrs. Bear's Secret Eggs Game

Now that their puppets and "forests" are ready, children use them to play the counting game described below.

SKILLS

- rote counting
- solving problems
- developing number sense
- recognizing and writing numerals

YOU'LL NEED:

- your Mrs. Bear counting puppet and your forest
- feely box of children's names
- your plastic eggs

EACH CHILD WILL NEED:

- his or her own Mrs. Bear counting puppet and forest
- individual chalkboard, chalk, and eraser
- ten paper eggs (Appendix B)
- scissors
- an envelope for storing the paper eggs

To introduce your children to Mrs. Bear's Secret Egg Game, explain that Mrs. Bear will hide some eggs inside her forest while they write the numbers 1-10 on their chalkboards. Turn your back to them while you hide a few eggs inside your "forest."

Teacher   Mrs. Bear has hidden some eggs in her forest. She wants you to try to guess how many. She says there are more than zero but less than ten. (Teacher drops seven plastic eggs into the forest while children write numbers from one to ten on their chalkboards.)

Children   It must be five. No, six! I think it's six. I bet it's ten because that's how many she really used. But she thought it was twenty. Maybe she has twenty in there. No, she said it was less than ten. It can't be twenty!

Teacher   Whew...hold on. Mrs. Bear can't hear so many guesses at once. Let's reach into the feely box for a name. That person can try to guess how many eggs she hid. Jimmy, your name came up first. Do you have a guess?

Jimmy   I think it's five.

Teacher   Mrs. Bear needs to peek. Just a minute. No, it's not five. Are there any numbers you could cross out on your chalkboards?

Children   Five! We can cross out five. Give us a hint. A clue!

Teacher   Good idea. Oops, I'd better give her a chance to peek inside. I think maybe she forgot how many were in there. (Have Mrs. Bear peek to figure it out.) She's ready. (Have her whisper in your ear.) She says it's more than five.

Children   Three. But it can't be three, she says it's more than five.

Teacher   Maybe it would help if we looked at our chalkboards again. Are there any other numbers on it we should cross off?

Children   We already crossed off five. Three. We just said it can't be three. Four! Two! One! We're ready.

Teacher   Let's pull another name for a guess. Tony, you get to guess.

Tony   I think it's nine.

Teacher   I'd better give her another chance to peek. It's hard for her to remember how many she put in there. (After Mrs. Bear peeks, have her whisper a new clue in your ear.)

Teacher   She says it's less than nine. Are there any other numbers we should cross out?

Children   So you mean it's not so much as nine? Is it lower?

Teacher   Yes, that's what less means.

Children   We can cross off nine. And ten. Ten is more than nine and her number isn't that many. It has to be six or seven or eight. I think it's eight. No, seven. Maybe six.

Teacher *I'll reach into my feely box. Mary, you get to guess.*

Mary *I think it's seven.*

Teacher *Mrs. Bear seems to be pretty excited. Maybe you're right. Is seven more than five? Is it less than nine? Let's take out the eggs and see if there are seven. (Let Tony lay out the eggs for children to count.)*

Children *We got it right! It is seven!*

Play the game again by reaching into the feely box and letting one of the children turn his or her back on the class and count some eggs into the forest. Meanwhile, have the other children erase their boards and write the numbers from one to ten again. Proceed as before, but have the child answer the questions and try to give the clues.

When most children understand how the game works, send them off to cut out their own ten eggs. As children finish cutting, partner them and ask them to take turns hiding eggs and figuring it out. They'll need their chalkboards, Mrs. Bear puppets, forests, and paper eggs.

Send the counting puppets and forests home when you feel the children have had enough time with them at school. Encourage them to play the secret eggs game with their families.

How Many Eggs?

Mrs. Bear's problems with counting are revisited. Rumor has it that the children will be preparing eggs and fruit for their very own special breakfast at the end of the unit. Will they be able to count the eggs better than Mrs. Bear? Here are some problems that may help.

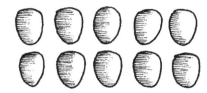

SKILLS

- counting
- comparing quantities
- playing out story problems with counters
- telling story problems

YOU'LL NEED:

- your plastic eggs with the yellow pom-poms inside
- a bowl

EACH CHILD WILL NEED:

- a chalkboard, chalk, and eraser
- twenty Unifix cubes

Explain that you'll be asking children to solve some egg problems like those that were so hard for poor Mrs. Bear. Encourage some discussion of how each problem can be solved and then ask them if they can find a way to show on their chalkboards or with Unifix cubes how they figured it out.

Teacher *Mrs. Bear very carefully cracked three eggs. How many shells did she have?*

Children *Three. No, six. Wait a minute! I can show you. Here, I'll draw it.*

Joshua *I did it, too. But I used some cubes. See! Two shells make one egg.*

Mr. Bear discovered that his favorite kind of cake was baking in the oven. The recipe called for two eggs. Mr. Bear counted two half shells on the counter. Did Mrs. Bear put in the right number of eggs?

Mrs. Bear was fixing breakfast again—scrambled eggs. She had six shells on the counter. How many eggs was she cooking?

Mrs. Bear cracked six eggs. How many shells did she have?

Continue with problems such as those above until the children begin to tire. Ask if someone can volunteer a problem for others to solve.

Exploring Twenties

In honor of the fact the Mrs. Bear used ten eggs for breakfast and produced twenty egg shells, children bring collections of twenty from home to share, count, sort, compare, and graph.

Gathering Collections of Twenty

Each child will need a collection of twenty small items—buttons, keys, baseball cards, pennies, and so on—which they've gathered at home. In this lesson, students help brainstorm a list of possibilities and prepare an envelope for the note which will go home.

SKILLS

- thinking about relative size and weight
- imagining twenty

YOU'LL NEED:

- chart paper
- a marking pen
- a small sack (Ziplock, lunch sack, or the like)

EACH CHILD WILL NEED:

- a copy of the finished letter
- an envelope

Gather the children together and explain that you would like them to collect twenty small items from home to bring to school for some more counting activities. Items should be easy to carry in a bag and all the same (twenty pennies or twenty baseball cards, rather than four buttons, five cars, one key, and ten paper clips). Work together to brainstorm a list of possibilities. This will require some thinking about size and possible weight. It might be helpful to display a small sack as you open the discussion. Record children's ideas on a chart and use their suggestions to compose a letter to families.

Distribute copies of the letter the next day for children to fold and seal inside envelopes. If you have time, let children decorate their envelopes—the greater their investment in the letters, the more likely they are to bring in collections.

Allow a day or two for children to collect items and bring them to school. Charting and sharing collections as they arrive will encourage and remind those who forgot the first day.

Be sure to collect objects of your own to share in case some students don't bring collections by the second day.

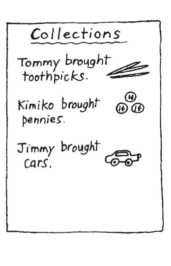

20 items – What can we fit in a bag?

20 little cars
20 keys
20 cheerios
20 shells
20 pennies
20 pieces of macaroni

20 toothpicks
20 plastic letters
20 stickers
20 baseball cards
20 screws

Are You Sure It's Twenty?

This activity allows children to enjoy one another's collecting efforts and exposes them to several counting strategies, as they check their collections to see if they really brought twenty items.

SKILLS

- counting with one-to-one correspondence
- using a variety of counting strategies
- using the vocabulary of "more," "less," and "the same"
- comparing quantities

My brother let me bring his baseball cards!

YOU'LL NEED:

- the ten plastic eggs from the story
- copies of the Working Space Paper (Appendix B)
- copies of the 1-20 Counting Grid (Appendix B)
- extra items for children who forgot their collections
- a few Ziplock sandwich bags

EACH CHILD WILL NEED:

- their twenty objects collected from home

Have all the children bring their collections to the meeting area. Ask them if they remember how many eggs Mrs. Bear used for breakfast. Lay out the ten plastic eggs in a long line.

Teacher *How can you use these ten plastic eggs to show that you have brought twenty things?*

Children *Count them. Yeah, count yours and then count ours. Yeah, mine is twenty...so is mine.*

Teacher *Okay. Let's count my plastic eggs. Ready? One, two, three, four, five, six, seven, eight, nine, ten. I only have ten eggs here—and some of you brought twenty things.*

Children *I brought twenty little cars. You told us to bring twenty. I brought twenty Cheerios!*

Teacher *Hmmm...I have ten eggs and you brought twenty objects. What shall we do?*

Nick *Get more eggs! You don't have enough!*

Kimiko *No, wait! Break your eggs in half like Mrs. Bear did when she was making breakfast.*

Teacher   Okay. (Takes all the eggs apart and lines up the half shells.) *Now how many shells do I have?*

(Children count)

Children   *Twenty! Now you have the right number!*

Teacher   *Counting is a good way to find out if you've brought twenty things. Does someone have a different idea?*

Kimiko   *Teacher, I can put my toothpicks down right next to your eggs.*

Teacher   *Kimiko, could you show us what you mean?*

Kimiko places one toothpick next to each half egg shell. When she is finished each toothpick has a shell partner.

Teacher   *How many half shells did I put down?*

Children   *Twenty!*

Teacher   *How do we know that?*

Children   *We counted them.*

Jennifer and Tony move up to the shells and toothpicks and begin counting again.

Jennifer   *Yes, there are twenty!*

Teacher   *How many toothpicks does Kimiko have?*

Children   *Twenty!*

Tony   *Yeah, it's twenty all right.*

Teacher   *Here is a working space paper. Can you see how many half shells are on the paper?*

Karrie   *I know. There are ten.*

Teacher   *Right—ten eggs, but how many half shells?*

Michael   *Oh, this is like the plastic eggs! Ten eggs and twenty egg shells.*

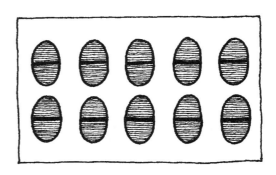

Teacher   *Is there any way you could use this paper to help see if you brought twenty things?*

Joey   *Sure—just put a thing in each side of the egg here—I'll try it with microcars. (Joey sets two tiny cars on each egg.) See? Two cars for every egg.*

It's twenty!

Next, show the children counting grids.

Teacher *How could you use these counting papers to prove you have twenty items?*

Kim *The grid has twenty numbers, so I could just put one of my barrettes on each number. Then you'd know I have twenty.*

Kim checks her idea and finds that it works.

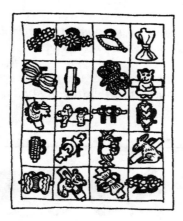

Ask all the children to use one of the methods you have just explored or invent one of their own to see if they have twenty things. Some may find that, in fact, they don't have twenty after all.

How Many Children Have Twenty?

Children discuss the reasons why some of the collections have more or less than twenty items. They use a graph to determine which have exactly twenty and which don't. Once the collections are identified, children help plan ways to fix them.

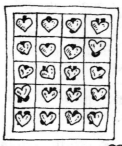

"Oops, too many!"

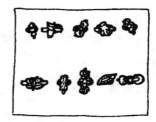

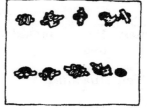

" I must have lost one!"

SKILLS

- constructing and reading a real graph
- discussing graph data
- discussing various solutions to problems
  helping others

YOU'LL NEED:

- two construction paper labels, one marked "Exactly Twenty" and the other marked "Not Twenty"
- 1-20 Counting Grids (Appendix B)

EACH CHILD WILL NEED:

- their collection of items

In one of the classrooms where this unit was first tried, about a third of the children had gathered their items without adult help and their collections numbered significantly more or less than twenty. It was clear that an activity was needed that would honor their collection and counting efforts and enlist the group's help in "fixing" those assortments. We decided a simple graph would provide some order and, perhaps, lead to some problem solving to adjust their collections. If this activity is needed in your classroom, be sure to commend children once again for their efforts in gathering items and assure them that it takes a lot of practice to learn how to count large quantities easily and accurately.

Teacher *I can't believe all the fine work you've done to gather your items and count them. I saw people helping one another and lots of excellent effort from everyone.*

Children *Mine wasn't twenty. Yeah...those two bags of pennies both had more than twenty! I just brought all my pennies. Mine was twenty! So was mine. I lost some...I used to have twenty!*

Teacher *Wait! You're all so excited but it's hard to hear everyone at once. How many of you found you didn't have exactly twenty today?*

A few hands go up and some faces look puzzled; they're not sure. They believed they had twenty in their bags even though it didn't work out that way when they were counted.

Teacher *I noticed that not all the bags had exactly twenty as I watched you working so hard to count them. While you were counting, I made these labels so we can set our collections out and see how many bags will need a few more or a few less items so they too will have exactly twenty.*

Call children a few at a time to place their collections beside the appropriate label.

Most children are able to set their collections in the correct spot but occasionally wishful thinking ("I thought it was twenty.") takes over and you'll note that some "not twenty" collections may get misplaced. If other children are aware, they may say something. If not, you may wish to leave well enough alone until the second portion of this activity, when those collections might be moved voluntarily.

Continue to call children until all the collections have been set by the graphing labels.

Teacher It's hard to tell for sure how many collections we have by each label. Can you think of ways we could make it easier to see?

Children Yeah... spread 'em out! No, put them in lines. Count 'em!

Teacher Hermon. You seem to have an idea in mind. Could you show us what you mean?

Hermon begins to spread things out into lines, but there seems to be no relationship between the lines.

Children Yep! Lots of "Exactly Twenty"s... not so many "Not Twenty"s.

Teacher How can you be sure?

Children It's more on that side. Yeah, lots more.

Lonson Those "Exactly Twenty" bags are real close together.

Teacher How could we fix it, Lonson?

A discussion ensues and finally a few children help Lonson adjust the columns so that there is a one-to-one correspondence.

Teacher Is it easier to tell how many are in each column now?

Children Yeah. There are only eight in the "Not Twenty" line. There are lots of bags in the "Exactly Twenty" line. Twenty-one! No, twenty-two!

Count the columns and talk about how many more and how many fewer in each column. Then help the group figure out how to fix the collections that aren't exactly twenty.

Teacher Let's do a little problem solving for the "Not Twenty" collections. How can we help people fix their collections so there will be twenty items in every person's bag?

Children Let's just dump them out and count them. Some have lots more than twenty. Mine does. Not mine—it was only seventeen.

Teacher Do all of you whose bags weren't exactly twenty remember how many items you had?

Katey Mine was more than twenty, but I don't know how many 'cause I filled all my spaces on that numbers paper and there were still more.

Teacher   *How could we help these folks?*

Michael   *What if they laid their stuff out on those number sheets and we could figure out whether they have too many or not enough?*

Ask your children to help the owners of the "Not Twenty" bags lay things out on counting grids for the group to see. Discuss how each collection could be adjusted and make plans to help children who need to gather more items.

Do All Twenties Weigh the Same?

After children are satisfied that all the collections have twenty items, it's fun to take a side trip to try some weighing and comparing tasks. Some children will assume that all the bags weigh the same because each has twenty. They've had too few experiences to consider that other variables might affect weight. In the following activities, children explore simple scales, compare their collections, and, ultimately, identify the heaviest collections in the room. As these investigations proceed, the teacher asks children to consider what makes some twenties heavier or lighter than others.

SKILLS

- sharing and taking turns
- using various scales for weighing
- using the vocabulary of "more," "less," and "the same"
- exploring the concepts of "heavier" and "lighter"

YOU'LL NEED:

- balance scales (Appendix A)
- milk box scales (Appendix A)
- A half-class set of Heavier/Lighter labels run on construction paper (Appendix B)

EACH CHILD WILL NEED:

- their collection of twenty items

Note: If your students haven't had a chance to use scales extensively, be sure to set them out in the play area several days before these lessons, along with some items to weigh (blocks, toy cars, plastic animals or other figures, a box of crayons, a rock, a large shell, etc.). It's very difficult to get children to focus on weight comparison until they've had a chance to explore the scales. Much of their initial response will involve piling as many things as possible into the pans, seeing "how far down" they'll go, and simply having a good time with the wonder of weight.

Ask the children if they think all of their collections will weigh the same and why. Show children the scales you've constructed and gathered, including those that have been out for exploration. What do scales tell us? How can we tell which collection is heavier and which is lighter? How would the scales look if two collections weighed the same? Do all the scales work the same way?

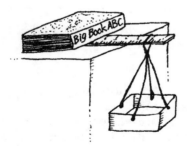

Teacher *You're all going to use the scales to find out how each kind works as you weigh and compare your collections. Let's look at Jimmy's collection of macaroni shells in our balance scales. Jimmy, would you put your collection on this side?*

Children *Wow! That sure goes down. Do mine. No, mine!*

Teacher *Let's see what happens if we put Amanda's collection in the other pan. Amanda, will you set your collection in this pan?*

Children *Whew! Her pennies went down more than Jimmy's macaroni. His macaroni went up!*

Teacher *What do you think that means?*

156

Children Pennies are heavy. Maybe the pennies weigh more than the macaroni? But both bags have twenty. Yeah, but not everything weighs the same.

Teacher You're right about the number of items in each bag. Something besides how many items must make a difference. What do you think might be happening?

Mandy Maybe it's how they're made. How do people make macaroni and pennies?

Children My mom cooks macaroni in hot water. Yeah and puts in cheese. My mom's purse has lots of pennies. I've got some in my pocket.

Young children often haven't had enough encounters with weight or how things are made to consider our questions in the ways we hope they'll respond. We believe, however, that it's important to keep asking and assisting where needed.

Teacher You know how and where macaroni and pennies are used. Do you have any idea how people made the macaroni that is in Jimmy's bag?

Kimiko My grandma makes noodles. Is that like macaroni?

Teacher I think the ingredients used to make macaroni and noodles are alike. What does your grandma use in her noodles?

Kimiko She pours in some flour and I think she uses some eggs and maybe some water.

Teacher That sounds about right, Kimiko. What about pennies, class? Do you have any idea how they're made?

Jimmy I think they've got hard stuff in them like my toy cars, yeah...metal stuff.

Teacher Your guess is mighty close, Jimmy. Pennies are made of metals. Class, do you think flour, eggs, and water weigh the same as metal?

Children No, metal's real heavy. Yeah, and our new van is made of metal and it's really heavy!

Teacher But Hermon's wearing a new metal ring. How heavy is it?

Hermon It's not heavy.

Teacher Metal things can be heavy or light. Do you think the size of each piece of macaroni and each penny would make a difference in the weights?

Children Each penny and each piece of macaroni is almost the same size so maybe they'll be the same when we weigh them. I think it'll be the same. Let's try it. Let's weigh the penny and the piece of macaroni.

Teacher Okay, watch carefully.

Children The penny went down and the macaroni went up.

Teacher What does that mean?

Children I think the pennies are heavier. The pennies weigh more.

Teacher What if we try Gini's leaf collection?

Children Maybe Jimmy's macaroni will go down more. Maybe it'll be heavier. No, I think the leaves will be heavier 'cause they're bigger than those little macaroni pieces. No, I think the leaves won't be heavy 'cause they feel soft in your hand. We jumped in the leaf pile at our house and they got all over us.

Teacher Let's compare them on our scales. Gini, would you place your leaf collection in this pan?

Children Wow! Gee! Now the macaroni went down.

Teacher Do you think the pennies are heavier or lighter than the leaves?

Continue modeling long enough to demonstrate comparing weights on all the scales and then make the scales and collections available during choosing. When you think children have had adequate time to experiment, distribute copies of the Heavier/Lighter Labels, and pair off the children to weigh and compare their collections one more time. After the results are determined, their collections will be stored on the labels until the next activity.

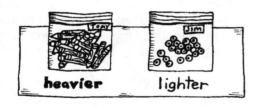

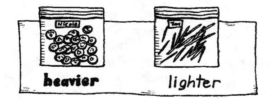

Which Collection Is the Heaviest?

After children have tried out a variety of scales and compared their collections, they investigate some of the variables that affect weight and find the heaviest collection in the room.

SKILLS

- comparing weight
- determining the heaviest
- understanding concepts of "more" and "less"
- reasoning

YOU'LL NEED:

- a balance scale

PARTNERS WILL NEED:

- their collections from the previous day on the Heavier/Lighter Labels

Teacher Today, we're going to try to find out which collection is the heaviest of all. As you look at our collections on the labels, can you think of any way we can find out which one is heaviest?

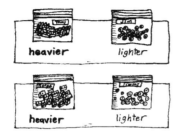

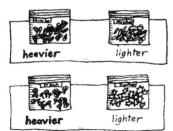

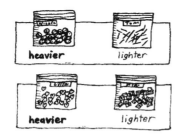

Children Mine's gonna be heaviest 'cause it's pennies. We could weigh them all again. I want to play with those scales again. That was fun!

Teacher Those pennies were very heavy but can you be sure they'll be the heaviest of all the collections?

Gerge My screws were real heavy, too.

Teacher We could weigh them all again but you'd probably get too wiggly for us to check every bag. Can you think of any faster way?

Kimiko What if we weighed just the ones that are on the heavier side of our cards?

Teacher Class, what do you think?

Michael Let's put the pennies on one side of the scale and try other heavy bags on the other side.

Teacher Okay, I'll put the pennies on this side.

Children Wow! The pennies make the pan go way down!

Teacher Do you think any of our other collections are heavier?

Gerge I think mine is 'cause it's fatter than the pennies.

Teacher Okay, come and put your bag on this side of the scale (indicating the other pan).

Gerge The side with my bag went way down. Mine's heavier.

Children Yeah, Gerge's collection of screws is heavier.

Teacher Now what? Gerge's collection is heavier than the pennies. Do you suppose his is the heaviest of all?

Children Yeah! No! Try some others! Try the bolts—they're real heavy!

Teacher How can we find out whether the bolts weigh more than Gerge's screws?

Children Try it on the scale!

This is a tough problem. If your class is too wiggly to solve it in one sitting, come back to it a second time, weighing the chosen bags until the heaviest collection has been determined. **Be sure to leave the bags and scales for independent investigation.**

The Ending

Mrs. Bear's egg dilemmas have provided children with an assortment of learning opportunities in which they've dramatized the story and estimated, counted, sorted, and compared weights. They've applied their growing counting skills to games and problem solving as well. The unit comes to an end with children preparing eggs and fruit for their own breakfast at school and illustrating an activity they especially enjoyed for a class big book.

Making Breakfast at School

Now that your children have worked so hard solving many problems and sharpening their counting skills, it seems only fair to end with a simple breakfast at school. The Fruit for Breakfast problem is best solved the day before and helps in knowing how much fruit to purchase and prepare. The actual breakfast might be prepared and served the next day. It's a lot of work but it's so much fun.

SKILLS

- counting to twenty
- one-to-one correspondence
- making choices
- solving problems

YOU'LL NEED (during the next two days):

- one egg for each child
- one slice of bread for each child
- margarine
- an electric skillet or griddle
- spatula
- small bowls into which children can crack their eggs
- one orange for each three-four children (cut into sixteenths)
- one apple for each three-four children (cut into sixteenths)
- one banana for each three-four children (cut into sixteenths)
- one paper plate for each child
- one plastic fork and one plastic knife for each child
- one napkin per child
- a copy of the Fruit for Breakfast worksheet (Appendix B)
- 20 Unifix cubes for each child
- a pencil for each child

Explain that the children will get to prepare breakfast at school tomorrow. Each child will get to crack an egg into a "nest" of bread, to cook, and to select twenty pieces of fruit. However, since you need to know how much fruit to buy, each child must plan how many pieces of each fruit he or she will choose in order to have twenty pieces altogether.

Teacher   *Tomorrow for our Eggs for Breakfast celebration, you may each have twenty pieces of fruit. Some of your fruit can be orange chunks, some can be apple chunks, and some can be slices of banana, but you can only have twenty pieces altogether. You'll each need a worksheet like mine and 20*

Unifix cubes. Does anyone have any idea how they might plan their fruit choices?

Danny *I want twenty of each kind, especially apples. They're the best!*

Teacher *I'm afraid that might be more fruit than I can afford at this time. I need you to figure out how many pieces of apple, how many pieces of orange, and how many pieces of banana you'd like, but it can't be more than twenty altogether. Here are twenty Unifix cubes. Does anyone have an idea how they might help us figure it out?*

Jose *I like oranges best. I want most of mine to be oranges.*

Teacher *That would be all right. How many chunks of orange would you like?*

Jose *Ten.*

Teacher *Let's set out ten cubes for Jose's orange chunks. How could we show that on his paper?*

Children *We could draw ten cubes by the orange. We could write ten by the orange. We could make ten triangles by the orange...that would look like chunks.*

Teacher *Good ideas! How many more pieces of fruit can Jose choose?*

Continue in this manner until you feel most children know how to begin and then ask each of them to count out twenty cubes and take a paper to a table to plan their fruit choices for tomorrow. Circulate and help where needed and ask children to help one another until everyone has a successful plan.

If you can arrange for a parent volunteer to help with the breakfast the next day, it will go more smoothly. Set up your room in such a way that you have an egg cracking area, a cooking area, a fruit counting area, and an eating area. Create a fifth area for children who are awaiting their turns or who have finished up. We have children move through the areas two or three at a time. At the first station they crack an egg into a small bowl, which they then carry to the cooking area. At the cooking area, they each cut a hole out of the center of a slice of bread with a biscuit or donut cutter, butter the "frame," and with some adult help fry their egg inside the bread frame. After their eggs are cooked, children proceed to the fruit station to count out twenty pieces of fruit, using their planning sheets for reference. Finally they eat and clean up.

Be sure to include a bit of health instruction in this session so everyone has clean hands before they handle food and each child understands his or her responsibility to throw away garbage after he or she has finished eating.

Are You Sure It's Twenty? Our Favorite Things

After breakfast, take time to help children remember the unit's activities. Children then illustrate their happy memories. Their finished pages are bound into a big book.

SKILLS

- reviewing what children have learned from the unit
- illustrating and writing about favorite activities

YOU'LL NEED:

- chart paper and marking pen
- poster board for book covers (See Appendix A)

EACH CHILD WILL NEED:

- one 10" X 16" sheet of white construction paper
- crayons

Teacher *Now that we've had our special breakfast, let's take some time to remember our favorite things about this unit. Who would like to tell us about an activity that was your favorite?*

Kimi *I liked making the eggs!*

Hermon *I liked when we weighed our collections.*

Jimmy *I liked when I got to be Rabbit and helped Mrs. Bear.*

Kimiko *I liked the store. It was fun!*

As children contribute their memories, list them quickly on a chart. Add simple illustrations where appropriate, to help those who still find print a mystery.

Show children the paper you've cut and ask them to make a picture of their favorite activity so that you can make a class big book. Depending upon the maturity of your group, you may want them to write a few words or a sentence about the activity in their invented spelling or dictate to an adult or older student. Assemble the pages into a big book (see Appendix A) to be enjoyed over and over.

I liked weighing our collections.

I liked being Rabbit and helping Mrs. Bear.

I liked the store. It was fun!

TONY

I LK MI PT

I liked my puppet.

JIMMY

HEAVY

I liked it when my rocks were the heaviest.

UNIT **5**

Teddy Bears
Catch a Cold

UNIT 5

Teddy Bears Catch a Cold: A Preview

What Will Happen in This Unit?

Children will explore measurement, geometry, sorting, and counting, while learning how to care for bears with colds.

Teddy Bears Catch a Cold Planning Sheet

	Day 1	Day 2	Day 3	Day 4	Day 5	Day 6	Day 7	Day 8	Day 9	Day 10	Day 11
Sharing, Choosing, Special Classes (Library, Music)										Children role-play bear care in the dramatic play corner	
Calendar											
Reading and Language Arts		Writing an "I Need" Letter		Read *Teddy Bears Cure a Cold*							
Unit Work — Science, Social Studies, Art					Bears Catch a Cold: Children all make beds for their bears	Making Teddy Bear Quilts	Temperature Taking (Optional)	Helping Bears Get Well			
Math	Mystery Box Sorting		Sorting and Graphing Teddy Bears	Making a Bed for Cinnamon					Bear Story Problems		
Closing											
Notes	Collect 4 toilet paper tubes per student. Obtain 6 student scientific thermometers.		Get heavy posterboard or other cardboard for bears' beds. (You'll need a 22" x 28" sheet for every two children in your class.)	Purchase one package of print giftwrap. Cut into two hundred 2" squares. Select two colors of construction paper that complement the gift wrap and cut two hundred 2" squares in each color.	Prepare Quilt Block Blackline as shown in Preparation section and run a copy for each student plus a few extra.	(If you're planning to do the "Taking Temperatures" Activity tomorrow.) Prepare a bowl of Jello and a thermos of crushed ice. Also prepare and make copies of a temperatures record sheet as shown in "Preparation" section.	Gather magazines with pictures of food, and large paper plates.				

What Do I Need to Know to Begin?

A teddy bear emerges from the mystery box and exhibits symptoms of a cold. The children are challenged to help it get better. They read about William the bear, in *Teddy Bears Cure a Cold* by Susanna Gretz and Allison Sage (1984), and how the other bears took care of him and helped him get well. They learn how to make a bed for the sick bear so he will be more comfortable. They bring their own bears to school and these are immediately stricken with the cold as well. The classroom becomes a teddy bear hospital and the children are each charged to make their bears comfortable so they will get better.

The major mathematical focus of this unit is on measurement. The children discuss size when they decide how large a bear to bring to school. They explore the idea of what it means to measure as they determine the size of the teacher's bear and then mark a piece of poster board to make an appropriate bed for the bear. They measure their own bears and make beds for them. They discuss measuring temperature and then experiment with thermometers.

Children also use their bears for sorting and classifying. They explore geometry as they make quilts to cover the bears. Story telling provides opportunities to count, add, and subtract.

The major social focus is on how to deal with illness. Students discuss the need to be warm and comfortable when one is sick. They talk about proper eating when one has a cold and find pictures of food to serve their bedridden bears. Finally, they role-play ways to tend the sick in the teddy bear hospital.

Preparation

This unit requires a copy of *Teddy Bears Cure a Cold* by Susanna Gretz and Allison Sage (1984), available from Scholastic Books or most libraries and children's bookstores.

You will also need four toilet paper tubes per student (100–150 tubes, depending on your class size), so you'll want to send a note home to parents before starting the unit (and begin collecting them from your friends).To do the "Taking Temperatures" activity, you will need to have at least six student *scientific* thermometers (as opposed to thermometers designed for home use) on hand. Your school may have them as part of a science kit or you could borrow them from a local junior or senior high. If you want your own, you can purchase them from Cuisenaire in sets of ten (see Appendix A).

In addition, you'll need to get some heavy poster board (6-ply is ideal) or cardboard (one 22" x 28" sheet for every two students), draw up a "Taking Temperatures" record sheet, and prepare materials for paper teddy bear quilts as described on the following pages.

Materials for Paper Teddy Bear Quilts

YOU'LL NEED:

- Quilt Block Blacklines Parts A, B, C, and D (see Appendix B)
- Scotch tape or gluestick
- the Teddy Bear Template Blackline (see Appendix B)
- one package (*not* roll) of giftwrap in an all-over floral print
- twelve sheets of 12" x 18" construction paper in two colors (6 sheets of each) that complement your giftwrap
- butcher paper in a color that complements the giftwrap and construction paper

To make the blackline children will use for their teddy bear quilts, locate Quilt Block Blacklines, Parts A, B, C, and D in Appendix B. Run one copy of each sheet. Then cut the quilt block pieces around their outer edges, match sides, and tape them together. Tape the assembled block onto a sheet of 8½" x 11" paper and copy to make a new master. Run a copy for each child plus a few extras.

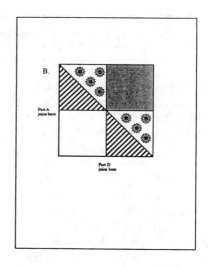

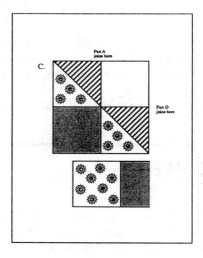

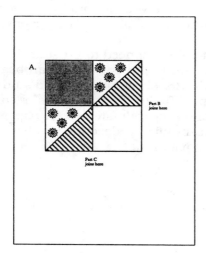

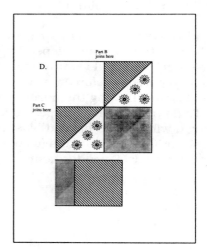

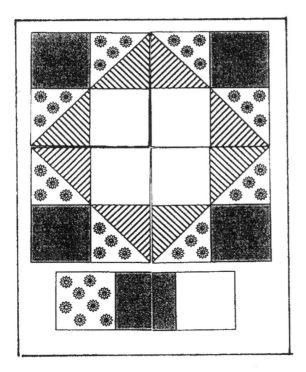

To make the paper 'patches' for children's quilts, cut your giftwrap into two hundred 2" squares. You can use a paper cutter to cut through the folded layers if you're careful, and one package of giftwrap (8 square feet or thereabouts) should be enough. Cut the construction paper into 2" squares also.

Run one copy of the Teddy Bear Template in Appendix B and use it to cut six to eight tagboard stencils for children to share when they decorate the middle sections of their quilts. An alternative is to simply have children draw freehand portraits of their bears on their quilts.

Finally, cut an 11" x 14" piece of butcher paper for each child to use as a quilt backing.

What Mathematical Skills Are Addressed?

Although the primary focus of this unit is on health, children use mathematics to sort and graph their bears, help set up the hospital, and pursue dramatic play. They measure bears to make beds that are the right size, then cut and piece together squares and triangles to form cheerful and attractive quilts. They investigate the concept of temperature, and by telling story problems, enhance their ability to role-play bear tending when the hospital is ready.

These intensive experiences may not lead to immediate, long-term mastery. Young learners need repeated contact with ideas in varying contexts throughout the early grades. In our own classrooms, we use *Box It Or Bag It Mathematics* (Burk et al. 1988) to teach and review these skills all year long, but we find "Teddy Bears Catch a Cold" an exciting way to introduce or reinforce some key concepts.

What Materials Will I Need?

General Math Materials (Appendix A)

- feely box of children's names
- Unifix cubes
- six student *scientific* thermometers

Classroom Supplies

- chart paper
- oak tag/tagboard
- white construction paper
- scissors
- crayons
- paste
- colored butcher paper
- felt-tip pens
- a 22" or larger paper cutter
- pencils
- white glue

Other Things You Will Need

- a teddy bear for the teacher
- a box large enough to hold the teacher's bear
- a teddy bear for every child
- a copy of *Teddy Bears Cure a Cold* by Susanna Gretz and Allison Sage (1988)
- 6-ply poster board or other heavy cardboard
- four toilet paper rolls per child
- one paper or Styrofoam coffee cup per child
- 2" squares of wrapping paper or colored construction paper in three colors
- a thermos of crushed ice
- a cup of warm to hot tap water
- a cup of cold tap water
- a bowl of Jello
- magazines that contain lots of pictures of foods
- fifty paper plates

Print Materials

- Teddy Bear Template (Run one copy and use as a pattern to cut a few teddy bear templates from oak tag for children to trace around as they make their quilts.)
- Quilt Blocks—parts A, B, C, and D (Run a copy of each, cut and tape together to form one master as described in "Preparation." Run a class set of quilt blocks from the master you create.)
- Temperature Record Sheets (Run a class set.)
- Attribute Signs (Run one set to hang during mystery box sorting.)

How Can I Fit This Unit into My Schedule?

The activities described in this unit take place over two weeks. Skim the entire unit before you begin, because many of the lessons are dependent upon one another.

We have included a planning sheet that was helpful in our classrooms. We hope it will assist you in charting your course.

Introducing Teddy Bears

In this section, you introduce your teddy bear and invite children to bring theirs to school.

Mystery Box Sorting

We often begin a new unit with Mystery Box Sorting. Something related to the unit, in this case a teddy bear, is hidden in a box and students ask questions to determine what it is. The activity provides experiences in collecting and using data to form a mental image of a hidden object. Although they have to think hard to figure it out, the magic of it all never fails to intrigue young learners.

YOU'LL NEED:

- a box
- a teddy bear
- chart paper
- access to a chalkboard
- Attribute Signs (Appendix B)

Have the children sit in a circle in the class meeting area. Show them the box with the teddy bear hidden inside. Explain that you have a secret item in the box and that you want them to find out what it is without peeking. Many things could

---

SKILLS

- listening
- taking turns
- building language
- thinking logically
- making predictions
- asking questions
- drawing conclusions

fit into your box, so they'll need to pretend they are detectives to collect clues about the hidden object. To do this, they need to ask questions that can be answered with a yes or no.

Tell children that they need to ask "about questions"—ones that investigate the object's color, size, or shape, or even how or where it is used. Kindergartners find it difficult to ask "about questions" and often want to know immediately if it's a mitten, candy, or whatever. Even when they ask an attribute question such as, "Is it a circle?" the answer often sparks other shape questions—"Is it a triangle" and so on. Many youngsters this age cannot rule out other shapes, even after one seems to be strongly affirmed. It takes many experiences before children will be able to attend to the information they've gathered.

You may need to stop occasionally and refocus their questions. We've included a set of Attribute Signs in Appendix B so you can hang simple signs showing color, size, shape, living/nonliving, function, and so on in order to help children with their questioning.

Don't give up. We do mystery box sorting every month because of the powerful problem-solving skills it teaches. The children get a little better at it every time.

Make a drawing on the chalkboard similar to the one below. Hang a piece of chart paper next to it. Explain that every time a child asks a question you will erase one part of the drawing. When the drawing is completely erased, the children may guess the name of what is in the box.

Teacher	*Does anyone have a question?*
Allen	*Is it small?*
Teacher	*How small?*
Allen	(indicating with his hands) *About this big.*
Teacher	*No* (writing "not small" on the chart). *It is not small.*

WHAT IS IN THE BOX ?
not small

| *Sarah* | (indicating the figure drawn on the chalkboard) *Is it as big as half the little man?* |
| *Teacher* | *Yes* (writing on the chart). *It is about that big.* |

WHAT IS IN THE BOX ?
not small
as big as ½ our little man

| *Mark* | *Does it move?* |
| *Teacher* | *No. It doesn't move.* |

WHAT IS IN THE BOX ?
not small
as big as ½ our little man
doesn't move

Karl   *Is it a machine?*

Teacher   *No. It is not a machine.*

```
WHAT  IS  IN  THE  BOX ?
not small
as big as ½ our little man
doesn't move
not a machine
```

Allow children to continue asking questions until the little drawn man has been completely erased.

Teacher   *Let's read over our chart and see what we know about the object in the box.*

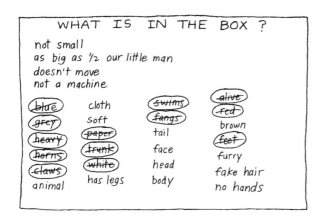

Teacher   *Does anyone think they know what is in the box?*

Tabi   *Is it a teddy bear?*

Teacher   *(writing Tabi's question on the chalkboard) Does anyone have another idea?*

```
Is  it  a teddy bear  ?
```

Michael   *Is it an otter?*

Teacher   *(writing Michael's question on the chalkboard) Are there any more ideas?*

```
Is  it  a  teddy bear  ?
Is  it  an  otter  ?
```

After you've recorded all the guesses, compare each idea to the list of attributes.

```
Is  it  a  teddy bear ?
Is  it  an  otter  ?
Is  it  a  puppet ?
Is  it  a  bunny puppet ?
Is  it  a  horse ?
Is  it  a  tiger ?
Is  it  a  stuffed bird ?
Is  it  a  stuffed dog ?
```

Teacher   *Let's start with the question "Is it a teddy bear?" Is a teddy bear "not small"?*

Yvonne   *It depends on the teddy bear. I have some teddy bears at home and some are small and some are big.*

Teacher	Could a teddy bear be "not small"?
Yvonne	Yes.
Teacher	Could a teddy bear be as big as half the chalk man?
Children	Yes.
Teacher	Does a teddy bear move?
Children	No.
Teacher	Is a teddy bear a machine?
Children	No.
Teacher	Could a teddy bear be "not blue"?
Children	My Care Bear is blue. But I have a bear that's not blue.

If more than one of their guesses matches all the attributes you'll need to help children refine their questioning a bit.

Teacher	The only idea we've been able to eliminate is the stuffed bird. All the rest of the ideas seem to fit, but I only have one object in the mystery box. Can anyone think of a question that would help us decide if it is an otter?
Annie	If it was alive, could it swim?
Teacher	Yes. It could swim.
Children	It's an otter!
Michael	I saw a bear swim once on T.V.
Karl	I saw a horse swim, too.
Jamal	My dog really likes water. He swims real good.
Teacher	I think tigers are good swimmers, too.
Jeffrey	Puppets can't swim. We can cross out the bunny puppet.

Annie	We can cross out puppet, too, I think. They aren't alive.
Teacher	Can anyone think of another question that will let us cross out more of these ideas?
Joseph	Can it trot?
Teacher	No it can't trot.
Children	Cross out horse. Horses trot.

Is it a teddy bear?
Is it an otter?
~~Is it a puppet?~~
~~Is it a bunny puppet?~~
~~Is it a horse?~~
Is it a tiger?
~~Is it a stuffed bird?~~
Is it a stuffed dog?

Roshan	Can it bark?
Teacher	No. It can't bark.
Children	Cross out dog!
Michael	I think otters bark like seals so cross out otters.
Tabi	Does it have stripes?
Teacher	No, it doesn't have stripes. So what do I need to cross out?
Children	Cross out tiger. It's a teddy bear! Yeah, a teddy bear!
Teacher	Are you all sure?
Children	Yes, it's a teddy bear!

Once your class has determined the contents of your mystery box, open the box and introduce your bear in such a way that he becomes *real* to the children.

Writing an "I Need" Letter

In this activity students help the teacher write a letter to their parents inviting teddy bears to school for a special math project.

SKILLS

- communication
- building language
- establishing size relationships

YOU'LL NEED:

- chart paper

Explain that the unit you are about to begin will be about teddy bears. In order to do the unit's activities, everyone will need to have a small to medium-sized teddy bear at school for two weeks. Have the children help compose a letter to grown-ups at home asking to bring a bear to school. If some of your children don't have a bear at home, ask the class to help solve that problem.

Teacher   *What should we say in our letter?*

Tabi   *We have to say that everyone who can needs to bring a medium-sized teddy bear to school. And we should say that some of us need to bring an extra bear for someone who doesn't have a bear.*

Teacher   *How will you know what medium is?*

Alan   *Medium is about this big. (He shows with his hands.)*

Teacher   *How will the rest of us remember how big that is?*

Michael   *We could use a ruler and measure.*

Jeffrey   *(jumping up to get a ruler and holding it between Alan's hands) It's bigger than one ruler.*

Yvonne   *(getting a second ruler and holding it next to Michael's) It's about two rulers.*

Teacher   *Should we say no bigger than two rulers?*

Children   *Yes.*

Other classes may tackle this size problem differently. In order to conserve poster board or cardboard you may want the bears to be smaller.

Michael   *Should we tell them it's because we're going to use our bears for math?*

Children   *Yes.*

Annie   *When do we have to bring the bears? That should be in the letter too.*

Teacher   *Annie's right. We need to say that the bears should come to school tomorrow. And since they need to stay for about two weeks, we also should say that they mustn't be special bears you need to have at home.*

There is much talk about what bear to bring and whether everyone can part with a bear for a few days.

Teacher   *How do we start a letter?*

Children   *Dear . . .*

Teacher (writing on the chart paper) *Yes, and I'll leave a space after "Dear" for each of you to write in the name of the grown-up to whom you will give the letter.*

Now we need to write the rest of the letter.

Once the letter is complete, duplicate it for children to take home.

Dear

Please remind us to bring a bear to school. We can't bring a bear bigger than 2 rulers. If we want, we can bring an extra bear for a friend. The bears will have to stay at school for two weeks, so they shouldn't be ones we need at home. We're going to use the bears for math. We need the bears tomorrow.

Love,

The Bears at School

The bears have arrived. If only they could know what lies ahead. The children sort them, recording the results onto a graph. Those poor bears then catch colds and the children measure them for beds that fit. To keep them warm, the children cover them with quilts they construct from paper squares. And to provide adequate care, the children take the bears' temperatures and discuss proper feeding. Finally, children tell and dramatize teddy bear story problems to help make the hospital run smoothly.

Sorting and Graphing Teddy Bears

This activity provides the children with an opportunity to share their bears with their classmates. They discuss how their bears are alike and how they are different, and then explore ways to group them.

SKILLS

- sorting by various attributes
- graphing
- comparing quantities
- sharing and taking turns
- problem solving
- identifying similarities and differences
- making predictions
- drawing conclusions

YOU'LL NEED:

- each child's teddy bear
- a 36" x 48" sheet of butcher paper to use as a graphing mat
- several 2" x 5" and one 2" x 24" oak-tag strips for labels
- felt-tip pens
- chart paper
- 9" x 12" white construction paper cut into "talking bubble" shapes (See p. 179.)

Gather children in a circle with their bears in their laps. Reintroduce your bear, then allow the children to introduce their bears in turn.

Teacher   *This is Cinnamon Bear. He was given to my little boy when he was a brand new baby. Cinnamon is now seven years old. He is wearing my son's first sun suit.*

Teacher turns to Alan.

Alan   *This bear belongs to my sister. I borrowed it. I don't know his name or how old he is, but I like his tall hat.*

Teacher   *Yes. He's very proper, isn't he!*

Annie   *What does* proper *mean?*

Teacher   *It means dressed just right. Michael, tell us about your bear.*

When all the introductions are finished, have the children place their bears in the center of the circle. Ask the children to look at the bears. Ask them to think of ways the teddy bears are alike and ways they are different. After they've had time to study the bears, have them tell you what they've discovered. List their observations on a piece of chart paper.

Teacher   *I want you to tell me how these bears are alike. I will write what you say on the chart paper.*

Tommy   *They all have two ears.*

Marta   *They all have two eyes.*

```
┌─────────────────────────────────┐
│ HOW  TEDDY  BEARS  ARE  ALIKE   │
│        2  ears                  │
│        2  eyes                  │
│        4  legs                  │
│                                 │
└─────────────────────────────────┘
```

Megan   *They all have four legs.*

Teacher   *You are really using your eyes! Now tell me ways these bears are different and I'll write your observations on the chart.*

Karl   *Some are twins, but not all.*

Sarah   *Some are grandmas and some are grandpas.*

Alan   *Some are wearing baseball caps and some aren't.*

Jamal   *Some are very proper and some aren't.*

Tabi   *Some are wearing clothes and some aren't.*

```
┌──────────────────────────────────────┐
│ HOW  TEDDY BEARS ARE  DIFFERENT       │
│  twins / not twins                    │
│  grandmas / grandpas / not either     │
│  baseball caps / no baseball caps     │
│  very proper / not proper             │
│  clothes / no clothes                 │
│                                       │
└──────────────────────────────────────┘
```

Compliment the children for all the differences they've found so far, and encourage them to look even harder.

Teacher   *Great job! What other differences can you find?*

Karl   *Some have ties and some don't.*

Yvonne   *Some have sort of mad faces and some are smiling.*

Continue recording differences children notice. It would be a good idea to take a break here and continue later.

Teacher *You all have been such good listeners, and you have thought of so many good ideas. Let's take a break before we choose a way to sort the bears.*

Children *Good! That's a good idea, I'm getting tired of sitting. Me too!*

Teacher *We'll just leave the bears right where they are for a while.*

When you resume this activity, review the list of differences and ask children to choose one of them to sort their bears.

Teacher *Let's pick one way to group our bears.*

Children *Boys and girls. T-shirts, no T-shirts. Big and little. Tails and no tails.*

Teacher *Are there any more ideas? (pauses) Let's take a vote to see which idea most children want to try.*

The children vote.

Teacher *So, we're going to group the bears by those with T-shirts and those without T-shirts. If your bear has a T-shirt, get it and put it here (indicating a spot near the edge of the rug).*

Have children collect their T-shirt bears and place them in the indicated spot.

Teacher *(indicating the bears with T-shirts) All these bears have . . .*

Children *T-shirts.*

Teacher *All the bears that are left have . . .*

Children *No T-shirts.*

Teacher *I'm going to make labels for our two groups. This one says "T-shirts" and this one says "no T-shirts." (Teacher places the 2" x 5" labels appropriately.)*

NO T-SHIRTS

T-SHIRTS

Teacher *Which group has more?*

Children *The ones without T-shirts.*

Teacher *How many more have no T-shirts?*

There is quiet while the children count the bears.

Alan *There are twenty bears with no T-shirts.*

Yvonne *There are seven with T-shirts.*

Teacher *How many more have no T-shirts?*

Children *Twenty.*

178

Teacher There are twenty without T-shirts. If there are twenty bears with no T-shirts and seven with T-shirts, how many more bears have no T-shirts?

The children talk among themselves for a while. But what is the answer? Finally, after much discussion, Sarah has an idea.

Sarah There are thirteen more bears with no T-shirts.

Teacher Can you show us how you figured that out?

Sarah I looked at the first line of bears with no T-shirts and matched them with bears with T-shirts until they all had partners. There were thirteen bears without T-shirts left.

Even though the teacher has the children help Sarah physically match the bears, many still don't see that the difference between the two groups is thirteen. It takes many experiences with this kind of question before most kindergartners begin to understand how to compare quantities.

Once they have finished organizing and comparing the numbers of bears, ask children to label the results.

Teacher (indicating the no T-shirt/T-shirt labels) Where shall I put these labels?

Children T-shirts here. No T-shirts over there.

Teacher I made another label to go with our groups. Can you help me read it?

Children help the teacher read the question.

Teacher What can you tell me about our graph?

Children The bears with no T-shirts group is more. Thirteen more!

As the children discuss their graph, record their comments on "talking bubbles." If you want to turn this into a picture graph for your wall, have each child illustrate his or her bear. Be sure to include the talking bubbles in your display.

Exploring The Book *Teddy Bears Cure a Cold*

After the bears have all been properly introduced and admired, your bear mysteriously develops a highly contagious cold. To gather information about the symptoms and treatment of a cold, the class reads *Teddy Bears Cure a Cold* and tries to use the information to help cure the sick bears.

SKILLS

- listening
- recalling a story
- recalling information
- story sequencing
- building language

YOU'LL NEED:

- *Teddy Bears Cure a Cold* (Gretz and Sage 1984)
- your teddy bear
- chart paper

Begin by holding your teddy bear on your lap.

Teacher   *This is my bear, Cinnamon. He was the bear hiding in the feely box. Do you remember?*

Children   Yes.

Teacher   (making the bear sneeze) *Oh, my goodness! My bear seems to have caught a cold. What could we do to help him get better?*

Children   *My mom makes me stay in bed when I have a bad cold 'cause I usually get an earache. I don't have to stay in bed, but I can't go to school. My mom won't let me drink milk. I go to school. My mom has to go to work.*

Teacher   *You all know a lot about what to do when you have a cold. I have a book to read that will give us even more ideas. It's called* Teddy Bears Cure a Cold.

Read *Teddy Bears Cure a Cold* to your class and discuss the story. How did they know William was sick? Why was this story called *Teddy Bears Cure a Cold*? Do they think the bears did a good job of taking care of William? Was it easy for William to sleep when he was sick? When did the bears first get the idea that William was getting better? What was it that finally made William want to get out of bed? Did Louise think the other bears would take care of her now that she was sick? Finally, ask your children what they might do to help your bear.

Teacher   *Do you know what we might do to help Cinnamon get better?*

Children   *We need to put him to bed.*

Tabi	*We need to feed him healthy food.*
Joey	*He needs to get lots of rest.*
Annie	*He should stay warm.*
Alan	*It didn't say that in the story.*
Annie	*But that's what my mom says.*
Teacher	*Let's make a list of all the things we can do to make Cinnamon better.*

Things That Will Make Cinnamon Better

Stay in Bed
Eat healthy food
Get lots of rest
Stay warm
Take his temperature
Don't let him walk around

Teacher	*What should we do first?*
Nancy	*We should put him in bed.*
Teacher	*But I don't have a bed for him.*
Children	*We could put him in the crib in the playhouse.*
Teacher	*I think if we put him in with the other babies they might catch a cold. We should have a separate bed for Cinnamon.*
Yvonne	*We could make a bed for Cinnamon.*
Teacher	*That's a great idea!*

Making a Bed for Cinnamon

This activity provides instruction in measurement as children help make a bed for the teacher's sick bear.

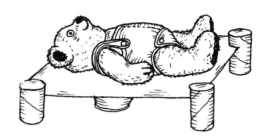

SKILLS

- counting
- measuring
- construction
- problem solving
- listening

YOU'LL NEED:

- a container of about two hundred Unifix cubes
- one 22" x 28" sheet of heavy poster board or other cardboard
- a paper cutter large enough to cut the poster board
- four toilet paper rolls
- one paper coffee cup
- teacher's bear
- scissors
- pencil, crayon, or other marking pen
- white glue

Gather the children in a circle at the rug to help as you make a bed for your bear.

Teacher I know of a way we can make a bed for Cinnamon. I have a big sheet of sturdy board to use (shows the poster board). *I want to cut this to "just fit" Cinnamon so I won't waste any board. What do I need to consider to make the bed just the right size?*

Michael *You need to know how big Cinnamon is.*

Teacher *How can we find out how big Cinnamon is?*

Allow the children to brainstorm ways to measure your bear.

Sarah *We could just lay him on the board and draw around him.*

This is a good suggestion, but the teacher wants them to explore measurement in a more formal sense.

Teacher *How could we find out how big Cinnamon is without drawing around him? Do you see anything in the room that you might use to help you?*

Alan *We could use our feet.* (The children have measured in the past with their feet tracings.)

Jamal *We could use a ruler. My daddy measures things with a ruler.*

Teacher *Feet, rulers—are there other possibilities?*

Roshan *We could use pencils. Then we could draw around the bear.*

Jeffrey *We could take the tiles and line them up next to Cinnamon and count how many.*

Teacher *That's another good idea.*

Jeffrey *We could count how many tiles.*

Children *We could use links. We could use blocks. Unifix cubes, they'd work! Yeah, use the cubes.*

Teacher *So many good ideas! We could use any of those things you suggested.*

Any of these materials will work for measuring, but the teacher chooses Unifix cubes because they are easy to handle and they stick together. It is important to remember to use other materials your students suggest for future measuring so they understand that each can be used as a measuring device.

Teacher *Let's try Unifix cubes this time. How could we use them to measure Cinnamon?*

Tabi *Can I show you?*

Teacher *Sure.*

Tabi *Take the cubes and stick them together until they are as long as Cinnamon.*

Nancy *You need to start right at the top of his head and end right at the bottom of his feet.*

The girls make a "train" of Unifix cubes as long as Cinnamon, carefully drawing lines with their hands at his head and his feet.

Teacher *What do you think boys and girls?*

Oona *The train isn't straight. I think it should be straight like a ruler.*

Teacher *Can you come and show us what you mean?*

Oona comes and straightens the train. It is now a little too long so after some discussion, she removes two cubes.

Teacher *How long is Cinnamon?*

Nancy (counting) *Twenty-three cubes.*

Teacher *Now we know how long Cinnamon is. Do we need to know anything else before we cut the board?*

There is much discussion among the group. Finally some hands go up.

Teacher *What do you think, Michael?*

Michael *We need to know how long Cinnamon is across.*

Teacher *What do you mean?*

Michael *We need to measure across. You know, this way.*

Teacher *What could we call that "across" measure? The up and down measure is the length. Does anyone know the name for measuring across something?*

Karl *I think it's how wide he is.*

Teacher *Good. Many people call that measurement width. It does mean how wide. What do we need to do to find out how wide Cinnamon is? Can someone show us?*

Michael links the Unifix cubes together and lays them across the bear from one paw to the other.

Teacher *Does everyone agree with what Michael has done?*

The teacher is somewhat concerned that the measure from paw to paw is not the width of the bear, but the children all feel the bear's arms must fit the bed, not dangle in space.

Teacher *How wide is Cinnamon from paw to paw?*

Children (all counting at once) *Eighteen cubes.*

Teacher *How can we use these trains to show how much poster board we will need?*

The children seem puzzled by the question; no one responds. The teacher places each train on the board creating a rectangle bordered on two sides by Unifix cubes.

Teacher *Let me set the cube trains on the board.*

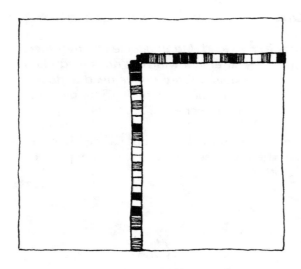

Teacher *How can we tell if this is the right size for Cinnamon?*

Alan picks up Cinnamon and places him inside the fence of Unifix cubes.

Alan *It's just right!*

The children all agree with Alan.

Teacher *What would be the best way to mark the poster board so I know where to cut?*

Jamal *Just draw a line right next to the line of Unifix cubes.*

Teacher *Should the line be on the inside or the outside of the cube train?*

Children *Outside. Yeah that will give him more room.*

Have a child draw lines along the train of Unifix cubes to indicate a cutting line. Use a very large paper cutter. Remind children that only an adult is allowed to use the paper cutter.

To hold up the center of the bed, especially for heavy bears, you will need to run a line of glue around the lip of a paper coffee cup and position the cup upside down in the center of the poster board.

Once this is finished, it's time to add the legs.

Teacher *I will show you how to make the legs for the bed. There is a little trick involved. First we need to decide how many legs a bed needs.*

Children *That's easy! A bed needs four legs!*

Teacher *Can someone come up and count four tubes out of this bag for me?*

What will happen if the legs of the bed are not all the same height?

Tabi *The bed will be tippy. Then Cinnamon will roll out.*

Teacher *How tall will the legs need to be so they won't be tippy?*

There is quiet for a moment as the children consider this question.

Yvonne   *I think they need to be real tall. My grandma has a tall bed. It's not tippy.*

Children   *But it shouldn't be taller than that cup. Yeah, make it the size of that cup. That's still pretty tall!*

Teacher   *We do want the cup to touch the ground so we'll need to consider its height as we figure out how tall to make the legs. I've figured out a good way to attach the legs.*

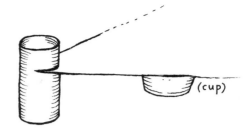

Show the children how to mark the tubes all the same height by placing them next to the cup and drawing a line.

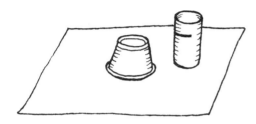

After you have marked all the tubes, cut a slit in each tube where you marked it.

Stick each corner of the poster board into the cut slit.

Voilà, Cinnamon has his bed!

In one of our field-test classrooms, one child was concerned about the teacher's bear being warm enough. She suggested covering him with a blanket from the doll corner. Once he was warm and comfortable, the children found a place to put him where he could rest.

Bears Catch a Cold

Your bear is very sick. He really shouldn't be at school. He is sneezing and coughing and blowing his nose. Oh, dear! The other bears have caught his cold! The only thing to do is put them all to bed. Children work in partners to measure their own bears and make beds.

Have the children gather on the rug with their bears. Look around the circle and point out sinister signs of colds in the bear. Ham it up. Pick up a few bears. My goodness, they're sneezing and coughing!

Teacher   *Oh, dear! It seems your bears have caught Cinnamon's cold. What should we do?*

Adam   *We should put them to bed till they get better.*

Teacher   *But we only have one bed.*

Joey   *We could make beds like we did for Cinnamon.*

Teacher   *What a good idea! Do you remember how we made Cinnamon's bed?*

Children   (all talking at once) *We measured. Yes, and we made a box with the cubes and drew lines to show where to cut. And put a cup under it. And used toilet paper tubes for legs.*

Teacher   *You tell me what we did and I will make a list of the steps on the chalkboard. (See next page.)*

You have such good memories. I think your chart shows every-thing we did. Now I would like you to get your bears and a partner to help you make beds for your sick bears.

The children will need a lot of space to work. It may be easier to put all the materials in one place, allow partners to come and take what they need, and then find a place in the room where they can work comfortably. As children finish marking the lines to show where the poster board is to be cut, send them to the paper cutter where an adult will do the cutting. Walk around as they are working. Remind

SKILLS

- counting
- measuring
- constructing
- problem solving
- listening
- cooperating

EVERY TWO CHILDREN WILL NEED:

- a container of about one hundred Unifix cubes
- one 22" x 28" sheet of heavy poster board or other cardboard
- eight toilet paper rolls
- two paper coffee cups
- white glue
- scissors
- pencil, crayon, or marking pen

YOU'LL NEED:

- a large paper cutter
- an adult helper

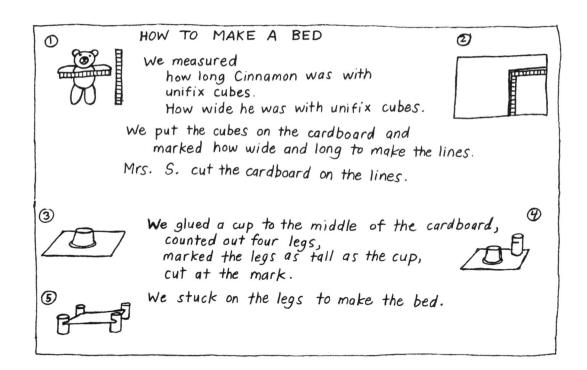

HOW TO MAKE A BED

① We measured
   how long Cinnamon was with
   unifix cubes.
   How wide he was with unifix cubes.

We put the cubes on the cardboard and
   marked how wide and long to make the lines.

Mrs. S. cut the cardboard on the lines.

③ We glued a cup to the middle of the cardboard,
   counted out four legs,
   marked the legs as tall as the cup,
   cut at the mark.

⑤ We stuck on the legs to make the bed.

them of the steps to make the bed and help as needed. They may need some help cutting the slits in the tubes. The beds do not have to look perfect; children will be very happy with their own work as long as it stands up.

Alan   *I'm all finished with my bed and Jeffrey is too. We need covers for our bears.*

Teacher   *Let's wait until everyone is finished. Then we can figure out what to do. We'll call this the hospital corner (indicating a corner in the room). You can leave your bears on their beds over here.*

Making Teddy Bear Quilts

Children need covers for their bears. In this activity involving patterns, symmetry, and geometry, children cut squares into triangles and arrange their squares and triangles into symmetrical quilt blocks.

SKILLS

- working with patterns
- manipulating geometrical shapes
- problem solving
- following directions

EACH CHILD WILL NEED:

- a copy of the assembled Quilt Block Blackline (see Preparation)
- 11" x 14" piece of butcher paper in a color that complements your quilt paper colors (see Preparation)
- scissors
- pencil
- colored pens or crayons
- paste

YOU'LL NEED:

- six to eight teddy bear templates (see Preparation)
- a copy of the assembled Quilt Block Blackline
- two hundred 2" squares of giftwrap (see Preparation)
- two hundred 2" squares of construction paper in each of two complementary colors (four hundred in all—see Preparation)
- 11" by 14" butcher paper

Have the children sit in a circle. Tell them that since there are not enough covers in the house corner to share, they will need to *make* quilts for their bears. (Allow plenty of time for this activity.)

Ask the children how many of them have quilts at home and how many like to sleep with their quilt when they don't feel well. Discuss how comforting a quilt can be.

Place a quilt block black line in the center of the rug with the three colors of paper squares.

Teacher   *We are going to use these paper squares to make our own quilt block. Look at these squares at the bottom. How many different designs do you see?*

Children   *There are three different designs. I see the same designs on the top part too.*

Teacher   *These squares at the bottom tell us where to put each color we will use in our quilts.*

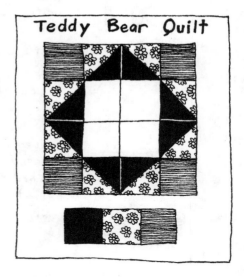

Adam   *I don't see any colors there. Just lines and stuff.*

Teacher   *Adam is right. There are no colors yet, just designs. We have to decide which color to glue over each one. Can anyone help me?*

Children   *Cover that first one with red. Yeah, red. That's my best color.*

As the children discuss which color to use for each design, select the 2" paper squares and lay them below the appropriate pattern squares.

Teacher *I want to paste these over the design squares so I will remember which colors I've chosen for my quilt but I don't want to cover the whole square. I still need to see the design underneath. I'm going to cut these squares so they cover only half of each design. I want to cut them to make triangles. Can anyone show me how to cut one of these squares into two triangles (indicating one of the three paper squares)?*

Susie *I can! See.*

She takes a pair of scissors and cuts the square on the diagonal from corner to corner.

Teacher *You are very clever. Can someone else cut these other squares?*

Children volunteer and come up to cut each of the other two squares into triangles.

Teacher *I'm going to glue a different triangle over half of each design square here at the bottom (indicating the three squares at the bottom of the sheet). Now I know what colors to make each part of my quilt block.*

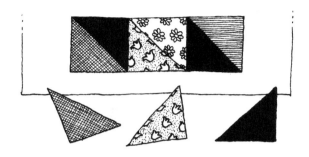

Who can show me what parts of my block should be this color (indicating the square covered partially by the red triangle)?

Children raise their hands and a volunteer is chosen. She indicates which places should be red.

Teacher *Shall I just put red squares in all these places?*

Children *No! You need to cut the squares to make triangles.*

Teacher *Yvonne, can you cut these squares into triangles for me? (Yvonne cuts the squares.) Now, who can put these triangles where they go?*

Peter comes up and, with a bit of trial and error, places the triangles correctly.

Repeat this procedure for each of the other colors.

Notice that the color to be placed in the corners could be left square. The children may not notice this and choose to cut each into triangles. That's okay. If they do this type of activity again, they might realize that if the whole square is one color, it could be formed by leaving the square whole instead of cutting it into two triangles.

Point out that the middle of the quilt block is to be left empty for something special.

Once the children see how the quilt block is to be completed, give them their own copy. Remind them that they need not match the colors to the same designs as yours (for example, they can decide to make the second design red instead of the first). Send them away to the tables where you have placed containers of colored squares and scissors. Have the children cut one triangle of each color and glue it into place at the bottom of the sheet to serve as their color key. As soon as their color keys are finished, encourage them to cut and glue their quilt block.

Have children write their names on the back of the completed quilt blocks and set them aside to dry.

At a later time, gather children at the rug. Show them how to place the bear template in the center of their quilt block, trace it with a pencil, and retrace the pencil line with a dark crayon or pen. Tell the children they can decorate the bear they draw any way they choose. They should try to make it look like their own bear.

Set out tracing templates for students to share. As they finish, have each child trim around his or her blocks and glue the blocks to the center of the 11" x 14" sheet of butcher paper. They can then cover their bears in the hospital corner with the finished quilts.

Note: **You may wish to have your youngsters simply draw and color their teddy bears' heads without using a template.**

Taking Temperatures

In this activity, children explore thermometers in order to understand their use when someone is sick.

SKILLS

- investigating temperature
- reading a thermometer
- making a graph
- conducting an experiment
- working together
- using a clock

YOU'LL NEED:

- six student scientific thermometers (See Appendix A)
- the children's bears
- a thermos filled with crushed ice
- a cup of cold tap water
- one temperatures record sheet for each child (See Appendix B)
- pencils
- red crayons
- adult helper, if possible

Have the children sit in a circle. Show them the cover of the book *Teddy Bears Cure a Cold*. Ask them to look at the chart taped to the foot of William's bed.

Teacher Can you see the chart at the foot of Williams' bed?

Children Yes.

Teacher Does anyone have an idea what it is for?

Hands go up. There is some discussion back and forth.

Roshan It has lots of numbers on it. Is it for counting the days William is sick?

Teacher Yes it does have something on it about days. Good observation.

Jonathon In the story I remember it was called a temperature chart.

Teacher You have a very good memory, Jonathon. That is exactly what it is.

Engage the children in a discussion about the temperature chart. Why did the bears keep track of William's temperature?

Teacher The very dark line shows what William's temperature should be if he were not sick. The red line shows what it is when he is sick. When his temperature is above the line, it is higher than it should be. Can your mom tell if you have a fever without taking your temperature?

Theresa My mom feels my head. If it feels hot, she checks it with a thermometer.

Teacher So when you are sick sometimes your temperature goes up? You get hot?

Children Yes. That's right! It makes you feel tired.

Teacher What happens to your temperature as you get better?

Alan Your temperature goes away, and them you're all better.

Tabi You have a fever when you are sick. My mom always says that.

Teacher You know a lot about illnesses. So, why did the bears keep track of William's temperature?

Children To see when his termperature went away. No, his fever. To see if it went up or down.

It's time to conduct some experiments to see how thermometers work. Show students one of the thermometers and the bowl of ice water. Ask what temperature they think the ice will be. Cool, cold, warm? Ask if anyone knows how to use a thermometer to find the answer.

Teacher Does anyone know how to read a thermometer?

Michael When I got to the doctor he puts the thermometer in my ear and it says numbers on the little box.

Alan My doctor puts little covers on the thermometer and puts it in my mouth.

Yvonne My mom puts the thermometer in my mouth and looks at a red line that runs up the stick.

Theresa Our room thermometer has a red line. It has numbers right next to the red line, too.

Jamal My mom said that the number where the red line stops tells what my temperature is.

Teacher If you are sick and have a fever, what happens to the red line?

Jamal I think the line gets longer. It goes way up the thermometer.

Teacher What happens to the red line on our room thermometer when it is a very hot day?

Children The red line goes up. Yeah, it goes up.

Teacher What would happen to the red line on the room thermometer if we out it outside on a very cold day?

Tabi The red line would go down.

Teacher What do you think will happen to the red line on this thermometer if we put it into this container of ice water?

Children The red line would go down. Ice is cold.

Teacher Let's put it into the ice water and see what happens. Watch the clock. I want to leave it in for two minutes; that's as long as it takes the red hand on our clock to go around two times.

Place the thermometer in the ice water and ask the children to watch the clock. After two full sweeps of the second hand, they should signal that the thermometer can be removed from the ice.

Teacher What do you notice?

Children The red line went way down! It got shorter!

Karl It went all the way down!

Teacher Is the ice cold?

Children Yes!

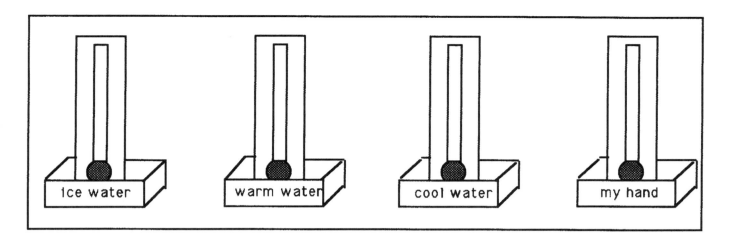

| ice water | warm water | cool water | my hand |

Show the children the record sheet. Ask a child to help you record the results of the first experiment by placing the thermometer beside the first drawing. Show him or her how to color a line with red crayon to match the height of the red line on the thermometer.

Teacher   *What did Oona do?*

Roshan   *She put the thermometer beside the first drawing and drew a red line to match.*

Teacher   *Why did she put it beside the first drawing?*

Carlo   *The first one has an ice cube under it.*

Children   *She made the line just as high as the red line. It's not very high.*

Have the children identify the picture below each thermometer tracing.

Teacher   *What picture do you see under this thermometer?*

Children   *A person. Are we going to take your temperature?*

Teacher   *Not mine, your own.*

Jonathan   *Are we supposed to put the thermometer in our mouth?*

Teacher   *No. At school you can spread a lot of germs around if you put the thermometers in your mouths. So instead I want you to wrap your hand around the thermometer for two whole minutes. Most of your hands are nice and warm.*

Once the children understand what they are to do, set out the materials. The children will work in partners; one partner will watch the red hand go around the clock two times while the other takes the temperature. They need to take turns. Each child will keep his or her own record. Six children can work at a time, while the rest of the class is otherwise engaged. It is a good idea to have a parent volunteer, older student, or an instructional aide at the table to supervise.

Once all the children have finished their investigations, it is important to gather everyone to talk about what happened. Make a chart of the results.

> What We Learned
>
> Ice is very cold.
>
> Our temperature is higher than ice.
>
> Warm water was about the same as us.
>
> Cold water isn't as cold as ice.
>
> Thermometers are fun!

Many children also enjoy constructing make-believe thermometers and adding make-believe temperature charts to the foot of their sick bear's beds. We set out a hole punch, oak tag strips, and string along with red marking pens. Children figure out their own designs.

Helping Bears Get Well

In this activity, children discuss what foods help them feel better when they are sick. They use magazines to find healthful food to feed their sick bears.

SKILLS

- practicing good nutrition
- sorting

YOU'LL NEED:

- magazines that contain lots of pictures of foods
- paste and/or glue
- scissors
- chart paper
- paper plates (one per student plus extras)

Gather the children close to you on the rug. Ask if they have any ideas about what foods people with colds should eat to help them feel better. List their suggestions on chart paper.

> Food To Cure A Cold
>
> mashed potatoes
> no milk!
> ice cream - if you have a sore throat
> lots to drink - juice, water
>
> 7-up makes your tummy feel better
> dry toast so you won't throw up
> tea
> scrambled eggs
> crackers
> jello
> chicken soup
> an icey

Tell children they're going to work together to find foods that will help their bears feel better. Their job is to look through magazines to find pictures of foods that would be good for bears (or people) with colds. After they have cut out these foods, they are to glue or paste them onto the paper plates. When the plates of "food" are finished and dried, set them in the hospital corner. Have children help design a sign.

Encourage children to use the plates of foods as they play in the hospital corner. Perhaps the food will help their bears feel a little better.

Bear Story Problems

To enhance their dramatic play in the hospital corner, children use their bears to act out story problems suggested by the teacher and themselves.

SKILLS
• adding and subtracting • problem solving • acting out story problems

YOU'LL NEED:

- each child's sick bear in bed
- 12" x 18" white construction paper
- crayons or marking pens
- feely box (see Appendix A) containing name cards for each of the children

Have all the children sit in a circle on the rug.

Teacher	*Today we are going to use our sick bears for counting stories. I'm going to reach into the feely box and pull out some names. Jeremy, Teddy, Kimberly, Kimiko, and Joey. Will you get your bears and their beds from our bear hospital and place them in the center of the circle?*

The five children place their bears in their beds in the center.

Teacher	*Listen very carefully to our story so you will know how to act it out. Some bears did not feel very well so they went to bed. They were coughing and sneezing.*

Children make their bears cough and sneeze.

Teacher	*How many bears were not feeling well?*
Children	*One, two, three, four, five! Five were not feeling well.*
Teacher	*Great. Let's make a record of our story. Can someone tell me the story again while I draw a picture of it?*
Yvonne	*Five bears were feeling sick. So they went to bed. They were really coughing and sneezing!*

Teacher draws five beds.

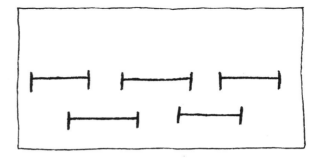

Michael *You just drew the beds. You forgot the bears.*

Teacher *I left the bears out on purpose so you could help to finish these pictures later. I need to write the story above the picture. What was it again?*

Oona *Five bears didn't feel well so they went to bed. They coughed and sneezed!*

Teacher writes the story as the child dictates.

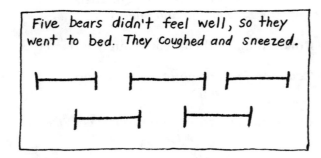

Teacher *There was a bear in the house that was not sick. (Pulls a name from the feely box.) Tabi.*

Tabi gets her bear and brings it to the circle.

Teacher *What should Tabi's bear do?*

Children *He could bring tissues. He could make sure they are all tucked in. He could take their temperatures.*

Teacher *This bear who was not sick took their temperatures, blew their noses, and tucked them in.*

Tabi makes her bear do as asked.

Teacher *I need to draw a new picture to go with this part of the story. Can someone retell the story so I know what to draw?*

Jeffrey *There was a bear who was not sick. He took care of the other bears. He blew their noses, tucked them in, and took their temperatures.*

Teacher *How many bears were sick?*

Children *Five bears were sick.*

Teacher *This time I'll draw the helper bear, but I'll only draw the beds for the sick bears so you can help draw in the sick bears later.*

Alan *There are six bears now!*

Teacher *How did you figure that out?*

Alan *I counted Tabi's not sick bear. That's one. Five more are sick. So, one and five more is six.*

Teacher *Good thinking! How should I write the story?*

Alan *There are six bears now. One is helping and five are sick.*

Teacher   *Tabi's bear is doing such a good job of taking care of the sick bears. Two of them feel so much better, they are ready to get up. Jeremy and Kimberly.*

The children come up and help their bears show how much better they feel. The bears get out of bed and begin to help Tabi's bear with the other sick bears.

Teacher   *What good helper bears! Can someone retell the story to help me remember what I should draw in my picture?*

Oona   *Two bears were feeling much better, so they got up to help Tabi's bear.*

Teacher   *Now how many bears are in bed?*

Children   *There are three bears in bed.*

Teacher   *How many bears are helping now?*

Children   *Three are helping. Hey, three are helping and three are still sick.*

Alan   *Three and three make six. There are still six bears!*

Teacher   *So in my picture I'll need to draw how many beds this time?*

Children   *Three.*

Continue in this way, inventing and recording the stories. From time to time draw the names of a new set of players from the feely box so as many children

as possible can have a turn. The structure of the stories supplies the children with many ideas for later play in the hospital corner. The more varied your stories, the more ideas the children accumulate. Be sure to include the idea of serving healthful foods to the bears.

Save the story records to be illustrated by interested children and then assemble them into a big book (see Appendix A) of number stories. Add the book to your classroom library to be read and enjoyed.

Unlike the other units in this book, "Teddy Bears Catch a Cold" does not have a definite ending. After the beds and quilts are made and a hospital corner set up, encourage children to tend sick bears, drawing on the language generated by the story problems, discussions, the temperature experiments, the plates of food, and, of course, *Teddy Bears Cure a Cold.* A few may even create temperature charts, pretend thermometers, bedside tables, trays, tiny books, and additional props.

Appendix A: Materials

Unifix Cubes

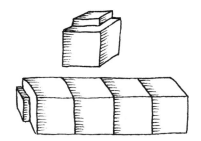

How many?

500–1,000 cubes

Where do I get them?

These can be ordered from:

The Math Learning Center
P.O. Box 3226
Salem, Oregon 97302
(503) 370-8130

How do I prepare them?

Pour cubes into a tub or box

Feely Box

How many?

Two

To make, you'll need:

- a very large, stretchy adult sock or leg warmer
- a plastic quart refrigerator container or a one-pound coffee can

How do I prepare it?

Cover the can or container with contact paper.

If you're using a leg warmer, use Tacky glue or a hot glue gun to attach it to the top of your covered container. (If you're using a large stretchy sock, cut off the foot portion and use the leg portion only.) Tape with filament tape around the outside to reduce eventual raveling.

Place small cards with each student's name folded in half inside. You'll need a second feely box for some of the units. Leave it empty for now.

Individual Student Chalkboards

How many?

One per student

Where will I get them?

These can be purchased from the the Math Learning Center or you can search out black Nat-Mat and cut it on a very large paper cutter.

Use felt or school erasers to clean them. (School erasers can be cut in half with a table saw.)

How do I prepare them?

Have children thoroughly rub these down in both directions with chalk, then erase and they're ready for use.

Scales

How many?

One, two, or more

- Balance
- Pan balance

Where do I get them?

Scales of various types can be ordered from:
Cuisenaire Company of America, Inc.
12 Church Street
P.O. Box D
New Rochelle, NY 10802
(800) 237-3142

Many other school supply catalogs carry scales as well.

Milk Box Scales

How many?

Two pair

Where do I get them?

Make them yourself or ask a parent to make them.

You'll need:

- string
- scissors
- rubber bands
- a hole punch
- plastic or cardboard milk containers

How do I prepare them?

Use scissors to trim your containers down to about a 2" height.

Punch a hole in the center of each of the four sides about $1/3$" down from the top edge.

Cut two 25" lengths of string. Thread the string through one hole, under the container and up through the opposite side's hole. Repeat for the other pair of holes.

Hold the scale up and balance it on the strings. Tie a slip knot at the top of the strings. Use filament tape to tape the strings in place on the bottom of the box.

Slip a school rubber band (not heavy duty) under the knot at the top and loop one end through the other to secure it.

Do the same for your other box trying to get the strings the same length as your first scale. Be sure to use the same size and thickness of rubber band.

Extend rulers out from top of table or desk and anchor the rulers with books. Suspend the scales from the rulers by their rubber band loops. Don't worry about rubber band breakage—the bands can easily be replaced and bear more weight than you might think.

Student Scientific Thermometers

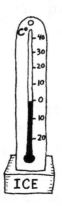

Big Books

How many?

Six

Where do I get them?

Student thermometers can be ordered from:

Cuisenaire Company of America, Inc.
12 Church Street, Box D
New Rochelle, NY 10802
(800) 237-3142

These thermometers come in sets of ten. They're filled with red alcohol rather than mercury and come attached to blank or calibrated cards.

How do I assemble them?

You'll need:

- children's memory pages from "Are You Sure It's Twenty?" and bear story problems from "Teddy Bears Catch a Cold" units
- poster board for covers
- a commercial book binder (available at many school or curriculum centers, or print/copy centers). If you are unable to use a bookbinder, punch several holes along the left side and bind with metal binder rings or plastic "chicken rings."

Appendix B: Black-Line Masters

Unit 1—Buttons
  Story Bibs
  Starred Paper
  8" Diameter Circle for Buttons—Cutting Pattern
  6" Diameter Circle for Buttons—Cutting Pattern
  1$\frac{1}{2}$" Diameter Circles for Buttonholes—Cutting Pattern

Unit 2—A House for a Hedgehog
  Large Shape Templates
  Small Shapes Template
  Starred Paper
  Counting Mat Price Labels
  Circles to Cones
  Triangles to Pyramids
  Rectangles to Boxes

Unit 3—Hansel and Gretel's Path
  Tree Outline
  Teacher's Pattern Cards
  Candy Shape Patterns
  The Small Path Gameboard
  Children's Pattern Cards
  Sorting Sheet
  Game Instruction Sheet for Families

Unit 4—Are You Sure It's Twenty?
  Working Space Paper
  1-20 Counting Grid
  Heavier/Lighter Labels
  Mrs. Bear Counting Puppet
  Forest Trees
  Animal Homes
  Paper Eggs
  Story Bibs
  Attribute Signs

Unit 5—Teddy Bears Catch a Cold
  Teddy Bear Template
  Quilt Block—Parts A, B, C, and D
  Temperatures Chart

Are You Sure It's Twenty?
Buttons
Story Bib

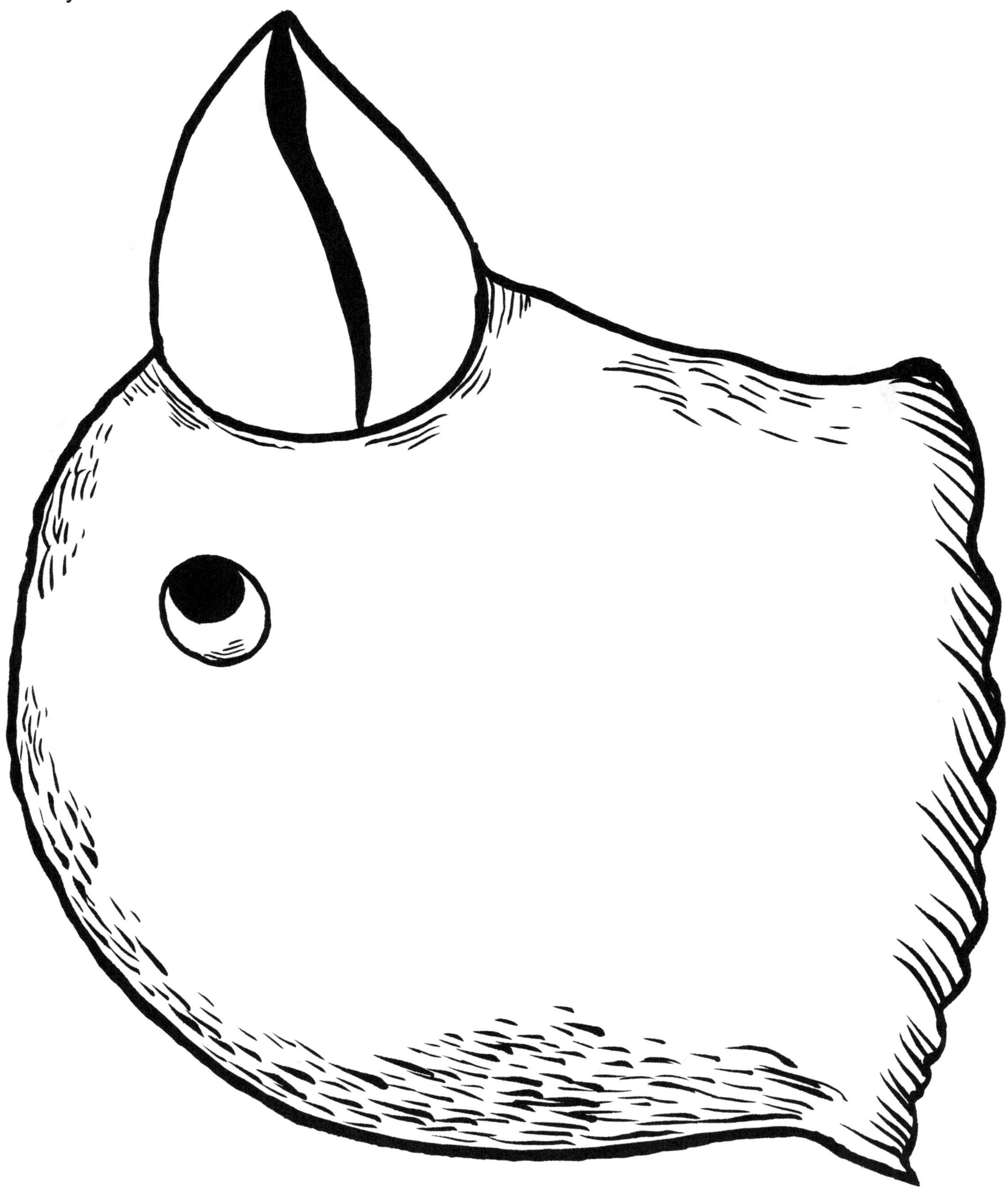

Buttons
Story Bib

Buttons
Story Bib

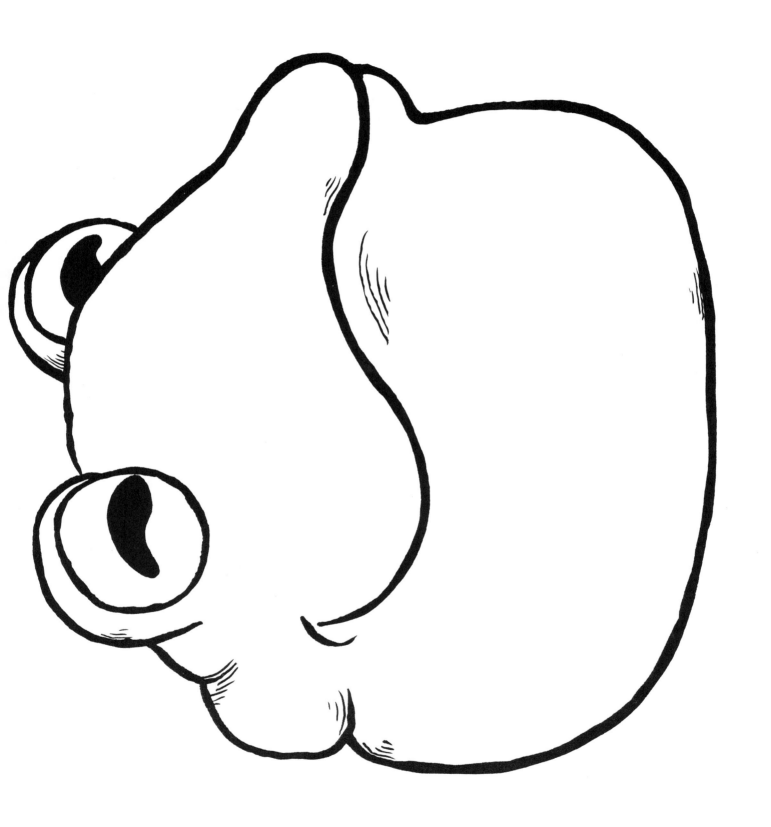

Buttons
Starred Paper

Buttons
8" Diameter Circle for Buttons—Cutting Pattern

Buttons
6" Diameter Circle for Buttons—Cutting Pattern
1½" Diameter Circle for Buttonholes—Cutting Pattern

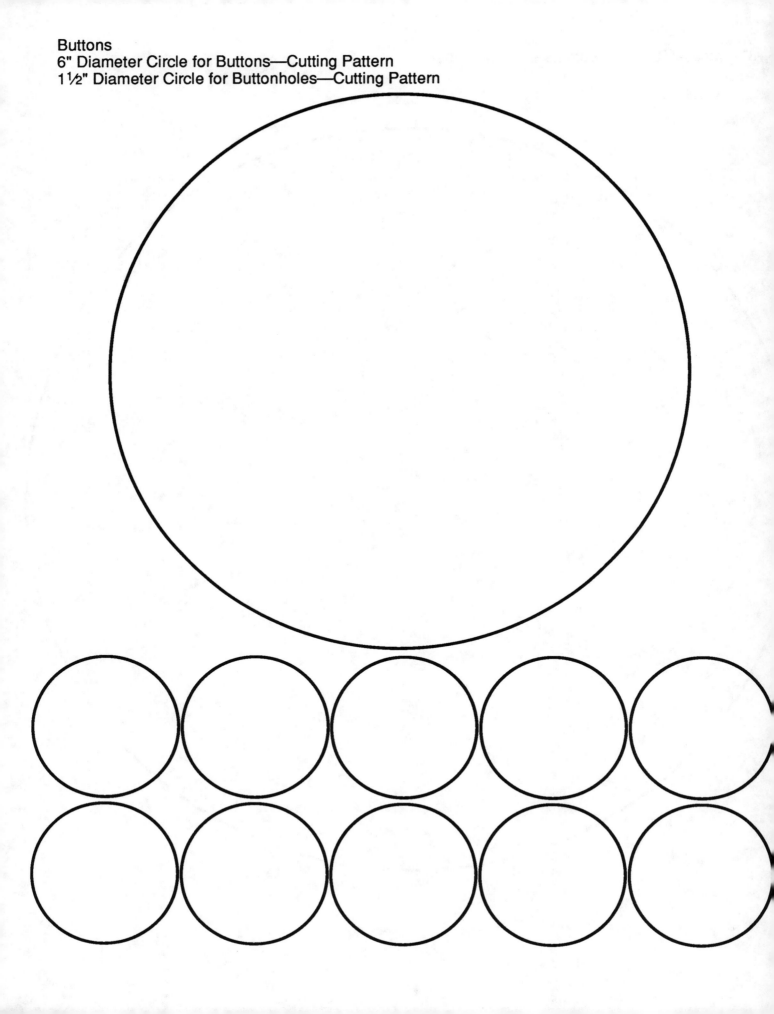

A House for a Hedgehog
Large Shape Template
Square

A House for a Hedgehog
Large Shape Template
Oval

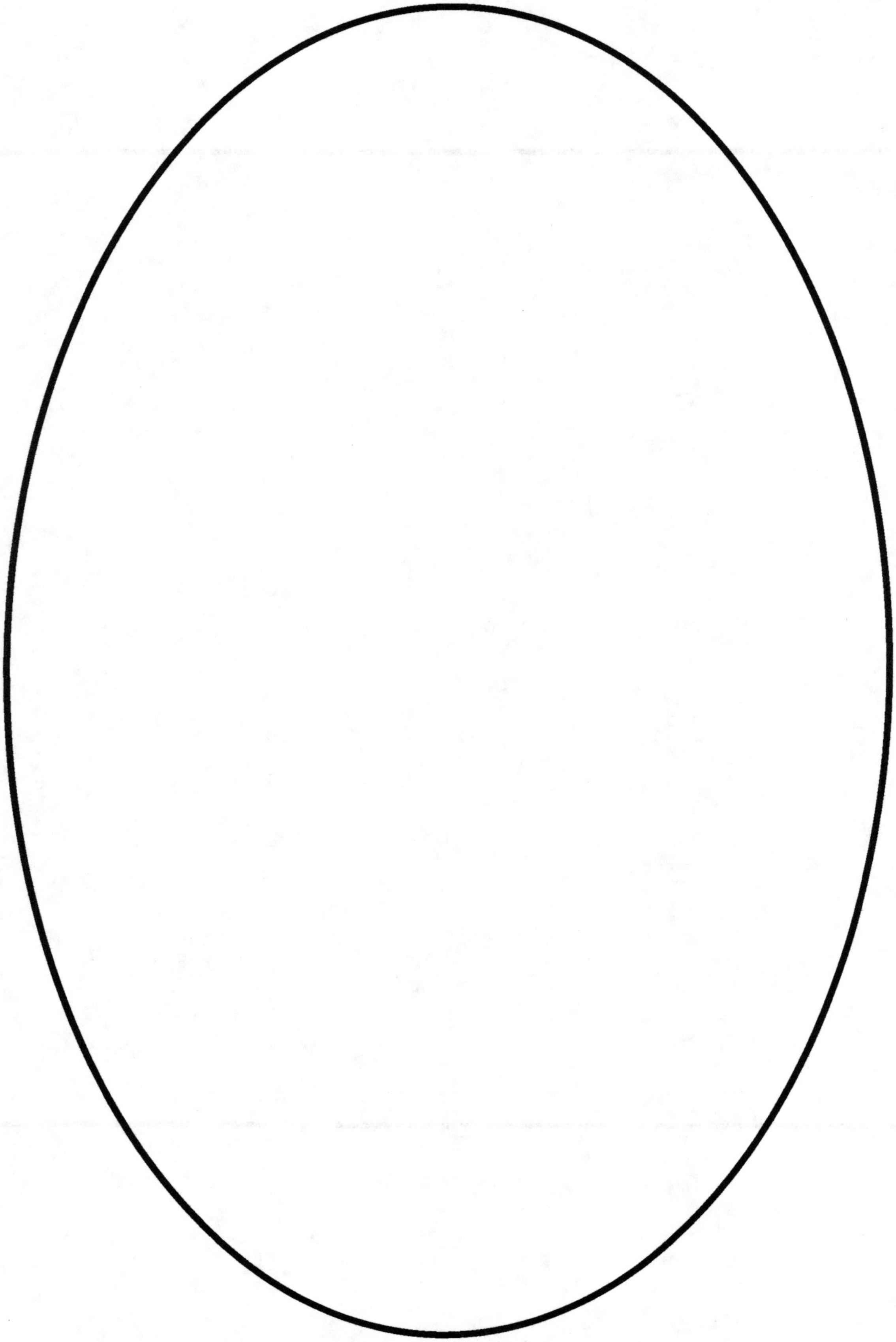

A House for a Hedgehog
Large Shape Template
Circle

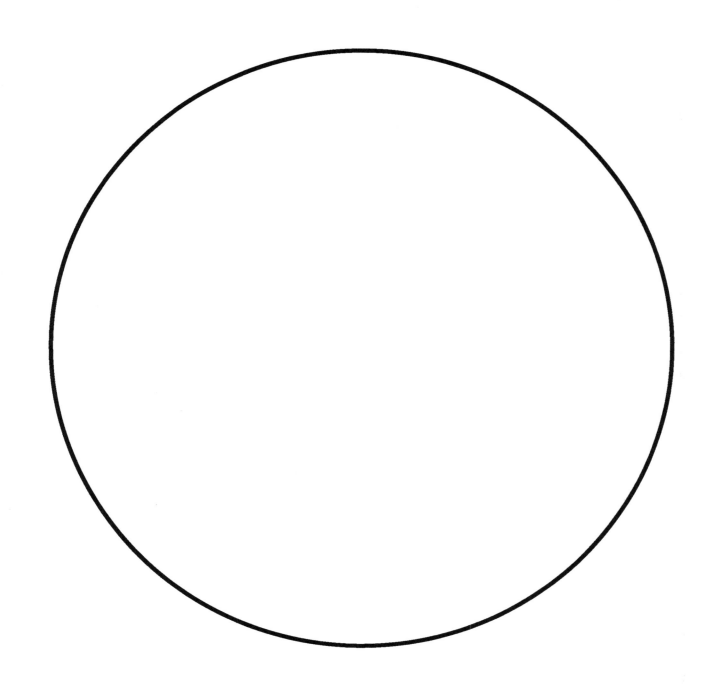

A House for a Hedgehog
Large Shape Template
Triangle

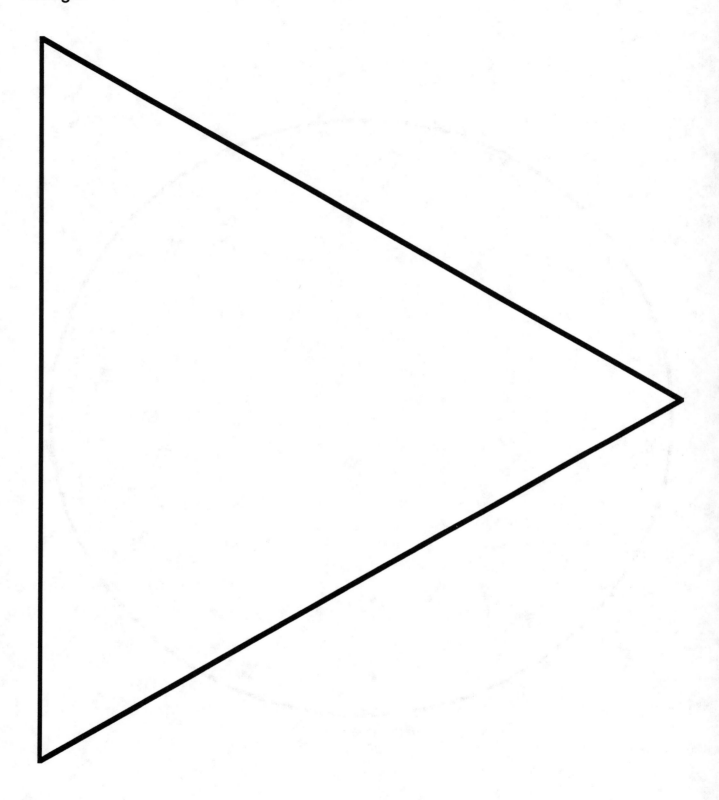

A House for a Hedgehog
Large Shape Template
Diamond

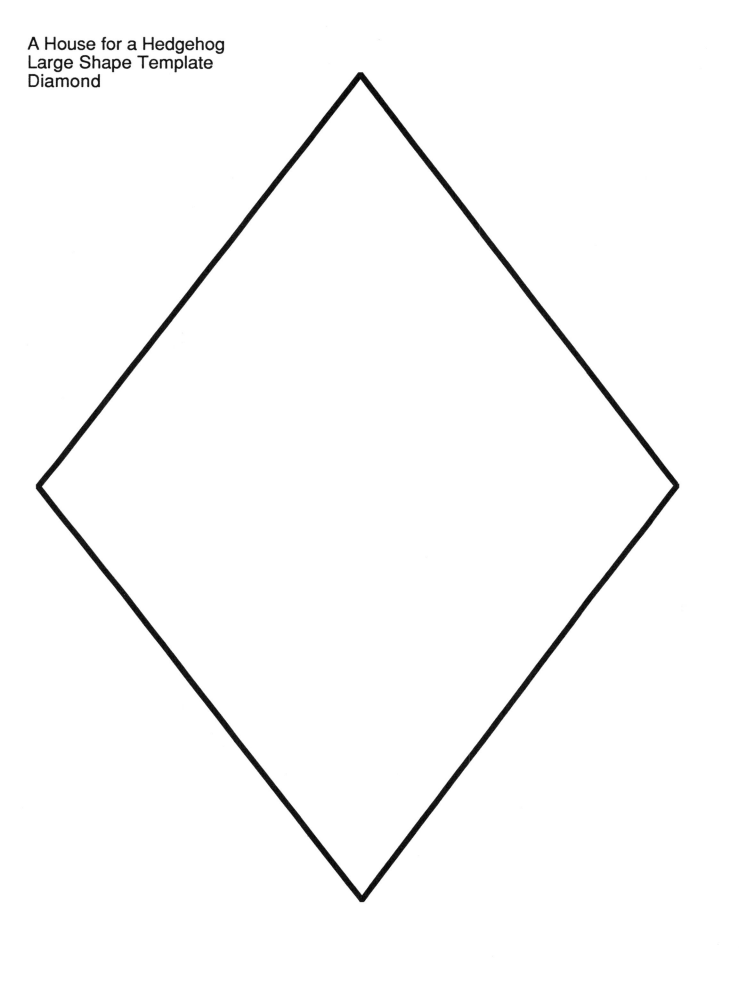

A House for a Hedgehog
Large Shape Template
Octagon

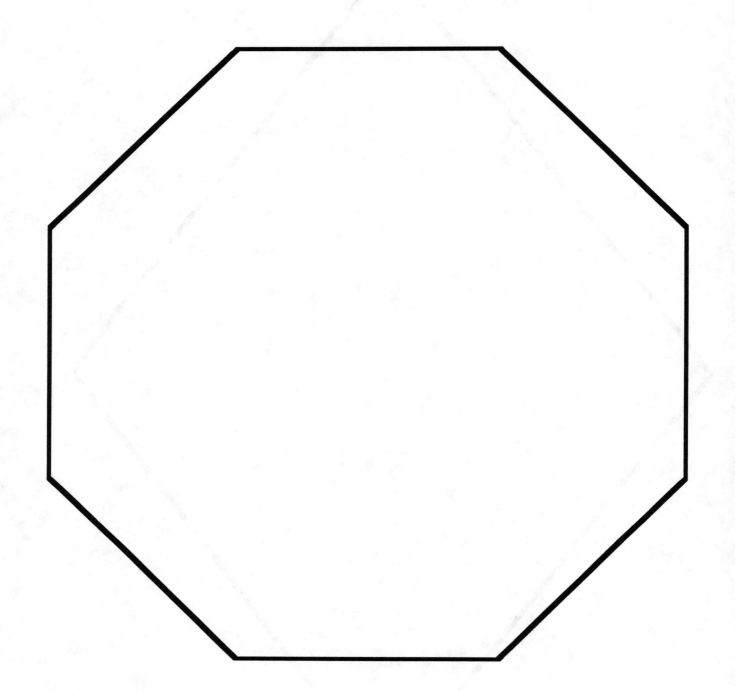

A House for a Hedgehog
Large Shape Template
Rectangle

A House for a Hedgehog
Small Shapes Template

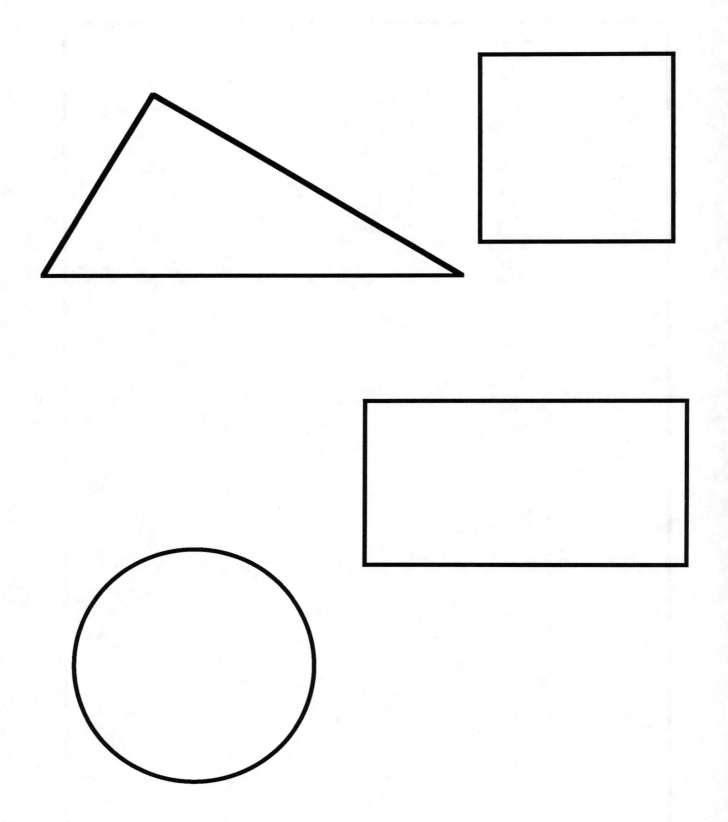

A House for a Hedgehog
Starred Paper

raisins   **3**   **for 1¢**

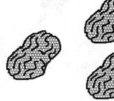

corn nuts   **2**   **for 1¢**

marshmallows   **1**   **for 1¢**

peanuts   **3**   **for 1¢**

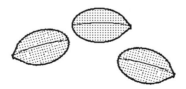

sunflowers seeds   **5**   **for 1¢**

carob chips   **2**   **for 1¢**

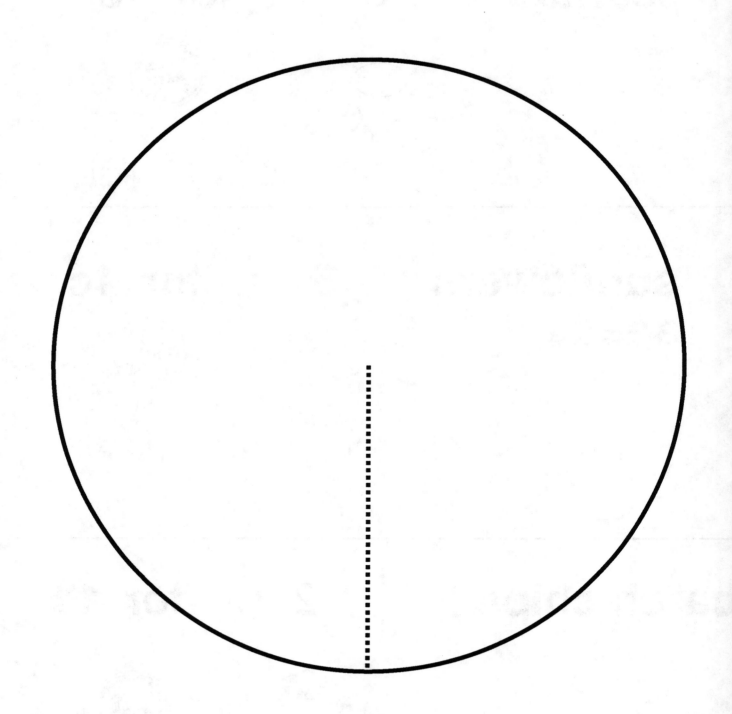

A House for a Hedgehog
Triangles to Pyramids

A House for a Hedgehog
Rectangles to Boxes

Hansel and Gretel's Path
Tree Outline

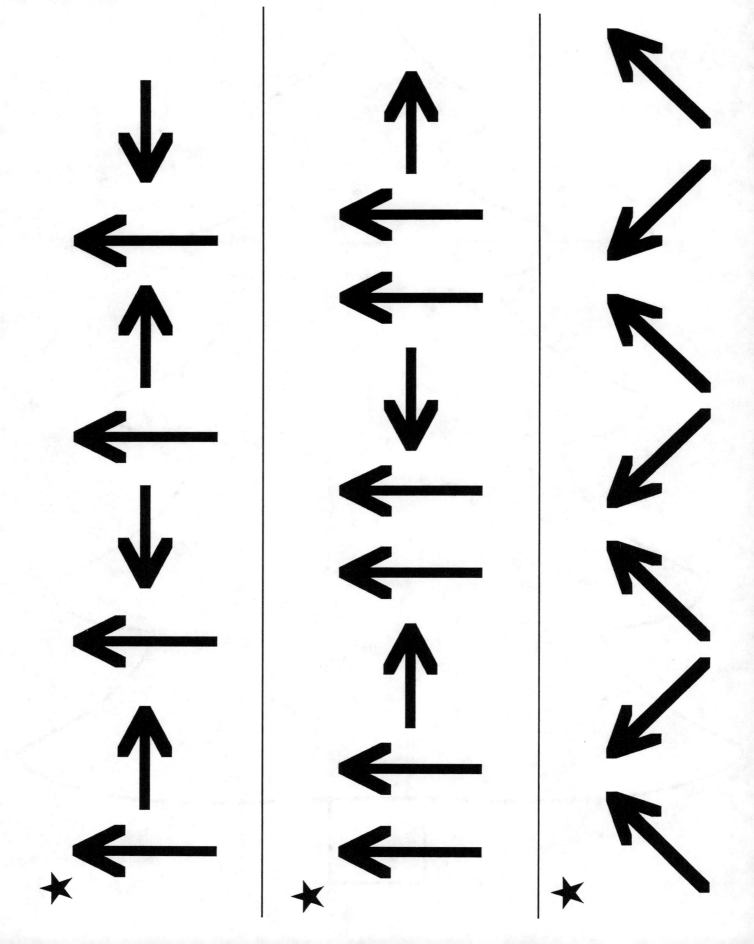

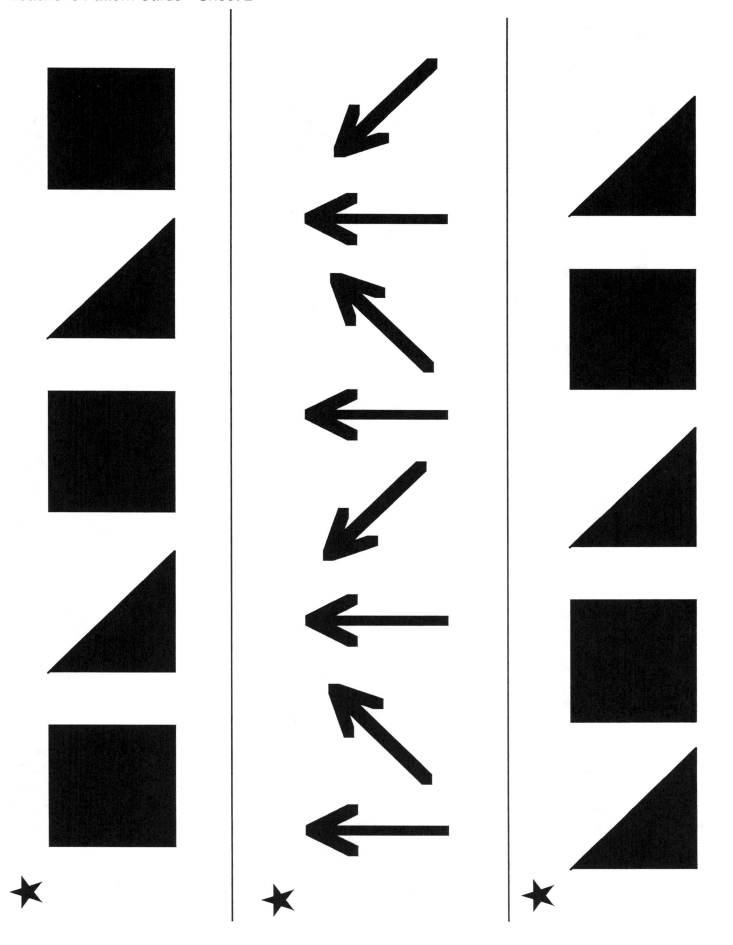

Hansel and Gretel's Path
Teacher's Pattern Cards—Sheet 5

Hansel and Gretel's Path
Teacher's Pattern Cards—Sheet 6

Hansel and Gretel's Path
Teacher's Pattern Cards—Sheet 7

Hansel and Gretel's Path
Candy Shape Patterns

Hearts

Cut 50 of each size from red construction paper

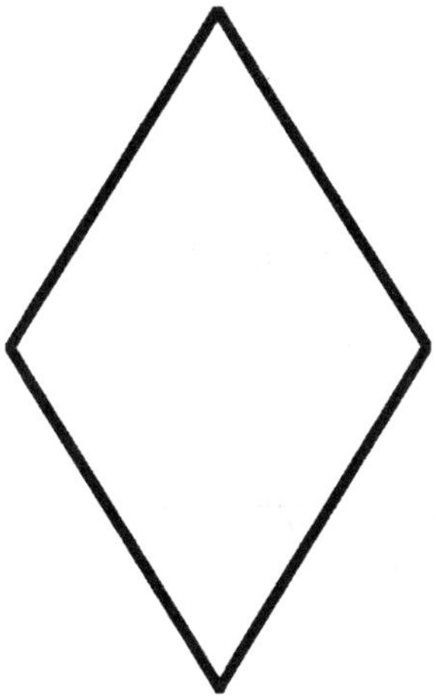

Diamonds

Cut 50 purple and 50 yellow

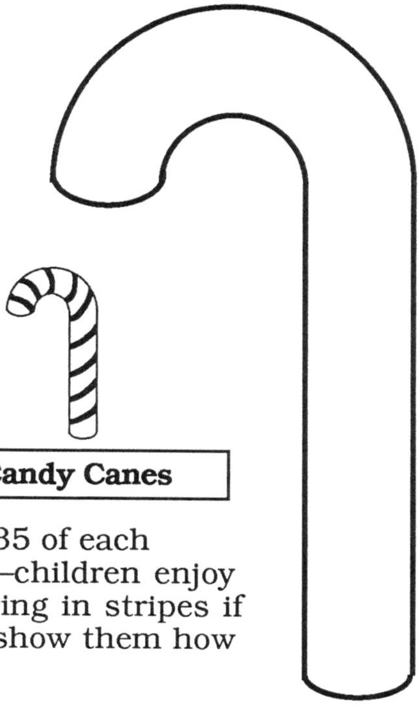

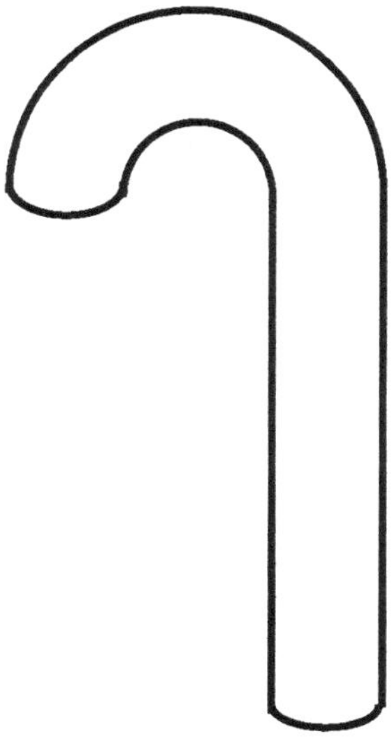

Candy Canes

Cut 35 of each size—children enjoy coloring in stripes if you show them how

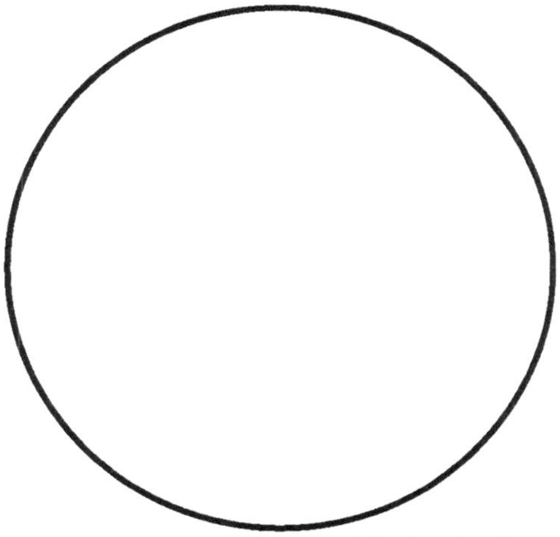

Large circles

Cut 50 in white for round peppermint candies—show children how to color "swirls"

Use these shapes as patterns to cut construction paper candy shapes for your cardboard gingerbread house. You may want to design other shapes too, depending on what your class wants.

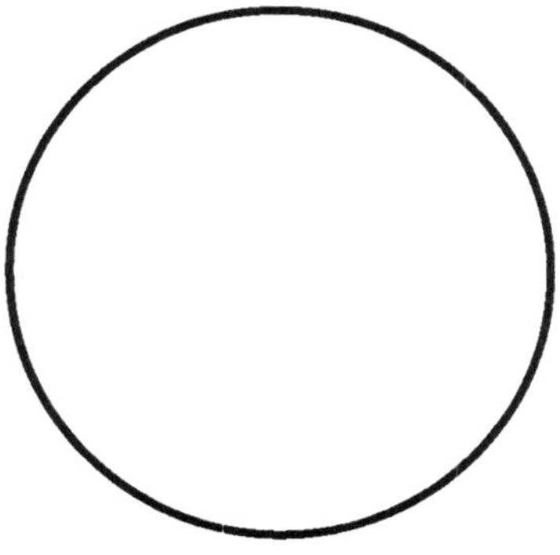

Small circles

m

Cut about 100 in a variety of colors—red, green, yellow, orange—for M&M's and other round candies.

Hansel and Gretel's Path
The Small Path Game Board

Run on 8 1/2" x 14" paper so children have room to draw in gingerbread houses at the bottom of the gameboards.

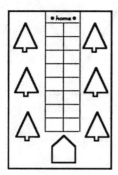

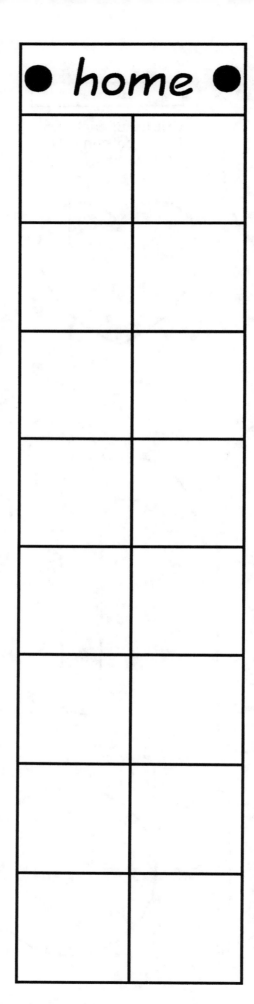

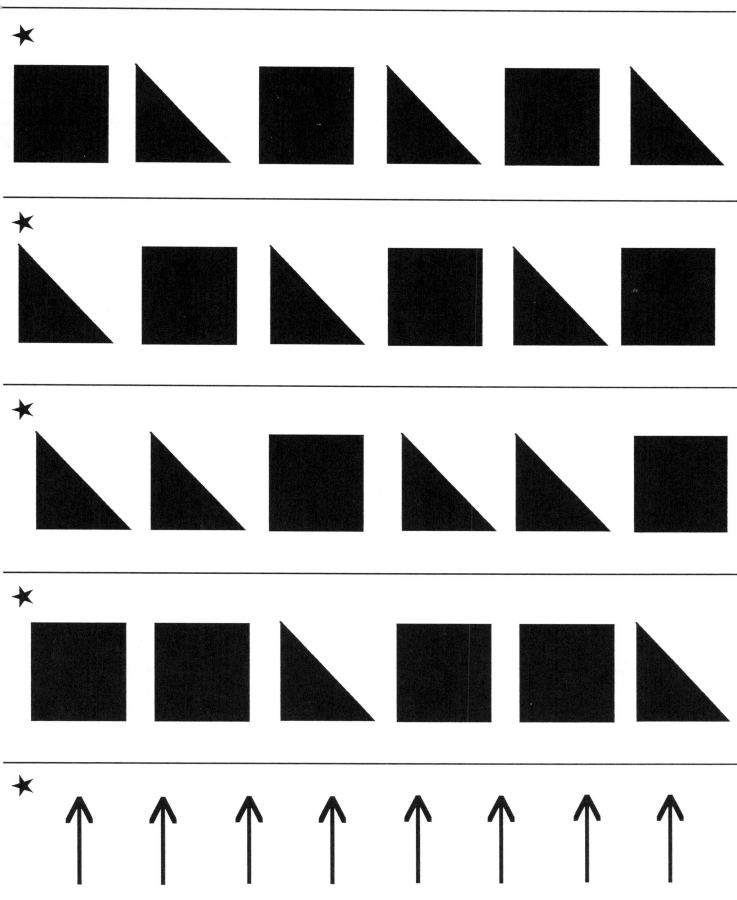

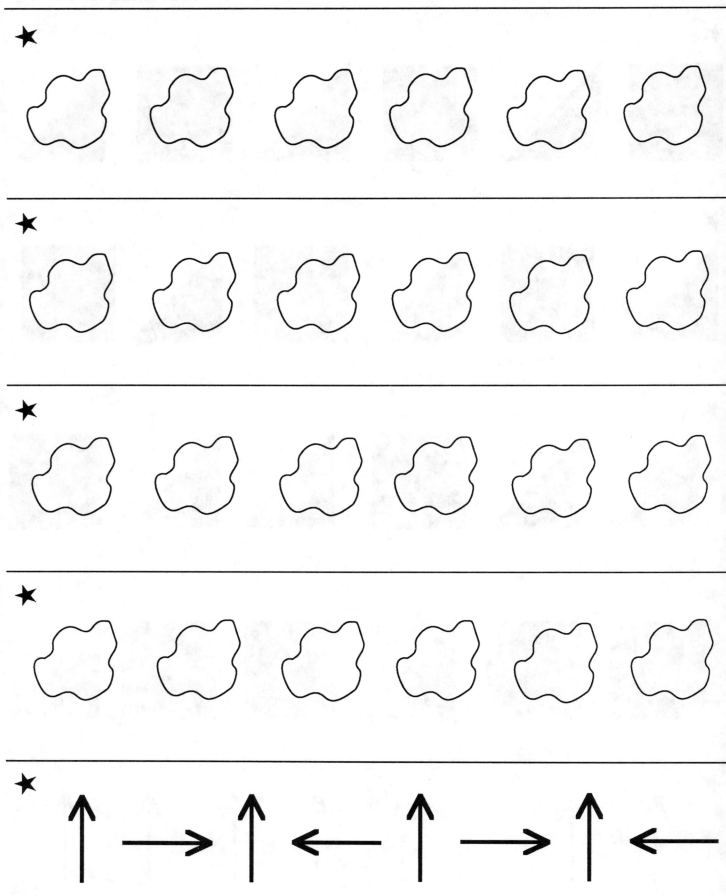

Hansel and Gretel's Path
Children's Pattern Cards—
Optional Sheet

Run copies of this sheet to send home with children's games if you want to provide an additional at-home challenge. Parents can help children create new pattern cards at home using the three blanks below.

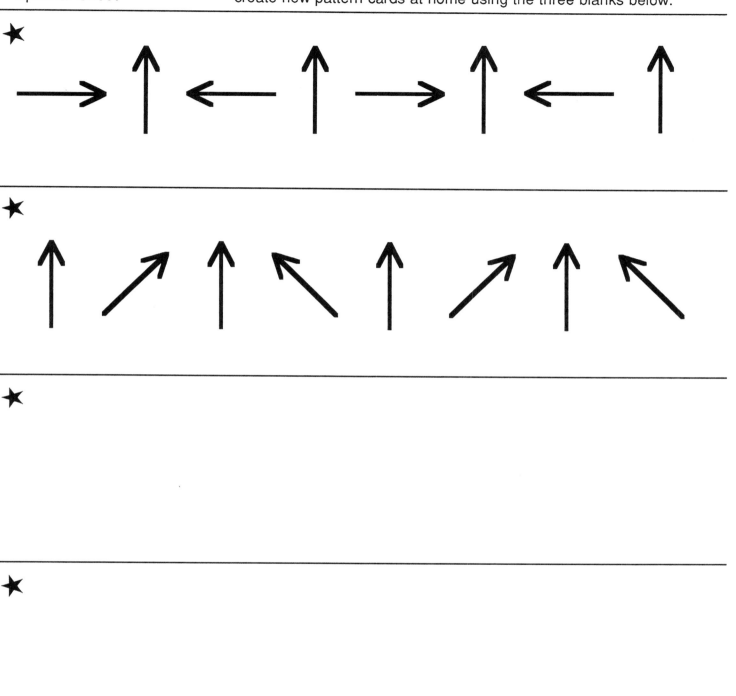

no

yes

Hansel and Gretel's Path—A Pattern Game

This is a game for two players. The object is to be the first one to get all three of your game markers (Hansel, Gretel, and the dove) home.

To play the game, you'll need:
- one path board
- a set of pattern cards
- three game markers for each person

Game Instructions:

1. Set out the path board. Place game markers on either side of the gingerbread house. One player should take all the blue markers; the other, all the orange.

2. Mix up the pattern cards. Stack them and place, <u>face down</u>, beside the path board.

3. Take turns. The first player takes the top <u>two</u> cards off the deck, sets them face up, and decides which one to use. Both cards may work, but the player must choose just one. (A card "works" if the player can move his or her marker all the way up the path to home using the pattern shown. Game markers can be moved forward, backward, sideways, and diagonally to follow a pattern, but you can't skip a row of stepping stones or the path will "disappear"!)

If only one card works but the player chooses incorrectly, both cards go to the bottom of the stack and the player must wait for his or her next turn to try again. If <u>neither</u> card works, both go to the bottom of the stack, and the player must wait for his or her next turn to try again.

If a player chooses a card that <u>does</u> work and is able to move one of his or her game markers home, then it's the other player's turn. Play continues until one of the players gets all three of his or her markers home.

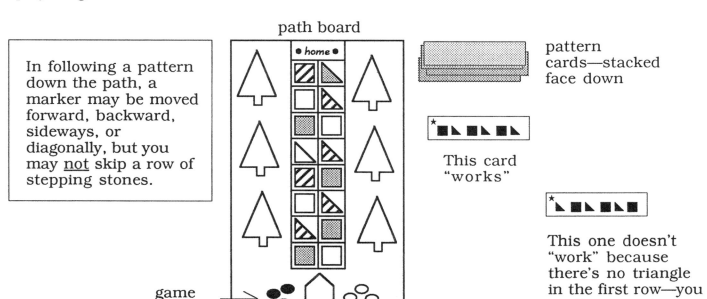

In following a pattern down the path, a marker may be moved forward, backward, sideways, or diagonally, but you may <u>not</u> skip a row of stepping stones.

path board

pattern cards—stacked face down

This card "works"

This one doesn't "work" because there's no triangle in the first row—you can't even get started.

game markers

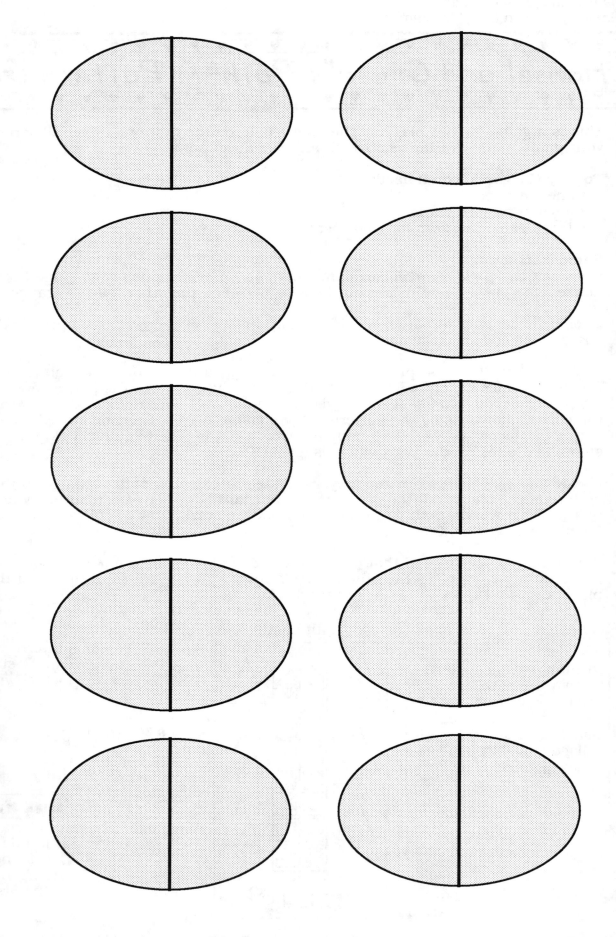

1	2	3	4
5	6	7	8
9	10	11	12
13	14	15	16
17	18	19	20

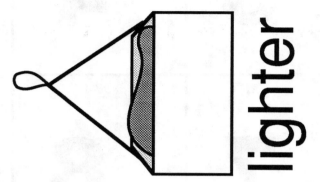

lighter

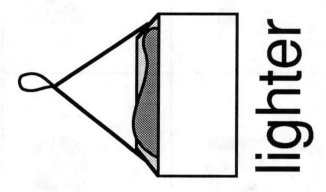

lighter

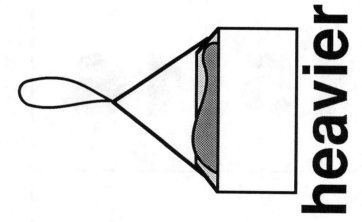

heavier

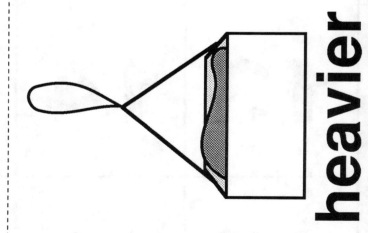

heavier

Are You Sure It's 20?
Mrs. Bear Counting Puppet

WELCOME

Are You Sure It's 20?
Paper Eggs

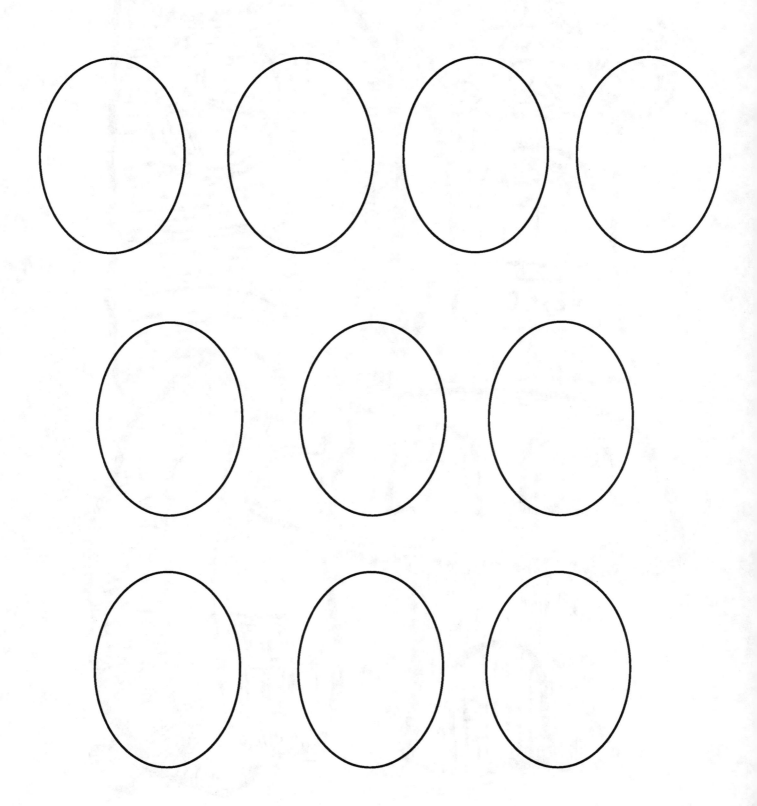

Are You Sure It's 20?
Rabbit Story Bib

Are You Sure It's 20?
Owl Story Bib

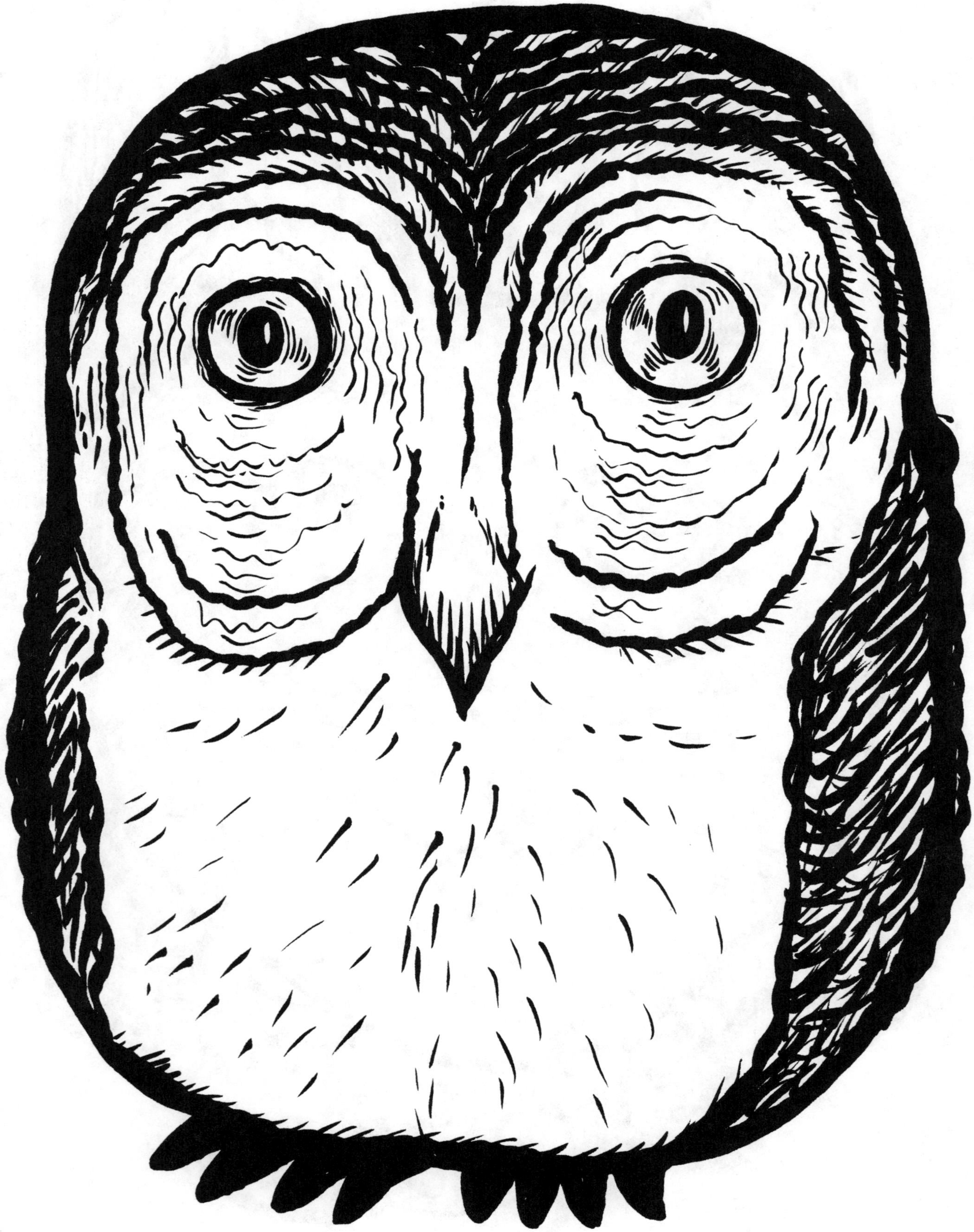

Are You Sure It's 20?
Fox Story Bib

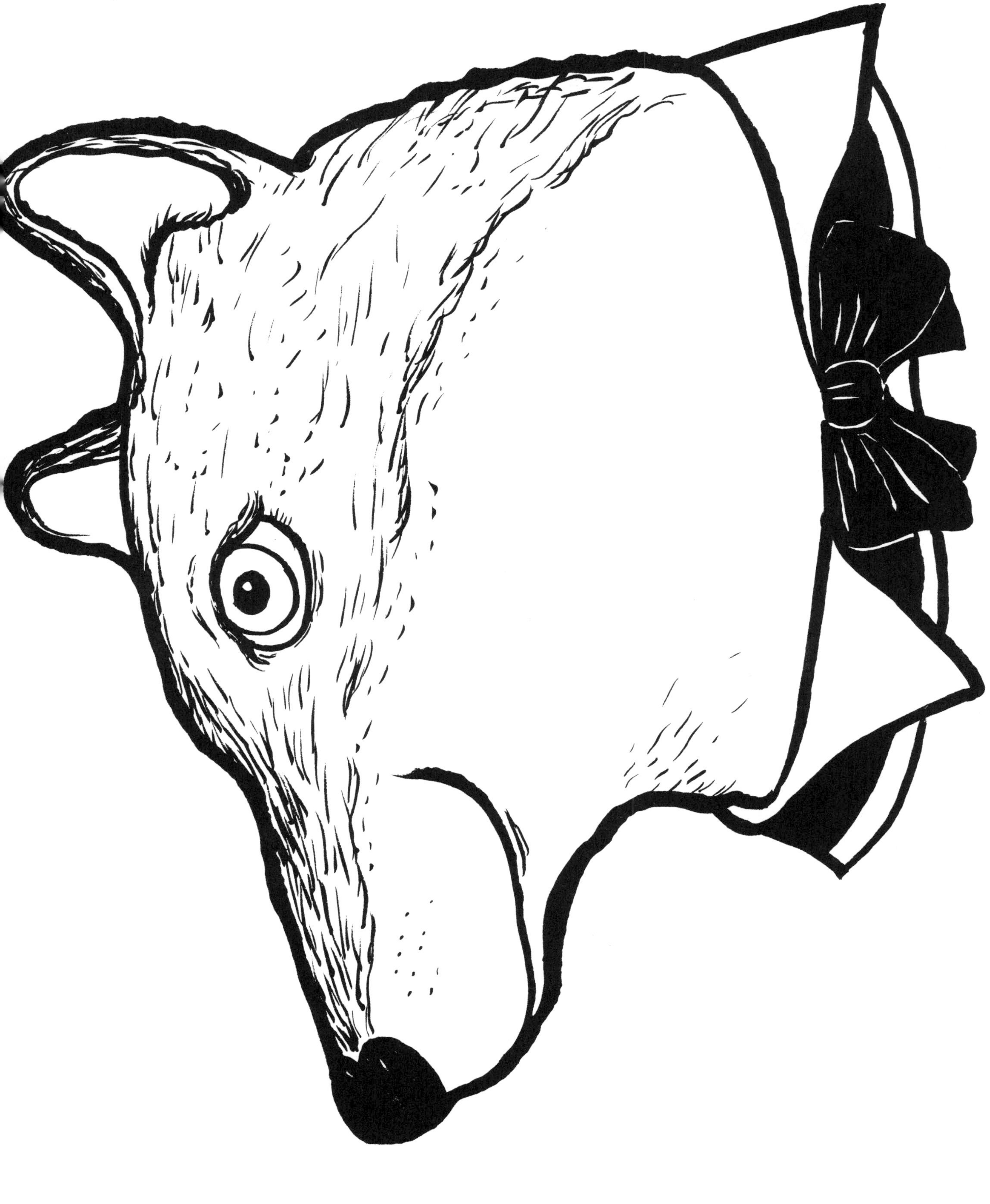

name _____

Teddy Bears Catch a Cold
Temperatures

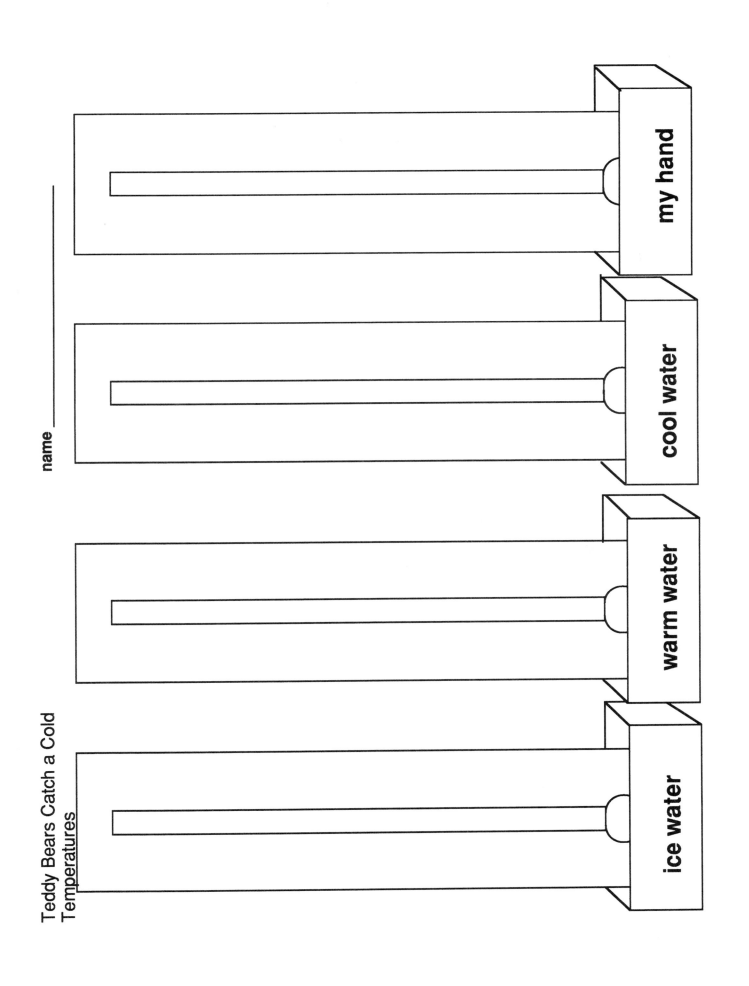

ice water

warm water

cool water

my hand

color

red

yellow

blue

size

big

little

shape

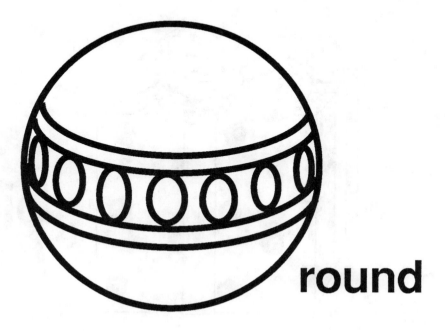

round

corners →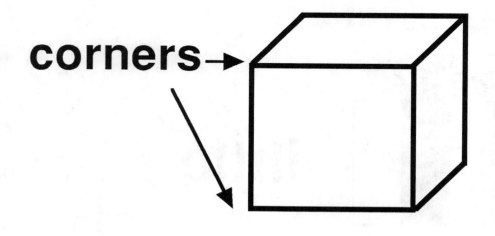

weight

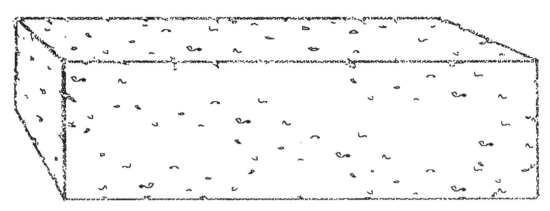

heavy

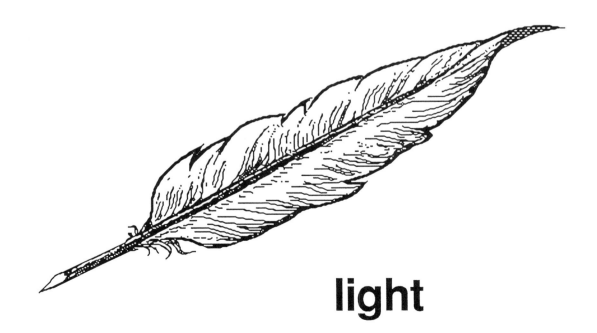

light

living or non-living?

**wild
rabbit**

**teddy
bear**

use

eat it

**play
with it**

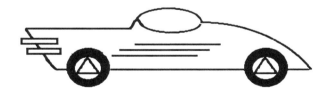

Teddy Bears Catch a Cold
Teddy Bear Template

A.

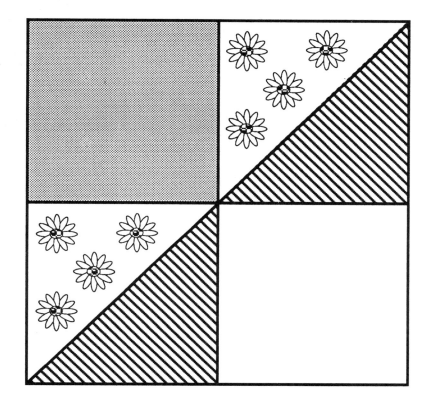

Part B
joins here

Part C
joins here

B.

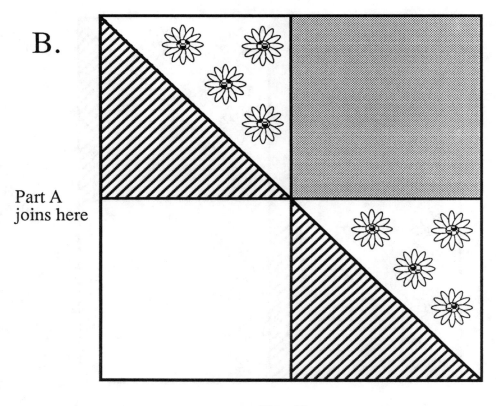

Part A
joins here

Part D
joins here

Teddy Bears Catch a Cold
Quilt Block—Part C

C.

Part A
joins here

Part D
joins here

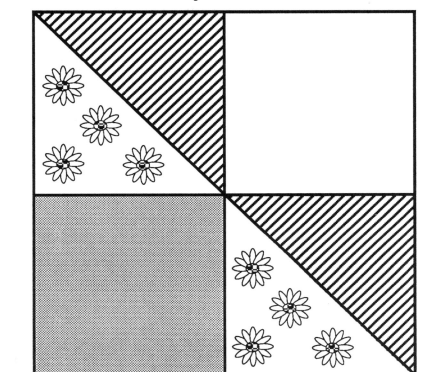

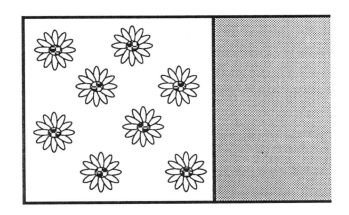

Teddy Bears Catch a Cold
Quilt Block—Part D

D.

Part B
joins here

Part C
joins here

References

Baratta-Lorton, Mary. 1976. *Mathematics Their Way*. Menlo Park, Calif.: Addison Wesley.

Barton, Byron. 1981. *Building a House*. New York, N.Y.: Mulberry Books.

Brett, Jan. 1989. *The Mitten*. New York, N.Y.: Putnam's.

Burk, Donna, Allyn Snider, and Paula Symonds. 1988. *Box It or Bag It Mathematics. Teacher's Resource Guide, Kindergarten*. Salem, Oreg.: MLC Publications.

Butler, M. Christina. 1988. *Too Many Eggs, A Counting Book*. Boston, Mass.: David R. Godine.

Carroll, Lewis. *Alice's Adventures in Wonderland*. 1989. Illustrated by S. Michelle Wiggins. N.Y.: Ariel Books/Alfred A. Knopf.

Carroll, Lewis. *Alice's Adventures in Wonderland*. 1985. Illustrated by Michael Hague. N.Y.: Henry Holt & Co., Inc.

Faunce-Brown, Daphne. 1983. *Snuffles' House*. Chicago, Ill.: Children's Press.

Gauch, Patricia Lee. 1971. *Christina Katerina and the Box*. New York, N.Y.: Coward-McCann, Inc.

Gretz, Susanna and Allison Sage. 1984. *Teddy Bears Cure a Cold*. New York, N.Y.: Scholastic Books.

Grimm, Brothers. 1985. *Hansel and Gretel*. Illustrated by John Wallner. Englewood Cliffs, N.J.: Prentice-Hall, Inc.

Grimm, Brothers. 1980. *Hansel and Gretel*. Illustrated by Susan Jeffers. New York, N.Y.: Dial Books.

Gross, Ruth Belov (retold by). 1988. *Hansel and Gretel*. New York, N.Y.: Scholastic.

Hoberman, May Ann. 1978. *A House Is a House for Me*. New York, N.Y.: Viking.

Johnson, Terry, and Daphne R. Louis. 1987. *Literacy Through Literature*. Portsmouth, N.H.: Heinemann.

Katz, Lillian G. and Sylvia C. Chard. 1989. *Engaging Children's Minds: The Project Approach*. Norwood, N.J.: Ablex.

Lobel, Arnold. 1985. *Frog and Toad Are Friends*. New York, N.Y.: Harper and Row.

Marshall, James. 1990. *Hansel and Gretel*. New York, N.Y.: Dial Books.

McDonald, M. 1990. *Hedgehog Bakes a Cake*. New York, N.Y.: Bantam Books.

Miller, Edna. 1964. *Mousekin's Golden House*. New York, N.Y.: Prentice-Hall.

National Council of Teachers of Mathematics. 1989. *Curriculum and Evaluation Standards for School Mathematics*. Reston, Va.: National Council of Teachers of Mathematics.

National Research Council. 1989. *Everybody Counts: A Report to the Nation on the Future of Mathematics Education*. Washington, D.C.: National Academy Press.

Pfanner, Louise. 1989. *Louise Builds a House*. New York, N.Y.: Orchard Books.

Potter, Beatrix. 1989. *The Tale of Mrs. Tiggywinkle*. New York, N.Y.: Viking Penguin.

Turner, A. 1989. *Hedgehog for Breakfast*. New York, N.Y.: Macmillan.